REVIEWS

"Dear reader, I am so glad you chose this book! In it you will find a fascinating story of a mother, who boards an emotional roller coaster that tests her in every way possible, while her precious longed-for baby struggles to survive. Walk with Olga as she relates her story of life, love, survival, and learning while on this path. Be uplifted..."

Marie Walters

"This was one of the most heart touching and hardest books to read. This book is not for the faint of heart. This book was a big eye opener for me as to understanding people who are going through a hard time in life. As I am related to Olga, as a sister, seeing them go through this scary time in their life, I did not fully comprehend the intensity of their pain and just how excruciating fragile everyday was for them until I read the book. It will be hard for you to read the book and not shed many tears. I can say their testimony forever changed my heart."

Lana Mchedlidze

"This book is a wonderful source of encouragement for anyone who is going through a difficult time in their life and struggling with their faith in God. Olga's story is a beautiful testament to the hope that exists in even the darkest of days."

Taylor Hooper

"This is a heartwarming story of a couple that struggle with tough decisions that I'm not sure I would be able to make concerning their 4th child. God's grace and love and their strong faith makes this a book that you'll not soon forget."

Sandie Hollister

"I did not have the honor of knowing Elijah, but I have come to know his mother, Olga, and learned of the amazing impact his life had upon his family and the medical personnel. As told in detail

by his mother, Elijah's story broke my heart and lifted my spirit on every page. He was a warrior sent here to teach all of us the value of life, and the power of families to find faith, love, and joy even in the most heart wrenching circumstances. Within the pages of this book you will mostly likely weep when Elijah struggles to survive, and his parents make life or death decisions. Yet, you will also be inspired by the courage and faith of this family as they triumph over tragedy and move forward to serve others with love and compassion in their community."

Kay Watson

"This book is a journey, filled with Love, Courage and Faith. Love not only for Elijah, but the love shown and shared by Olga and Oleg for each other and their children. Courage shown by Olga and Oleg to do everything in their power to save the life of their precious Elijah. Faith in our God that He would be with them through out this journey. This journey does not end with the final page... It continues."

Joe Amaya

"Life is full of good times, love, hope and, sometimes, hard choices. Hopefully those hard choices happen only once in a lifetime, an overwhelming challenge of hope and faith... Having worked in a Neonatal Intensive Care Unit (NICU) for 38 years, I met and cared for, not only infants, but whole families. One family I will never forget immigrated from the Ukraine and Russia and were put into a world so very foreign from anything they had ever had to experience before. They had to put their trust in what Doctors and Nurses had to say. Oleg and Olga and their entire family were dealt a card no-one would have wanted to deal with. I know this from my personal experience. Their story will capture your heart and soul, as they fought for the life of their premature son. Through this son, Elijah, they found more love and faith than they ever though was possible. I am honored to be part of this story."

Patti Dryden

The Puzzle of Elijah

Life is a puzzle.
You never know what the big picture is going to look like.
You may think, here is the end of life,
but in reality – it is only the beginning.

Olga Anischenko

The Puzzle of Elijah

Published in the United States of America
ISBN-13: 978-1987682960
ISBN-10: 1987682963
«CreateSpace»
4900 LaCross Road, North Charleston, SC 29406, USA
1-866-356-2153
Book editor: Kay Watson
Cover designer: dezaro.net

Website: www.olgaanischenko.com
YouTube: Olga Anischenko English Channel
Amazon books: Olga Anischenko or http://a.co/9QyldgZ
Facebook: https://www.facebook.com/olga.anischenko.3
To invite Olga as a speaker: 360–521–9240

INTRODUCTION

My name is Olga. This story is about my family, friends, and completely unfamiliar people, who miraculously appeared in our life and helped us during difficult times. I wrote this book for seven long years.

Writing this book has been everything but easy. It has taken time to reflect, understand, and to become completely at peace with the decisions we made and the actions we took. And to be completely honest, it was painful everyday as I recalled and wrote down memories, experiences, thoughts, and such personal conversation as we sometimes had to have. It was never easy for me to entrust my soul to paper. I even had to face family and friends who doubted the wisdom of sharing our story. They felt there were parts of the story which should not be told. I then faced a new dilemma: should I tell only part of our story or be truthful in every detail. I chose the harder way, to share our journey as openly and completely as possible.

Ultimately, I realized my story, told sincerely, would help other families in similar situations. This approach inspired me and gave me confidence I was doing the right thing. I know what parents feel in the midst of continuing crises. I have experienced their fears and their pleas for mercy in their prayers. I know they do not need pity. They need help and encouragement; support and assurance they are doing the right thing for their child; and never-ending love which gives them confidence to keep going.

Every page of this book was written by me with tears. In the process of working and examining what we experienced, I discovered a lot in myself, in my loved ones, and in my God. It is God that Oleg and I are grateful to for the experience and support we received throughout such a difficult time for our family. We have discovered that serious trials can become the foundation for future growth and success. Passing through the limits of physical and moral strength, we moved forward. Accepting from God both good and bad, we decided to rely entirely on Him, believing that He will lead us to a better future.

In fact, my book is a story of faith, hope, love, courage and, at the same time, worry for the future of our family. Under the weight of unimaginable stress, we made important and irreversible life and death decisions. It was a struggle and a challenge to everything we believed in and how we lived. Now, years later, we realize who we are and why we have experienced this life lesson. Over time, there was a clear understanding that we survived largely due to our large family, and the upbringing we received in our childhood. Our parents instilled the qualities in us which helped us cope with the tragedy. We realized that our life is firmly entwined with the subtle and inextricable thread of the past.

....

1

*Find out about your ancestors and you
will learn a lot about yourself.*

My husband Oleg and I are immigrants to America. In 2007, ten years into our marriage, our journey began...

One evening, when Oleg, I and our three children knelt to pray to God, I heard Oleg say: **"God, I am so tired of being a "lukewarm" Christian. I want to have a personal relationship with You! Please send a situation into my life that will show me WHO YOU REALLY ARE!"**

For a moment, I felt scared and thought what is my husband talking about? But because I loved him and trusted him, I thought he knew what he was asking for. As I understood later, our words have power because God heard my husband's prayer. He came and knocked at our door, and we began a very hard journey. Only a few years later, when we read a following statement in a full Bible, we understood what had actually happened.

In the book of Sirach, 2:1-5, it is written: *"My child, if you aspire to serve the Lord, prepare yourself for an ordeal... Be sincere of heart, be steadfast, and do not be alarmed when disaster comes. Whatever happens to you, accept it, and in the uncertainties of your humble state, be patient, since GOLD IS TESTED IN THE FIRE, and the CHOSEN IN THE FURNACE OF HUMILIATION."*

I am about to tell you what happened after Oleg's prayer. I am not blaming my husband or God. Today, seven years later, Oleg and I thank God for every second of our life, for God's miracles, lessons and for revealing Himself to us. God's work in our life was painful, but worth every moment of it. It was the time of spiritual growth and learning Who really God is. Today, we love God, each other, and our children so much more than we ever did before. We value our family and know the price of health and happiness. And most important, we know the difference between religion and the real God!

This story begins with our family. We, as individuals, are a product of our family and of other people, who influence us. Therefore, to understand our decisions, you have to understand us as a family. The decisions we make today are connected to the past.

....

My family is from Ukraine. Grandmothers and Grandfathers grew up in wealthy families, but during the revolution, the communists took away most of their property and distributed it between the poor people. Life in the Soviet Ukraine under the communist regime was hard: less food being produced, hunger and some deaths from starvation.

During World War II, in 1942, the Germans invaded our country. My Grandfather, Alexander Lapin, was drafted into the Red Army. He helped to defend the city of Leningrad and was among the troops who entered Berlin. He believed his faith in God kept him safe, when so many people died during the war.

When Alexander came home, he fell in love with a beautiful girl, Anna, and married her. They lived in the urban-settlement, Rakitno, seventy miles from Kiev, the Capitol of the Ukraine. Alexander was a generous man and people were drawn to him. He was originally a member of the Baptist church. After returning from the war, his faith had changed. He became a pastor of a Pentecostal church, serving his community and seven surrounding villages. He rode his bicycle to see people, bringing honey and other gifts with him. At the same time, Alexander worked as a machinist of a local train company. With time, their family grew to nine children. My Father, Anatoliy, is their second child.

Alexander & Anna Lapin   *My Father – Anatoliy Lapin*

....

My Mother's Father, Peter Lysenko, was also drafted into World War II. One battle became so intense that many of his fellow soldiers were injured or killed. Wounded and fearing death, he cried out to the Lord, "If you exist, help me survive and I will serve you to the end." He survived, but was captured by Germans and put on a train to Auschwitz, a concentration camp. On the way, he and two other soldiers crawled up to the roof and tried to escape. The two soldiers were shot and killed; Peter was the only one to escape.

Several months later he returned home. His life was still in danger, as the Germans were in every village of the Ukraine. He joined the Baptist church, where he met a beautiful girl, Maria, and married her. At first, he worked at a grocery store. Later, he became a supervisor of agricultural workers. During evenings he would do wood work and build furniture. Peter also became a pastor of a Pentecostal church in his village. With Maria, they had eleven children. My Mom, Vera, is their third child.

Peter & Maria Lysenko   *My Mother – Vera Lysenko*

Several years later, Peter developed a tumor in his head and almost died. His wife and children prayed for him, and God healed him. Disabled, Peter could no longer work and stayed home with the children.

Maria worked as a nurse to support the family. At that time, to practice one's Christian faith was unacceptable to the communist government. Because Maria was a Christian, she was sent far from her village to work with disabled patients, so she would not tell people about God. Soon, she lost her job. Peter went to Kiev and talked to the governor. He told him that he defended his country and became disabled. His wife, Maria, was the only source of income, but she lost her job because she is a Christian. He asked for help. The governor was not happy about this situation. He promised to write a letter to Maria's employer. Soon, she got her job back.

The police actively searched for people practicing their faith. If caught by the government, they were subject to fines, persecution, even imprisonment. The government threatened to take away the children of Christian families, if they kept teaching them about God. In order to worship God together, families had to gather in secret at someone's house, in the woods, or in another village, where they were less known. Freedom of religion, as we practice it in the United States today, was prohibited. Something as simple as a church building was not allowed to exist. To protect the church and its members, parents strongly encouraged their children to marry within the faith. Therefore, it was important for Christian families to know each other and to rely upon each other. Mom's and Dad's families lived thirty minutes apart and my parents met during church activities.

Christian children were generally not accepted into college. Only those, who had straight A's and didn't have to take an exam, were accepted. Still they were always oppressed. My Mom was one of the lucky few, accepted into college and allowed to complete a degree as an Engineer/Technologist. My Dad received his training through college and later through his job, and had professions as a Diesel Locomotive Engineer, Electrician, Welder and Plumber.

....

My Dad knew and loved my Mom since she was thirteen, but he had never told her. Upon returning from the Soviet Army during 1970's, at age twenty-one, he asked my Mom to marry him. She agreed, and they have been very happy together. They lived by his parents, who divided their land into four plots and gave a plot to their three oldest children, including my Father. Dad was a machinist at a train station, and Mom supervised a meat company. The first few years of their marriage, with the help of relatives, they built their house, while keeping full-time jobs.

My parents first had two daughters. When time came for me to be born, the doctor and Mom were the first ones to welcome me into this world. At that time, Fathers were not allowed into the delivery room. When Dad came to visit Mom and the baby, the nurse greeted him,

"Congratulations, you have a baby girl!"

"A girl? I really wanted a boy!" responded my Dad.

"It is a girl and you are taking her home!" the nurse answered firmly.

After ten days of hospitalization, Dad brought Mom and me home. They had two weeks to register the name of a newborn child.

"What name should we give to our daughter? Maybe Oksana or Natasha?" my Mom asked my Father.

Dad left to register the name. When he came home in the evening, my Mom was surprised to see that the name on the birth certificate was Olga.

"Why did you choose the name Olga?" she asked my Dad.

"It is beautiful and easy to say. It will sound beautiful when she is young and as she gets older," Dad answered.

The name Olga means "Holy, Blessed and Successful." I was lucky to be born to parents who loved me, cared for me, gave me values, taught me right from wrong, and provided me with a faith to guide my life. Even today, they continue to provide a point of reference, answer my questions, tell me what they think and give me honest advice. I value their opinion and their love.

When my parents had a fourth child, they were considered a large family, so the government gave Mom a two-year maternity leave. She stayed home, and Dad continued working. One day, while doing a repair at his job, Dad injured his right wrist. It was cracked, became very sore, swollen and infected, and eventually turned into cancer. The doctor told my Father, in order to live, his arm needed to be amputated.

Everyone prayed for our Father. No one thought he deserved it. He was a good Christian and a youth leader in their church. My Father's parents believed God was powerful to heal their son and tried to talk him out of the surgery. They also worried how our Father would be able to support his family.

I remember one evening, when our Father sat on a bed and hugged us all, there was a big lump on his right arm. That was the last time I saw him with both arms. He agreed to amputate his right arm above the elbow, so that the infection would not spread to his whole body. His surgery was done on his 30th birthday. My Grandfather could not visit my Father for a whole month. It was too painful for him to see his now disabled son. In addition to pain, the newly acquired disability cost my Father his career.

Both of my Grandmothers had big families and could not help much. So, Great-Aunt Hanna, who never married and loved our Dad since he was a little boy, helped our Mom. She watched the children, while Mom visited Dad at a regional hospital, riding the train two hours each way, three times a week. Hanna stayed with us, cooked meals and washed our laundry. She sent us to school and gave us lots of love.

Great–Aunt Hanna   *My Mother and I*

Even though we were little, I remember seeing my Mom praying many times and asking God to heal our Father. We prayed with her. Our Father stayed at the hospital for a few months and then came home to complete his recovery.

When people came to visit him, some of them encouraged my Mom,

"Stay strong. Believe, God will heal him."

But others didn't see any hope for the recovery.

"Prepare for the funeral," they whispered in Mom's ear.

When Mom's maternity leave ended, she could not return to her previous job because of her ill husband, four small children and cattle to feed. She requested a transfer to a closer location. Mom was offered her a job at the office, but she chose to work as an operator, three shifts: morning, evening, or night. It was a walking distance from our home. She was able to come home during her lunch hour to feed us and the livestock.

Our Mom's love helped our Father to recover, get up each day and continue living. Great-Aunt Hanna and all the relatives helped us as much as they could. Sometimes we had no money for food. In those times, it seemed people were always willing to help us. We even received a parcel from Germany, from people whom we didn't know. We accepted it as from the hand of God.

Our Father could no longer be a machinist. With tears in his eyes, he would watch the passing trains near our home. As he became stronger, he started a bee farm and sold honey. Our family grew tulips in a hot house and sold them on March 8th, the International Women's Day. We also grew produce for our family and lots of radishes, which we sold every season. My Father was creative and did more work than many men with two arms did. Both my parents worked very hard and never complained.

Attending church for the first time after the illness, a very religious member of the church told my Father he had a message for him from God, **"What happened to you was My will. Don't ask why. A long way lies before you. Your feet will step where you have never been before. Your**

family will always have food and clothes, and I will take care of you." At that time our parents had no idea what this prophecy meant. It came true eleven years later, when we emigrated from Ukraine to America.

My parents, brothers & sisters. I am the second one on the right.

While Mom worked, we spent time with Dad. We raised produce for food, helped in the garden, picked berries and cared for animals. My Dad made work fun. Often, we played with our cousins, swam at the lake or river and played games.

In school we were polite Christian children. We always earned good grades and excelled in art. The Principal often praised us at school assemblies. At the end of her speech, she always added a conclusion, "There is no God. Whoever believes in God will lose a lot in this life." The school children made fun of us, as Christians. Acts like these were accepted as normal social rules of conduct, never spoken, but always understood.

In the 1980's only a few people in our village had cars. You had to have cash and be on a waiting list, in order to buy a new car. Because our parents had many children and our Dad was disabled, the government let our family buy a car without being on a waiting list! Amazingly, with one arm Dad was able to drive his car. He frequently helped friends and neighbors with rides. Later, he drove his Father to churches in surrounding villages and supported Christians there. Our Father was a respected man in our community. He was always kind, quiet, helpful, happy and had a heart full of love.

My parents' religion taught them to have all the children that God would give them. Even though they worried how they would financially support a larger family, they had four more healthy children in Ukraine and were able to provide for all our needs. We were a large and happy family, never viewing our Father as disabled. Mom loved him so much! At that time, many individuals having amputations did not survive – our Dad was among the lucky ones.

....

16

2

In 1979, because of religious persecution, many Jews and Christians were seeking permission from the Russian government to leave the country. By the late 1980's, the government began issuing Visas. Our family applied for a Visa to immigrate to America. We traveled to Moscow and stayed there for two weeks, waiting to be interviewed by the American Embassy. After approval by the Russian government, in 1990, we received a Visa that would permit our family, our Uncle Peter, and other relatives to immigrate to America.

We were required to have a sponsor to immigrate. Our sponsor was Jacob Lapin, a person we did not know, even though he had the same last name. Because we did not understand the immigration process, we were afraid to go. Uncle Peter chose to immigrate to America first. A year later, he became our sponsor and sent us a new Visa. This was a difficult decision for our parents. Being in America would allow us to freely practice our religion. If we remained, we would continue to be persecuted. Language would be a barrier and the future unknown.

Our ties to family in Ukraine were difficult to let go. Since Mom's parents had immigrated to America after Uncle Peter, she really wanted to go. But Father's parents and Great-Aunt Hanna were still in Ukraine. "I am old and want to spend the rest of my life in my homeland," Great-Aunt Hanna said. Father's parents also had no plans to leave their country.

My parents, brothers & sisters. I am the second one on the right.

I was fourteen years old and excited about going to America, but I didn't know that being in a foreign country, unable to speak the native language, would be so challenging. The freedoms that we would enjoy in America, would allow our family religious, educational and economic opportunities. People who have always had those freedoms, cannot understand what it is like not to have them. We chose freedom.

We sold our house and car and used the money for our immigration. On January 22, 1992, we said good-bye to our family and friends. Our Father kissed the corner of our house, which he had built, knowing he would likely never see it again. We loaded our luggage on a private bus that we rented and drove 600 miles to Moscow International Airport. After thirteen hours of flight, we landed in New York. Six hour later, we boarded another airplane and flew to Portland, Oregon. Because some of our friends and relatives immigrated before us, they were there to greet us. We were excited to see each other.

The first two weeks we stayed with our Uncle Vlad's family in Vancouver, Washington, in his three-bedroom house. One bedroom was for our uncle, his wife and their five children. The second bedroom was for our parents and their two youngest children, and the third bedroom was for us, four older girls. Our two brothers slept on couches in the living room. We slept during the day and were awake at night; it took a few days to adjust to the 12-hour time difference.

When Uncle Vlad drove us to the grocery store for the first time, I could not believe what I saw: ice cream in plastic buckets, and so many different fruits and vegetables! Our food selection in the Ukraine was not even close to what America had to offer. We were happy in Ukraine with what we had because we knew no better. In America, we thanked God for everything: food on the table, a place to live, and warm clothes.

For a while, we found oranges underneath my sister's pillow. "Why do you keep oranges under your pillow?" we asked. "Because I love oranges so much and worry that I may not have them tomorrow," answered our sister. She had hard time believing that she was in America and could eat oranges whenever she wanted.

The two weeks passed, and we were ready to move into our own place. It had not been easy to find a space given that there were ten of us and little money. Finally, we found a two-bedroom apartment. It was challenging with one bathroom and a small space, but we were in America! God had blessed us!

At one point the principal of a school came to talk with my parents about my brother's behavior. When he saw our tiny space and our lack of furniture, he left and came back in one hour with a truck full of used furniture, lamps and other items that would improve our life. We are still grateful for his kindness! It made a difference in our lives.

As I think of it today, I am so thankful to our Uncle Peter, for helping us immigrate to America. I am thankful to Uncle Vlad for letting us stay with his family in a foreign country, even though it wasn't simple for seventeen people to live together. I also thank God for the good people who helped us, and for the welfare program, which gave us food stamps and cash for living. From the bottom of my heart, I thank this country for accepting us, the Immigrants!

....

We were happy, excited and ready for a new start in America; then we started missing our old country. It was difficult to make friends. We missed our house and our native language which we understood. Most of Mom's relatives lived in Vancouver. She seemed to be happy, being close to her family. But our Father missed his family in Ukraine. (He never saw his Mother again, as she died shortly after he left, but he saw his Father ten years later.) Our parents worried about how we were going to live in America. They did not have jobs and language was a barrier. Our Father stayed home with the younger children and received Social Security disability.

English was taught in my Mom's school, but that had been twenty years before, therefore, she had limited English skills. It was difficult to function in America, and Mom understood that she would need to get a job requiring English. She constantly tried to learn the English language. I remember seeing her often fall asleep with an English/Russian dictionary in her hands.

My Father had learned German in the Ukrainian school as had the rest of the family, so we all had to start learning English. When shopping, Father carried a pencil and paper with him and drew a picture of what he needed. We, three older girls, were placed in ninth grade in the English as a Second Language (ESL) program. At our school many immigrants spoke Russian, so we did not feel lonely.

Our Mom became pregnant with her ninth child. We desperately needed a larger home. My parents looked at a few houses, but no one would rent to such a big family. One day they were buying a newspaper at a gas station and met a lady named Patricia.

"Come back in two hours. I will give you the key to my two-story, three-bedroom rental house," Patricia said.

"Thank you so much. We see your kind act as help from God," my Mom answered.

Our new house was in another part of Vancouver, therefore, we had to change schools. Because we knew very few students who spoke Russian, school became more challenging. I could not say in English what I wanted to say; if I said something wrong, I felt embarrassed. Most of the time I just remained quiet.

Making friends was difficult. I prayed to God to send me a good friend. Soon I met Katya, a new immigrant, who also did not speak English. We became friends. That day, I remember, I shared the news with Katya,

"My baby sister was born today. Her name is Vera. She is ninth in our family!"

Since then we are the best friends with Katya until today. It has been 25 years!

The first two years in High School I took English as a Second Language class. As a Junior, I took ninth grade's Standard English and received my first "A". I was so proud of myself! Those hard days with the dictionary in my hands finally paid off. During my last year in High School, I completed a Legal/Medical Office Applications program at

Clark County Skills Center. After graduating from high school, I started college.

Our school provided us with summer jobs. My first summer in America, I was 14 and working at a day care center for $4.25 per hour. With my earnings I could buy what I needed and give any extra money to my Father for the family. As children and now as adults, we have always had a great relationship with our parents. They were generous with us and we all shared our resources.

At age sixteen, I completed a traffic safety program at my high school and received my driver's license! It was not an easy accomplishment for me, but I managed to pass the test. Having a driver's license enabled me to help my Mom, as she did not drive at that time.

After four years in America, our Mom had her tenth child, our beautiful baby sister, Anna. Parents were praying to God to help them buy a small, affordable house. One day, they just drove around Vancouver and saw a "For Sale" sign on an old and inexpensive house on one acre of land. They had no credit history, no English language, and could only afford a small payment. They met with the owner.

"God tells me to sell this house to this man," the owner proclaimed pointing at my Father.

"Thank you so much for selling the house to us without even checking our credit history or income. We feel God's love to us through your action," my Father responded gratefully.

My parents bought the house and felt so lucky. The payment was low; once more God took care of us. At this time, man's word and a handshake was his bond. We remodeled the house and our Mom opened a child care business in it. We all helped her.

....

My husband's parents, Sergey and Olga Anischenko, lived in Sukhumi, in the country of Georgia, where Oleg was born. Within a year, they moved 6,300 miles to Nakhodka, Russia, by the Japanese Sea, to be closer to his Mother's family. Oleg was the second son in the family of five sons and one daughter. Both of his parents worked as tailors at a sewing company, and his Father had a second job, as a stoker at a coal company. They lived in their own house and had enough land to grow fruits, vegetables and berries. They worked hard to make a living.

The Christians in Russia and all the satellite countries were persecuted. In 1976, many Christian families sought to immigrate to America for religious reasons. Oleg's Father was persecuted and arrested for his religious, human rights work. When the iron curtain finally collapsed, Oleg's family was allowed to emigrate in 1988.

On a train, they rode 100 miles to Vladivostok. Then they flew 6,000 miles to Moscow, to get their immigration papers. Two weeks later they were able to board the train to Austria. Their family had purchased train tickets for a coupe wagon with beds, which is like a small room for the family. When Oleg's Father tried to enter the train, he was pushed out by a military commander.

"Go to the back of the train and ride with soldiers," – the commander said.

"But we have small children and bought the tickets for the coupe," – Oleg's Father objected.

"You will ride with soldiers today," – the commander answered rudely.

Oleg's family rushed to the back of the train, pushing their luggage on a metal cart. Oleg's younger brother was running in front of the cart. He tripped, fell and his leg was deeply cut by the cart. The family had no time to stop. They simply picked him up and rushed to the train, where two nice ladies helped them aboard and assisted in binding the wound.

Oleg's parents, brothers & sister. Oleg is the second tallest in the back

Oleg's family lived in Austria for two months and then immigrated to Italy. In Italy, they waited for another two months for a sponsor and documents, allowing them to enter the United States. Finally, they were able to take a plane to New York, and then to San Francisco. Due to a long flight and the time change, they were exhausted. On the flight to San Francisco, Oleg's sister went through the checkpoint, boarded the plane into the first-class seating, and fell asleep without her family knowing where she had gone. Oleg's fourteen-year-old brother, trying to be helpful, went to look for her with one of the airport security staff. Her parents found her sleeping inside the plane, but the older brother failed to make the flight. Thus, another flight for the brother had to be arranged by the sponsor.

You can only imagine the stress Oleg's parents went through while immigrating to America.

In San Francisco, earlier Russian immigrants from the church of Alexander A. Shevchenko, who came to America during 1940s, helped them. Oleg's family lived in their church for two months before renting a small apartment. At the school they attended, Oleg and his siblings were the only white students. The other students consisted of African Americans, Hispanics and Phillippinos. This was very different than Russia. As their cultural knowledge grew and their language skills improved, America became less foreign.

After two years, Oleg's family moved into the smaller, quieter and more affordable city of Modesto, California. Together, Oleg's parents sewed for themselves and for others. More Russian people immigrated to Modesto and established a Russian church there. Oleg's Mother taught Russian school, Bible school, and led a children's choir. She is a very positive and knowledgeable person. Oleg's Father was kind and had high expectations for his sons. Unfortunately, diabetes disabled him at the age of 35 and his health was weak.

....

3

Marriage is for life and divorce is a sin. If you have problems, you work them out.

Some of my cousins lived in Modesto. In time, my extended family became friends with Oleg's family. A year later, our cousins moved to live in Vancouver and Oleg came to visit them. The first time he saw me, he shared with my cousins that he liked me very much. They did not hesitate to report that news immediately to me. I was only fifteen years old and thought I was too young for love.

Two years later, one of my cousins opened an Auto Body shop in Vancouver. He knew that Oleg was responsible, so he invited him to come and work in his shop. Oleg thought this would be a great learning opportunity to improve his automotive skills. Plus, as he told me later, he could not wait to see me again. With the blessing of his parents, he moved to Vancouver to live and work. However, he had also promised his Father that he would return to Modesto after a year.

At this time, Oleg was nineteen years old and I was seventeen. We often saw each other in church and sometimes at my cousin's home. Soon, Oleg started calling me. The third time I talked to him on the phone, he shared his feelings about me.

"Olga, I really like you. I am serious about this, and with time, I would like to marry you. Would you like to be my girlfriend?"

Oleg's words really scared me. I barely knew him and wasn't ready for a relationship, much less marriage, so I kept answering, "I don't know."

"Olga, do you know anything?" Oleg asked, impatiently.

"Oleg, I just started college. Give me time to concentrate on my education. If you are very serious, call me back in a year," I answered politely.

That year hadn't been easy for both of us. For some reason, I could easily talk to other youth in church, but not to Oleg. I avoided him and did unkind things to him. For example, he would quietly wait in the hallway to speak to me after the service, but I would intentionally pass by without looking at him or greeting him. It was if he did not exist. I knew that Christians should not do this. Maybe I had those feelings of love for him inside me, but I did not want to recognize it.

During the year, Oleg had returned to Modesto, as he promised to his parents. Exactly one year after I asked Oleg to call me back in a year, he called me and said,

"Olga, the year has passed, but I still love you so much. Would you consider being my girlfriend?"

I was so shocked. During the year we had communicated very little. I was happy to hear his voice.

"I was not nice to you, Oleg. Would you ever forgive me?" I asked.

"I love you so much, Olga. I forgive you and would like to spend the rest of my life with you," Oleg said with a calming voice. "Would you consider dating me, please?"

"Give me a day to think and pray about this," I asked.

Oleg promised to call me the next day. With blond hair, blue eyes and a big beautiful smile, Oleg was the nicest young man I had ever met. He was always friendly and polite. I liked him, and my parents liked him, too. I knew if I entered a relationship with him, it was a serious step and promising basically to date him exclusively. Was I ready to do this? Did I want to do this? After much praying and asking for God's blessing, I agreed to enter into a friendship with Oleg. That relationship has grown into a great love.

For the next nine months, Oleg would drive to Vancouver once a month, twelve hours each way, to see me. While staying in Vancouver for three to four days, he would also pick up a job at my cousin's shop. On the first evening, Oleg came to see me with a huge bouquet of flowers. Our love was growing stronger every day. While he was in California, we would talk on the phone and write each other letters.

I believed that marriage is for life and divorce is a sin. If you have problems, you work them out. Things were becoming serious and I knew that if Oleg asked me to marry him, it was for life, if I said "Yes".

During one of his visits, Oleg took me out to a beautiful park besides the river and proposed to me on bended knee.

"Olga, would you marry me, please?"

"Yes!" I exclaimed with joy, and then continued, "Oleg, please get, up. You are embarrassing me on your bended knee. People are watching us!"

We were so happy together! I loved Oleg so much and he loved me. Shortly after this visit, Oleg, his parents, his pastor, and his relatives came to meet my parents and me. We celebrated our engagement. Oleg's parents brought a huge sweet Russian bread, called "Karavai", which they had made and decorated beautifully with dough flowers and a braid on top. Traditionally, a young man brings this bread to the girl he loves when he asks her to marry him. They eat this bread together. Oleg's family was wonderful. I felt their love towards me from the first day. It was a beautiful day and it just happened to be my 19th birthday.

On April 5th, 1997, Oleg and I were happily married. We promised each other to be faithful in happiness and sorrow, in richest and the poor, and stay together until death separates us. We felt deep love for each other and felt God's blessing upon us. One day I learned that Oleg's name meant "Holy and Faithful". To know that his name was connected with God only lifted up my heart more.

Our first year of marriage was a beautiful year of adjustments. We loved each other dearly, but had to find how to compromise on our different points of view. My values taught me to respect my husband and to listen to him as the head of the household, yet, we didn't always agree on what to do or how to do it. As the years pass, we have learned that we can have a difference of opinion and to respect that difference. The more freedom we give each other, the more our love and our respect for each other grows.

....

Oleg worked at an Auto Body shop, where he was a highly-skilled technician. I continued with college. A year after we were married, I completed my Associate Degree in Business Administration/Accounting. It took me three years to complete a two-year program because of my limited English skills. I was so proud of myself, being the first in my family to graduate from High School and college in America! After college, I took a job at the bank, but continued to look for a job where I could use my education.

Soon, I became pregnant. We were blessed with our first son, David, whose name means "Beloved by God". We loved being a young family, ready to assume greater responsibilities. Oleg and I came from large families and had helped our Mothers many times with child care. However, there is a process of growing into a mature parent, that nothing can teach you, except being a parent. I recognized how important it is to have parents who love you, help you, and are willing to share what they know. My parents already had three Granddaughters. David was the first Grandson for both sets of Grandparents, which gave him that special place in their hearts.

Eighteen months later, our beautiful daughter arrived. We named her Kristina, which means "Anointed, Follower of Christ". Oleg's Mother flew in from California to help us for two weeks. She was wonderful, letting me rest, recover and care for Kristina, while she took care of David, prepared meals and maintained the laundry. My Mom helped as much as she could but was limited because she was operating her business as a full-time child care provider.

When Oleg's Mom flew back to California, it was my first day alone with the two children. I remember sitting on a couch with a crying Kristina and David. I felt like they wanted to show me who could cry louder, each wanting my attention. As a young mother, I didn't know which child to take care of first, so I also started crying. Yes, it helped, and after couple of minutes, we all calmed down and understood that we were a team and needed to be nice to each other.

Most of the time, David was nice to Kristina, but sometimes he was jealous and didn't want to share his Mommy. In the mornings, when they woke up and saw each other, they were so happy, jumping on the bed and hugging each other. It was such a great blessing, seeing our children that God had given us.

Two months before Kristina was born, we bought our first house, thus Oleg worked more hours to provide additional money for our family. After work, he returned home tired and in need of rest, but the minute he saw David and Kristina, who were excited to see him, Oleg's tiredness disappeared. He picked up the children and played with them. Our love as a family and as a couple continued to grow.

....

When Kristina turned one, I decided to look for work. I was lucky. With my first application and first interview, I got a full-time job with the Women, Infants and Children (WIC) program. This became an important and rewarding endeavor in my life. The first four years I worked as a bi-lingual clerk at the front desk. I knew that with my degree I could have found a better job, but I was happy due to four elements: a good team, good pay, good benefits, and close to home. I learned job skills and more. I learned how to handle working relationships with the clients and co-workers, how to be patient, to respect each individual for who they are, and not to impose my personal judgments on others. Experience is a great teacher.

My Mom watched our children while Oleg and I worked. Often, when I came from work to pick up our children, she gave me freshly prepared food to take home. You just don't go home as a wife. You have a family to care for, you have a husband and children, and you have to prepare a meal.

One time, I came to Mom's house to pick up our children after work. She had just cooked vegetables for the potato salad. It only needed to be cut in pieces and mixed with a dressing. She gave it to me.

"Take it home and make salad for your family," she insisted.

"What about you?" I asked.

"I can cook more vegetables," Mom stated emphatically.

I thanked Mom, got into my car and cried. My Mom, who worked since nearly six o'clock in the morning, has given me her dinner, so I would not have to work as hard. I felt ashamed that I was not ready yet to do what she did. Thank you, Mom, for your loving heart!

....

The children were growing and were so different. With curly hair and dimples on his cheeks, David looked a lot like my Dad. With blond curly hair and big blue eyes Kristina looked more like Oleg. David was neat and liked to play alone. But Kristina was the happiest and bravest child on earth and needed company.

When they were growing up, they were such funny children. One time my Mom was crying. David came up to her and said, "Grandma, don't cry. I will buy you some ice cream."

And when Kristina was growing up, she thought she could reach the moon. One evening, Kristina and I sat on a swing. She saw the moon and asked, "Mom, what is it?" "The moon," I said. "Can I take it home?" Kristina asked.

Kristina loved ripping flowers and giving them to me. She would rip flowers in our garden, in our neighbor's garden, by the church, and I had to teach her where she could rip flowers and where she could not.

Oleg's birthday was coming up. "What present should we buy for Daddy?" I asked. "Chips and Pepsi!" Kristina said excited. "No, our Dad loves coffee!" David said seriously.

One evening Oleg came home late from work. David was already sleeping. Then I realized – it was too quiet, which meant that Kristina was creating trouble. Quietly I walked to the kitchen and saw her with scissors in her hands. Her beautiful curly blond hair was already cut off and on the floor. I didn't know how to react – to cry or to scream at her? With a wide-opened mouth I was speechless... I hugged her, put her to bed and took her to a hair dresser the next morning. Those beautiful curls are still in Kristina's baby book.

Our firstborn, David   Our daughter, Kristina

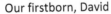

When Kristina was four years old, I became pregnant for the third time. After my ultrasound, I received a phone call from my doctor, while I was at work.

"I don't like your ultrasound results, Olga," the doctor announced. "It shows that your baby-boy could have Down's syndrome, Trisomy 18 or Spinal Bifida. Olga, your child may be born very ill, not able to walk, and not even look like a normal person. Come in to do more testing."

After I hung up the phone, my hands were sweaty and shaky, and tears covered my eyes. Good thing no one saw my pale face. I couldn't concentrate or tell anyone the terrible news. How could I? "I will have an ill child? It can't happen to me."

After few minutes, I calmed dawn, walked to my supervisor's office and asked for permission to leave work and see the doctor. She let me. It isn't safe to drive, when you are scared and can't concentrate, but I drove to the doctor's office.

"Olga, we can do an amniocentesis test to make sure the ultrasound results are correct," the doctor said.

"How do you perform this test?" I asked.

"With a needle we will poke your stomach and will take a small amount of amniotic fluid to check for genetic abnormalities. We don't have to do it today. You can talk to your husband and let me know of your decision."

The doctor gave me a brochure with this information. I spoke with Oleg at home. He was calm, but I worried.

"Our child is healthy. Everything will be okay," he said.

In the brochure I read that there is a 60% miscarriage chance after this test. I called the doctor.

"We will not do this test," I said. "Even if you did the test and it was abnormal, we would still not abort the baby. We know abortion is a sin. We will pray, and God will help us."

Oleg didn't show that he worried, but I did. I couldn't calm down. Being pregnant, I still had to continue working, drive children to Mom's house in early mornings and pick them up after work, clean, cook and take care of the children. At night I would wake up at 2 or 3 A.M. and pray to God, begging Him to heal our baby. Only Mom, one of my sister and few friends knew about this problem. I was embarrassed to tell this news to someone or ask for prayers. I kept it all to myself. "How can I go back to work and show him to my co-workers? How can I show a disabled child to my friends and family? What would this say about me?"

When the time came for our baby to be born, I was in tears and couldn't imagine what he would look like. But God heard our prayers and saw that we were not ready to accept a disabled child into our family. With tears of joy, we welcomed our healthy baby Michael. For us it was a miracle from God! Michael's name means "Who is like God".

When we brought Michael home, David and Kristina were happy to see him, but then they started acting up, crying and being jealous. Oleg was at work, and I thought, "What is going on?" Then I understood that they needed more of my attention, and I had to learn how to be a mother of three children.

Being parents of three is vastly different than being parents of two. I wanted to stay home to breastfeed Michael. WIC, my employer, supported my choice to combine maternity leave, saved sick and vacation leave, and time off without pay to enable me to be off work for eleven months.

....

When I returned to work, there were some changes at the WIC program due to budget constraints. This required all clerks to also be cross-trained as Nutrition Assistants. Thus, in addition to scheduling appointments, issuing WIC vouchers, and answering a multiple-lined phone, my new duties included diet and weight assessments, checking hemoglobin and teaching the nutrition classes.

This offered several challenges. I was scared of blood. To do a hemoglobin test, I had to poke a client's finger and deal with the blood. I also had to speak in front of people, but had no confidence to do so. How do you get up in front of a group of people when you have an accent and have no confidence in your ability to speak? I expressed these and other concerns to my boss.

"Olga, you have a choice. You either do it, or you quit," she said.

"I need a job. It is a good job with good income and benefits. I have no choice as to keep the job and learn my new duties," upset, I answered.

It is amazing what you can accomplish, if you put your mind to improving your skills. Two years later, in addition to my previous duties, I began teaching pregnant women about breastfeeding and helping them after delivery.

....

In 2007, ten years into our marriage, Oleg changed to another auto body shop. Our income and benefits dramatically increased. Our house was on a busy street and not safe for our children, so we decided to buy a bigger house in a better neighborhood. We also bought two new cars on credit. Our life was good. We thought the money would always flow and we would be fine forever.

Raising our children was fun, but it also required lots of work to assure that our children were getting the best that we could provide them. I even volunteered in our church to teach Russian language to a class, which David attended. I understood the importance of our children knowing two languages, so I taught them how to read, write and speak Russian.

We were involved parents, trying to provide every opportunity for our children, and especially those opportunities that we had not had as children. David was growing up as a serious and neat boy. Happy Kristina always helped Mom in the kitchen and took a good care of her younger brother, Michael. She loved doing his hair and dress him up. And Michael was growing as a happy and patient baby. It was like he understood that I had to care for his brother and sister as well. With the straight hair and blue eyes, Michael looked a lot like me. When Michael was growing up, we noticed that he was a very brave kid. At the age of four, he started riding his bike without training wheels, and two weeks later he rode a real dirt bike! Oleg loved children and provided what he could for them. Life with three children was so busy, but worth every moment of it!

Our third child, Michael

....

As a family, we regularly attended church and read the Bible. Serving God and being close to Him was important to us. Oleg and I often discussed what our parents taught us, what we saw in church, and what we hoped to have in our life. We were a little dissatisfied that we were Christians, but didn't experience God's big power in our life. In the Bible, the book of Revelation 3:15-17, we read that God preferred for people to be either "cold" or "hot", but not "lukewarm". It is better to be a non-believer, than to claim that you know God and profane His name with your bad deeds.

Up to this point in our marriage we were Christians, but we took being Christians for granted. For example, reading the Bible and attending church was something we did, but we weren't fully engaged. We didn't do it with joy or excitement, because we felt that we were obligated to do it. We never questioned the relationship of ourselves to our faith. We just accepted what we were told. But now Oleg and I wanted to experience more of God's love, power and presence in our life. So here, as I already said in the beginning of the book, our journey began...

One evening, when we knelt to pray to God, I heard Oleg pray, **"God, I am so tired of being a lukewarm Christian. I want to have a personal relationship with You! I want to experience more of Your love, more of Your power and more of Your presence in my life. Please send a situation into my life that will show me WHO YOU REALLY ARE!"** For a moment, I felt scared and wondered what Oleg was talking about. "How would this change our family and our life?" But I loved Oleg and trusted him. I thought he must know what he is asking for, but I had no idea what this would mean for our family. It struck me--it was an important moment in our lives.

From that day, Oleg totally changed. He began reading the Bible daily, sharing what he learned with us, and seeking answers for questions he had. It was like he was driven and wanted to know more. After he finished reading the book of Romans in the Bible, he did not understand it and had lots of questions. He wanted to know who the Apostle Paul wrote the book of Romans to, what he meant, and did it apply to us? We had been taught that certain parts of the Bible applied only to Gentiles, while other parts applied to Jews.

One day Oleg told me, "You know, Olga, if I want to know more about God, I probably have to learn more about the days of Moses, Jesus and His Apostles."

I wondered what information he will be able to find. Oleg used the internet for research and was excited to share with me daily what new insights he learned. His love and interest in the truth about God grew. He simply had to know more. As we discussed and thought about what he learned, we began to have questions about what we were taught and prayed to God to reveal us the Truth. I also read the Bible, but hearing what Oleg shared with me was very interesting and unknown to me before. **We began to question what God actually required of us, and what was the purpose of our life.** Each question would lead us to other questions, like an unwinding spool of yarn. As a family, we studied and grew together in our faith.

....

At the same time, significant changes happened in our life. Oleg's job with a good salary was an hour drive each way. He decided to switch to a closer location, to be able to spend more time with the family. Unfortunately, his new location was not as busy. Oleg's income decreased because there was less work and he was paid on a piece rate.

Oleg's Father passed away at the age of 54. It was a big hit for Oleg's whole family. It took them a while to accept it and move on.

At about the same time, I injured my shoulders, which led to pain for the next few years and frequent doctor visits. Also, the economy took a downfall and our WIC department received a layoff notice due to lack of funding. I was going to lose my job in a year.

Between the house payment, car payments, our credit cards and other expenses, I wondered if we would ever be able to pay off our debt. I often cried out to God that we didn't have the strength to handle this.

One day, my friend invited me to a prayer group, where God spoke to me, **"My daughter, give your worry to Me and I will help you. All I need from you is PRAISE!"** So, every time I worried, I praised God and His peace would come. It was such a wonderful feeling! Inside my heart I knew that God would help us.

The downturn in the economy also impacted my brothers and sisters. At that time, our parents started a family prayer time on Wednesday evenings at their house. Together with our children, we worshiped God and prayed for our needs and for needs of others.

One evening, my Aunt prophesied to most of the people in the group, and then to me, **"My daughter, prepare yourself for an ordeal. Pray often for strength when a disaster comes to your family."**

I was scared and thought that something bad would happen to Oleg. Later that evening, my Grandmother came up to me and said, **"Learn to be humble and patient."** I praised God often and prayed for His protection over our family.

....

One month was replaced by another and the time of my lay-off was getting closer. We made financial changes in our family. Unbelievably, our debt became smaller. We sold both cars, eliminating two big payments and bought cheaper cars. Saving every penny, we tried our hardest to pay off our credit cards. I stopped going shopping and sometimes even went to a food bank to get help with food. The year of lay-off notice gave us time to adjust to a lower income.

Surprisingly, a year and a half later, we were debt free, except the mortgage payment, which was still very high relative to our income. We sought a loan modification, which took about three years to be finalized. Looking back, we were amazed at how God had helped us. I stayed at home with David, Kristina, and Michael, who were 11, 10 and 6 years old. We were happy together and thanked God for blessing us.

....

4

You never know what your real values are until you are faced with difficult real-life choices.

We love children and were delighted to find out that I was pregnant with our fourth child. In the sixth week of the pregnancy I developed complications and went to see the doctor.

"Olga, the ultrasound shows two fetuses," the doctor said. "But one is smaller and not developing, and the other one is bigger and growing. This creates a risk of miscarriage. I need to prescribe strict bed rest for you."

"A miscarriage? Two babies? One is not developing?" A sense of dread descended over me like a shroud. Scared, I implored God to save our baby, if it was His will.

....

A few weeks later, I felt better and one of the fetuses survived. At four months of pregnancy I went for a second ultrasound.

"It is a BOY!" the nurse said. Then she paused, seemed worried. "Actually, let me go get the doctor," she said. "There seems to be a problem here."

The doctor came and very carefully examined the ultrasound images. The look of his face registered concern. I knew immediately, there were serious problems.

"Olga, when we do the ultrasound, we can see if the baby's heart is healthy. If a baby has Downs Syndrome or Hypoplastic Left Heart Syndrome, the heart looks different. I can see the left side of your baby's heart is not developing. It means he has Hypoplastic Left Heart Syndrome, which is not good news."

For a moment, I couldn't speak. My heart started beating rapidly and my hands started shaking.

"What? Our baby has health problems?" tears filled my eyes.

"This is a very rare heart defect which occurs in only 1 of 2,500 births. Usually, with this syndrome, 50% of babies also have Downs Syndrome. Your baby has no chance for life once born," the doctor explained.

"Is there anything you can do to fix this problem?" I asked shakely.

"Previously, these babies had been dying right after birth. But 30 years ago, the doctors began doing surgeries to correct such problems. Usually they do an open-heart surgery on the first day of the baby's life. Then, another surgery at six months, and the third one at the age of 3 years. The recovery is very difficult and not many babies survive these surgeries," the doctor answered with a sad tone.

I was devastated and shocked by the news and could not believe this was happening. Why had God allowed me to survive the risk of miscarriage, to let this happen to my child? I wasn't sure if I would be able to handle this situation, but just because I thought this, it didn't make the problems of my pregnancy go away. What if I could not handle this situation emotionally or physically? What about our other children? The questions raced through my mind. Then reality grabbed me. No matter how many questions I had, none of the answers would take away the harsh reality of this pregnancy.

"Olga, I am referring you to a high-risk pregnancy specialist, in case you consider an abortion," the doctor continued.

"I can't do an abortion. This is our baby, whom we already love so much."

All in tears I left the doctor's office. Outside, shaking, crying, and having a hard time concentrating, I called Oleg at work and told him the devastating news.

"Our baby is a boy, who is having many heart issues. He will die if we don't do the surgeries. Why did God let it happen to us?"

"Olga, God will help us. We should trust in His will," Oleg said with a calm voice.

But I thought, reality is reality and miracles just don't happen in today's world. Men often hide their feelings and don't talk about them as much as women do. I wondered whether this was Oleg' true feeling or if he was telling me what I needed to hear.

....

That minute I remembered the Bible story of Job that Oleg and I had recently read. Job was a blameless, upright person, who feared God and shunned evil. Satan thought that Job was righteous because God had blessed him.

"If you take everything away from Job, I will prove to You that Job will curse you," Satan told God.

"I let you test Job. I am sure he will not curse Me. He is a righteous and blameless person," God replied to Satan.

With God's permission Satan tested Job, by destroying his wealth, killing all his children and taking his health away from Job. But Job didn't curse God. He remained loyal to Him. Satan was proved wrong and God blessed Job even more than before, by giving him more children and wealth. I wondered if God was testing us, as He had tested Job?

I drove directly to Mom's house to see and talk to her. I knew her comfort would be forth coming.

"Our baby has very serious heart issues and may be born very ill," I broke in tears. "He may not even survive..."

"Daughter, please don't cry. Give your worry to God. He is in charge of everything and He will help you. We will be praying for your baby," hugging me, Mom tried to calm me down.

I picked up our children and went home. Later that evening, Oleg and I talked to our children.

"David, Kristina and Michael, we have news for you!"

The kids came and sat next to us, ready to listen.

"The baby in Mama's womb is a boy. You will have a little brother!" Oleg said.

David and Michael jumped up, being so happy about baby-brother.

"But I wanted a sister," Kristina started crying.

I comforted Kristina and shared the rest of the news, "We also have very sad news for you. Your baby-brother has many issues with his heart. When he is born, he may not even live long. He might require multiple surgeries and may not come home right away."

The children were scared. With tears on their eyes, they looked at us, not sure what to ask, how to react or what to answer.

"We need to pray to God and ask Him to heal our baby," Oleg said. "God is powerful. He heals people, if it is His will."

Oleg embraced the children in his arms. We all prayed and cried out to God, asking for His mercy.

....

One week later, while Oleg was at work, I had a second ultrasound at a high-risk Obstetrician/Gynecology clinic.

"Olga, this ultrasound confirms that all the problems with your baby's heart are real," summarized the doctor.

"Why did it happen to our baby? Did I do something wrong?" I asked through tears.

"No one knows why the Hypoplastic Left Heart Syndrome occurs. As with most congenital heart defects, there is no known cause."

"Can you tell me more about the surgery?" I asked.

"Sure," the doctor said. "It is a very complicated open-heart surgery. Eighty-five percent of babies survive the first surgery. Less babies survive the second surgery. And a lot less babies survive all three surgeries. With time, their heart becomes very weak. They require a heart transplant. If they can't wait long enough for the transplant, they die. Only a few individuals live up to thirty years."

The doctor paused, and I did not know what to say or ask. What a terrible dilemma for a parent to face. Our baby will die if we don't do the surgery. But, I also didn't want my baby to go through the pain of surgery…

"Olga, you may consider an abortion," the doctor said.

"No," quickly escaped my lips. "I love my baby so much already. There is no way we can do an abortion. I am also from a Christian family and we know that abortion is a sin. I feel that aborting my baby would be the same as killing him. I can't do that. His life is in God's hands. I will give my baby all chances for life, and I know God will help me."

The doctor looked at me, regretfully. He knew I had no idea what I was facing if I decided to go with open-heart surgeries on a newborn baby.

"I will refer you to a cardiologist," the doctor said. "They will do an echocardiogram, which will show more details of your baby's heart. Talk to your husband. You still have time to do an abortion, if you decide."

I left the doctor's office and called Oleg.

"The ultrasound confirmed again that our baby's heart is badly malformed and is not going to change," I said through tears.

"God will help us, Olga. Please don't cry," Oleg tried to calm me with little success.

"I can't accept it. I don't want to accept it. Why did God let it happen to our baby? Did we do something wrong? Is He punishing us for something?"

"Olga, we don't know why it happened. You know we didn't sin. I don't think God is punishing us. For some reason, He let it happen and He will help us through it," Oleg did his best to soothe me.

Until that day, I was hoping that it was a mistake, but it seemed that both Oleg and I were powerless, and that God had failed us. Driving home, I cried out to God, hardly seeing the freeway through tears. "Why, God, did You decide to give us an ill baby? Are you punishing us for something? Show me, what is it? I will do whatever it takes to fix it. I just want our baby to be healthy." But God was quiet. I didn't hear Him answer…

At home, I continued to cry and implore God to heal our baby. I could do this since Oleg was at work and the children were at school. I was home alone. No one could see me cry. After a while, I began to sense a different perspective. I felt as if through our experience with the third pregnancy, God prepared us to better handle the issues in the fourth pregnancy. The doctors predicted that our third child could be born with serious health problems, but he was a healthy baby. Could it happen again? Here we were, facing a decision: the doctors were telling us there was a huge problem and suggesting an abortion; our religious values said we should not do an abortion. How do you decide such a critical question? I knew Oleg and I needed to think and agree, and it had to come from our heart and values.

....

I knew our situation would be nearly unbearable and that we would need lots of advice, love, help, comfort and support, to be able to deal with this complicated pregnancy.

I first turned to my Father. We share a special connection; I know he will always be there for me. His words and guidance come from the heart. When I was a child, I always heard him pray every night and I knew God heard him. My Father also often told us how God healed others through the hands of his Grandfather. I knew we had to pray.

"Dad, our baby's heart issues are so serious. Can you please pray for us?" I asked my Father.

"Olga, the news is terrifying, but please, take care of yourself," my Father said. "Don't worry. God will take care of you and your baby. We will pray, and God will help. I love you, Daughter. Be strong."

I know he worried and wanted to help me. Even though there was little he could do, he could continue loving us and praying for us.

I also called my Mother-in-law to tell her the news and ask her to pray for us. She is such a wonderful lady. She tried to calm me down and asked me not to worry, reminding me that often the doctors are wrong. She promised to pray for us.

Next, I called our friends, relatives, co-workers and neighbors, and asked them to pray for us. The illness of our baby did not only add worry to Oleg and me. It affected our whole big family and the people who surrounded us. Everyone questioned why God let it happen. People didn't know what to tell us or how to comfort us, yet they promised to pray for us.

....

We sought support and comfort from the ministers of our church. We spoke to them about the serious problems of our baby, expecting prayers and the traditional anointing of the holy oil. Instead, we heard the opposite, "Check your lives. Maybe there is something for which God is punishing you. God doesn't usually give ill children to Christians."

Oleg and I were shocked. We expected support rather than more pain. We knew we had done nothing wrong. We thought God is merciful. Everything comes from God. Nothing is done without His will. It is only God who judges us. Returning home, we prayed asking God to heal our son and to give us strength and understanding to accept His will.

Every day I was in tears. Often, I called my best friend, Katya, with my questions. She knew I needed help.

"Call Pastor Ivan." she suggested. "He is a positive and a knowledgeable person. He will answer your questions."

One day, when I just couldn't find peace, I called the Pastor Ivan, whom I had never met. I asked him my questions. His answers were like a breath of fresh air that poured new life and strength into our lives.

"If you don't feel that you have done anything wrong before God, stop asking for forgiveness," the Pastor Ivan said. **"Praise God for everything that He is doing, even for what you don't understand today. The Bible says that everything comes from God and nothing is done without His will. It was His will to give you an ill baby. Maybe God is preparing you for something. He may do His work through you. Praise God for everything and be patient. It will not last forever. Usually, the sun comes out after a thunderstorm!"**

This unexpected word of encouragement strengthened our belief that everything comes from God. Although we did not understand everything, we felt relieved after our conversation with this minister. We thanked God that this minister inspired us and poured in us a positive energy. It's like he gave us life back. In our tormented heart God's peace appeared again, which is above all our thoughts and doubts.

....

In those days, our church fought for us in prayers. We also turned to different churches and asked them to pray for God to heal our baby. Once young people from a neighboring city came and gave us the prophetic word that they received in a prayer about our situation. It was said that our son will be healed in the mother's womb! With tears of joy we thanked God. We believed in prophecies and it was what we wanted to hear …

....

A month after my appointment with the high-risk Obstetrician/Gynecology specialist, I saw a cardiologist. Oleg came with me. We were hopeful that the change would be positive, but the echocardiogram showed no improvement. Our son would still need all the surgeries and spend his early life in the hospital.

"I would recommend you consider an abortion," said the cardiologist. "The surgery is very complicated, and your baby may not even survive."

The cardiologist gave us time to think and left the room. She was the third specialist who had recommended abortion. Oleg and I sat hand in hand. I didn't want our baby to go through the surgery, and I didn't want him to die either. I knew the abortion was same as killing a person. I couldn't stop our son's life.

"We believe in the God of Abraham, Isaac and Jacob, and He will help us," Oleg said. "There is no way we will do an abortion."

When the cardiologist came back, we told her our decision and left the hospital. On our way home, we prayed and wondered when God was going to step in and heal our baby. Our faith gave us hope.

Every month we met with the same cardiologist and had echocardiograms, which showed that the problems with our baby's heart were still there. As the fetus grew older, the option of an abortion would no longer exist. This didn't matter because we weren't willing to consider an abortion. **Every time, the doctors were telling us how severe our baby's heart defects were, Oleg and I loved our expected son more and more. We still had that hope that God would heal him.**

....

A normal pregnancy is forty weeks. Unfortunately, at twenty-six weeks, my blood sugar started rising. I developed Gestational Diabetes and didn't look or feel healthy at all.

"Olga, you need to start eating healthy," the doctor said. "I will refer you to a dietitian, who will tell you which diet to follow. Olga, you also need to start pricking your finger three times daily to check your blood sugar. I am afraid you may need to start insulin shots soon."

"I can poke my finger and check the sugar level, but I am so scared of insulin shots. I promise I will do everything possible to keep my blood sugar level in control," I said.

I have never had Diabetes. I was young and thought it only happened to old people. A week later, my blood sugar was still very high. The idea of shots scared me. I couldn't imagine giving myself a shot, so I tried even harder to eat healthy. Luckily, my blood sugar level dropped to an acceptable range.

At twenty-eight weeks, my blood pressure began to rise, and I started to retain water. My body seemed to fill up like a balloon, which made me even more uncomfortable. I had a doctor's visit again.

"Olga, I am worried that you may develop preeclampsia. We may need to hospitalize you," the doctor said.

"What is preeclampsia?" I asked. "How can I develop it?"

"It is a serious condition, characterized by high blood pressure and protein in the urine. It occurs when the placenta starts functioning improperly. This condition can cause respiratory problems and restriction of your baby's growth. It can also damage your liver and kidneys. The only cure for preeclampsia is to deliver the baby early."

"Our baby is sick and now my life and health is in danger? But, there is no way you can hospitalize me. My children need me at home."

"I hope we don't have to hospitalize you, but time will tell," the doctor said.

How do you believe the doctors if you feel fine? In truth, I tried to rationalize the problem away. At home, I tried harder to rest and follow the doctor's directions, hoping that my blood pressure would not rise.

....

A week later, I developed a bad headache and just felt awful. I drove to my Mom's house to check my blood pressure on her machine. It was 167/107. Normal is 120/80. At that time, I was thirty-two years old and had no idea that those numbers were very high for anyone, much less for a pregnant woman. My Mom worried and told me to call the doctor. I called and spoke with a nurse.

"Olga, lay on the left side for one hour and check again," the nurse instructed. "If the blood pressure does not decrease, go to the emergency room immediately. From such high blood pressure, your baby might die any minute, or you might have a stroke."

I laid on my left side for an hour. How do you stay calm when you are worried? I didn't know. I tried, but my blood pressure did not decrease. Oleg came home from work. He and I left the children at my Mom's house and went to the Southwest Washington Medical Center (SWMC) in Vancouver. After six hours at the hospital, the doctor prescribed me medications to lower my blood pressure and let me go home.

The next day, I was okay and just rested. The following morning my blood pressure was high again, so I called the nurse.

"Olga, get to the hospital as soon as possible because your baby and you can die any minute," the nurse instructed.

Oleg and I left our three children at my Mom's house and drove to the Emergency Room. The doctors immediately hospitalized me. They put an IV with medications in my arm to decrease my blood pressure. I felt normal, except for a terrible headache, but what the doctors were telling me made it sound like I was very sick and in a serious trouble.

Oleg stayed with me. He was calm, but worried. Late in the evening, he left to pick up the children and go home. He had to continue caring for our children and supporting our family. I don't know what he thought or told the children that evening. My Mom told me later that our children were scared and prayed that nothing bad would happen to me and the baby.

....

My evening at the hospital was quiet. The nurse attached a monitor to my stomach, so the nurse and I could hear my baby's heartbeat. The medications were working, and my blood pressure decreased slightly. Surprisingly, I was calm and accepted everything as it happened. I now was sure that my life and the life of our unborn son was in danger. I prayed to God for His help. Resting quietly, I read a book and made a few phone calls before I fell asleep.

Luckily, the next morning everything seemed to be okay. I thought I might be able to return home. Unfortunately, a test showed protein in my urine and the doctor said I should stay in the hospital another day. I was really disappointed because my oldest sister Tanya had asked me several months ago to save the date for a baby shower for me that evening. Even though my seven sisters, two sisters-in-law and I knew that our baby was very ill and might not survive, we rarely talked about it. Planning a baby shower for me was a normal process. That is what sisters and friends do for every expectant Mother. Tanya had worked very hard to have a baby shower for me that evening. All the guests were invited. I didn't want to disappoint her, but now I didn't think I was going to be able to attend. Surprisingly, later in the day, my blood pressure decreased.

"Olga, I will give you a two-hour pass to go to your baby shower," the doctor said. "Then you have to come back to the hospital. Be very careful."

"Thank you!" I exclaimed. "I am so happy you let me go. This means so much to me!"

Maybe the doctor let me go because if she told me I couldn't go, my blood pressure might rise higher than if I would go. In retrospect, it might seem crazy, but at the time the baby shower was very important to me. Sometimes, we get our priorities mixed up and just do things that in hindsight we would never do.

My friend, Katya, picked me up at the hospital and drove me to the party. The guests were waiting for me at my sister's house. Her living room was beautifully decorated in lime and brown colors. The sign "It's a Boy!" hung on the wall and delicious food filled the table. The party was wonderful. My family and friends came to support me. They knew I was ill and they prayed for me. I thanked everyone for coming and told them I had only a two-hour-pass from the doctor. We ate, opened presents and took pictures. My ten-year-old daughter Kristina brought me food, opened the presents for me, and was just happy I was with her. The time flew by quickly.

"Friends, I don't have time to read your cards," I said. "But I will read them at the hospital. I promise."

"It's okay, Olga. We wish you luck and we will pray for you," my friends and family answered. They prayed for me. It felt good to be surrounded by loved ones, who wanted our baby to live, and their gifts reflected it.

Happy that I could attend, I returned to the hospital. I was tired and went to bed. The nurse attached the monitor again to my belly. She turned it on every thirty minutes to check the baby's heartbeat. I felt normal with no pain or headache and fell asleep. At about 11 p.m., a beeping noise woke me up. Frightened, I opened my eyes wide, looked at the monitor and saw that our baby's heart beat had dropped dramatically from 150 to 56 beats per minute. In panic, I pressed the help button. The nurse ran into my room.

"Olga, turn to your left side!" she instructed.

I did. The baby's heart beat went up. I calmed down and fell asleep again. In the morning the nurse told me that during the night, my baby's heart beat had slowed down three more times.

....

5

Do not be afraid, for God is always with you,
even though you don't see Him.

The next morning, I called Oleg. This was the first day of school for the new year. Normally, we would drop our children at my Mom's house. Then the children would ride the school bus to the school near her house and in the afternoon, return for day care. But this year, because of the pregnancy and my plans to stay at home, I had transferred our children to the school nearest our house.

Oleg had no idea what it took to get David, Kristina and Michael ready for school in the morning. I was worried and wanted to know if he had survived, so I called him. He said it was hectic without me at home. He had to get the children ready for school, prepare breakfast and lunch for them, figure out the bus routine and get to work on time. He thought he did okay, but wished I was home to do that. I also wished I had been there to help him, but secretly was glad he now would find out what I did every day.

After talking to Oleg, I sat on my hospital bed and started reading the cards from my baby shower. After reading a few, my eyes paused on the third card:

"How all the *Angels* must have smiled
When *Jesus* chose this newborn *Child*
For you to love and *cuddle*, too -
A *miracle* that's all for you!"

Tears filled my eyes as I thought, "Why did Jesus choose an ill baby for me?" I felt my baby move... He probably felt my worries and wanted to let me know that everything would be okay.

The doctors came to my room and said, "Olga, it would be better for us to transfer you to Oregon Health and Science University (OHSU) in Portland. They specialize in heart surgeries that your baby would need right after delivery. We worry that your baby might be born early."

"I still have ten weeks to be pregnant," I said. "I can't have my baby today. I just want everything to return to normal and go home."

"Olga, you will be safer at OHSU. We need your permission to transfer you there."

"It's okay," I said. "You can transfer me there."

I knew it would be best for me and my baby. I called my husband again and told him the news. Then, I got ready for the transfer.

"Riding in an ambulance is a new experience for me. I am scared because I always associate the ambulance with people who have serious medical problems or are dying," I told the doctor my concern.

"You will be safe," the doctor assured me. "Everything will be okay."

"We need you to lay on the stretcher," the paramedic said.

"I can walk to the ambulance myself," I answered.

"Olga, it is for your and our safety. You need to lie on the stretcher."

I did. They wheeled me out through the halls of the hospital. I didn't look or feel like I was sick. Someone young like me shouldn't need to be in a stretcher. I was the center of attention and it embarrassed me.

The ride was smooth with no sirens and no flashing lights. Inside the ambulance, my blood pressure increased and the nurse worried. When we arrived at OHSU, the driver wheeled me out from the ambulance. On a stretcher, I met the faces of new doctors, nurses and patients. Again, I could not believe it was me on that stretcher. Embarrassed, I was ready to hide my face under the blanket.

The paramedics took me to the intensive care room of the delivery unit. Two nurses gave me medications, started IVs, measured my blood pressure, and took blood for several tests. Then, the cardiologist, neonatologist and medical students came to introduce themselves.

The cardiologist said, "Olga, we will try to keep you pregnant as long as possible, because it is too early for you baby to be born."

"I know. I still have ten weeks to be pregnant. I can't have my baby born today," I answered, not even thinking of all the things that can really go wrong...

The nurses monitored the baby's heartbeat. During the day, the monitor would often beep to show that the baby's heart rate was dropping and then it would recover. I did not know a lot about Preeclampsia and did not ask many questions because the nurses were busy. They were completing doctor's orders, trying to decide if I should eat or not. I was very hungry, but had to wait and didn't know why. Later, I understood that they did not want me to eat before the surgery. They were not sure how soon they might have to do the C-section. I was given a shot with steroids, which was supposed to help our baby's lungs open, in case he was born early.

In the evening, Oleg and the children came to visit me. The children told me about their first day at school and then asked, "How soon you are coming home, Mama?"

"I hope, very soon," I said.

"Today after work it took me two hours to read all the papers that our children brought from school," Oleg said. "I had to sign so many of them and wished you were home to do that."

I just smiled and said, "It is good for you, honey, to see what mothers usually do, all the things which seem to be easy."

After about an hour, Oleg and the children left for home. Tired, I fell asleep.

....

Just before midnight, a worried nurse woke me up.

"Olga, your baby's heart is stopping about every five minutes," she said. "The doctors are deciding whether to do the C-section or not."

Frightened and sleepy, I was trying to wake up and realize what was happening. Three doctors walked into my room.

"Why is my baby's heart stopping every five minutes?" I asked, confused.

"Your high blood pressure and the protein in your urine is causing your baby's heart to stop," the first doctor explained. **"His heart defect is not the problem. It is you, Olga, who developed not only preeclampsia, but eclampsia, the final and most severe phase. Your placenta started to secrete substances that can cause dysfunction in your blood vessels. You may start having seizures or go into a coma. It also can damage your liver and kidneys. Both you and the baby can die. Basically, your body is killing your baby."**

"Olga, with his heart defect, your baby has less than 1% chance to survive," added the second doctor. "You have two options. One is to let the nature take its course and let your baby die. We will induce you and remove the baby from your womb without surgery. The second option is to do an emergency C-section. We would not recommend the

C-section because it's a major surgery and your baby has such a small chance to live."

Even though the doctors had warned me, I didn't really believe that it would come to this. Let my baby die? What is happening? Where is Oleg? I need his help and support! I thought.

"Do I have time to call my husband?" I asked.

"Yes, you do," the doctor answered and stepped out to the hall.

I called Oleg and told him as fast as I could, "Our baby's heart is stopping every 5 minutes. He is dying. The doctors are asking if we should let him die or do an emergency C-section on me. I need you to come to the hospital as soon as possible, please. I will call my Father and ask him to come and spend the night with our children. I will call you back."

I quickly called my Father and asked if he could spend the night with our children. My Father said he will and promised to pray for us.

I called Oleg back to ask him what to do, but for some reason he didn't pick up the phone. I tried again. No answer warned me.

"Where is Oleg? Why he doesn't answer?" I sat on my hospital bed, confused. Every minute counted. I thought to myself, "How can I say, 'I am willing to let my baby die?'" Even if he has a 1% chance to survive, I should give it to him. The doctors should do the C-section. Even if my baby does not survive, I will have a scar to remember him by. **THERE IS GOD IN HEAVEN, WHO GIVES LIFE AND WHO TAKES IT AWAY. I will give my baby all his chances. I know he will live!"**

The doctors came back into my room and asked again, "So, Olga, what have you decided?"

"My husband is on his way here," I answered with a shaky voice. "Please do the C-section. I will give my baby all his chances for life. God will make that final decision about our baby's life."

"Are you sure, Olga? This surgery is a major procedure, which we would prefer not to do on you."

"Yes, I am sure."

"Would you like us to save your baby when he is born?" the doctor asked.

"What do you mean?" I asked confused.

"Would you like us to let him die or provide him with breathing help and medications for his heart?"

"I would like you to do everything possible to save his life. God will take his life, if it is time, but I will do everything possible to help our son live."

The doctors were quiet for a minute and then left the room. They knew what I didn't want to accept. Only later, I realized that if they told me that my baby had no chance for life, I would not be asking them to save him. But because they gave him that 1%, I asked them to save him. I knew miracles happen.

After about thirty-five minutes, which seemed an eternity to me, Oleg was finally with me in the room.

"Olga, I am sorry it took me a while to get here," he said. "The main entrance door of the hospital was locked, so, the security guard had to let me in through the back door."

Oleg's face was pale. Only God knows what my husband experienced.

"I have agreed to the surgery. I want to give my baby all his chances for life," I said with tears.

"Olga, God will help us. No matter what happens, I just need you alive," Oleg said, hugging me and trying to hold his tears.

That night I turned thirty weeks pregnant; two and a half months early for our baby to be born. The nurses transported me to the operating room, while Oleg had to stay and change into a surgery outfit. Surprisingly, I felt an unusual peace and knew God was with me during that critical time. I felt like He was gently holding me in His hands with His angels surrounding me. I was doing everything possible to give our baby his chance for life and left the final decision up to God. What more could I do?

When Oleg came into the operating room, the doctor had already made the incision cut for the C-section. Oleg told me later that he had seen blood before, but not that much of it. It made him feel sick when he paused and looked at the surgery.

"Sir, please sit down," the nurse said.

"I am fine," Oleg answered.

"You have to sit down," the nurse repeated.

"I am fine," Oleg answered again.

"Sir, you have to sit down because you can faint from seeing so much blood and we cannot be responsible for you."

Oleg sat on the chair next to me, hugged me, kissed me on my head and prayed quietly. The surgery went on for about an hour. I could not see anything behind the curtain. I felt the doctors pushing on my stomach. I felt no pain, no fear and did not cry. I didn't feel like myself. Usually, I would be so scared, but I was calm. I quietly prayed for God to be in charge and for His will to be done. After about ten minutes, the doctor delivered the baby and asked the nurses to take him to the Neonatal Intensive Care Unit (NICU). I could not see the baby or hear him cry. Oleg couldn't tell if the baby was alive. The doctors continued finishing my surgery.

After the surgery, I was taken to the recovery room for one hour. The nurse gave me medications and made sure I was okay. Oleg sat by me and held my hand. Another nurse came and asked if he wanted to go see our newborn son.

My husband left with her and shortly came back.

"Our son is alive!" he said relieved and excited. "Olga, when you called me, I was under the impression that he had already died. All the way to the hospital I cried out to God because I wasn't sure what was happening. Olga, I was worried about you, too. My son is alive! He is moving his hands! Praise God!"

I only now understood why Oleg hadn't answered my second phone call. Only God saw his tears and heard his questions. Oleg sat by me, held my hand and kept thanking God that our baby was alive.

"The nurses started medications through an IV for our son's heart and provided him with breathing help," he explained. "Our baby is in NICU in a warm incubator."

I was glad to see Oleg happy, even though he still worried. I was glad to hear that our baby was alive, and the doctors were taking good care of him. But after the anesthesia my mind was foggy, and I was in pain. Thank God, I was in one of the best hospitals in Oregon with good doctors and nurses, taking gentle care of me.

....

After an hour in the recovery room, I was taken to the Intensive Care Unit for postpartum mothers after a high-risk delivery. The nurses put my surgery bed next to the bed that I was to use in the room and asked, "Olga, can you try to scoot from your bed to the one in this room?"

I tried, but felt terrible pain from the C-section incision. Also, due to the anesthesia, I couldn't feel my legs at all. It was impossible to move. How do you move, when you don't feel your legs and experience severe pain? I became scared and started crying.

"I am in lots of pain and can't feel my legs," I said.

Oleg offered to help the nurses move me, but they did not let him. They asked for help from a male nurse. They wrapped me in sheets and used them to move me from my surgery bed to the bed in the room. Then, the nurse gave me extra pain medications.

That night there wasn't a room available with a sleeping couch for Oleg. So, he slept on two chairs, sitting on one and resting his feet on another. I wanted to sleep, but I couldn't. The anesthesia medications made my whole body itch the minute I began falling asleep. I told the nurse, but she answered that it was a side effect of the medications.

In the morning, a room with a couch became available, so the nurses with my husband's help transported me there in a wheel chair. Oleg fell asleep on a couch right away. The nurses changed my wound dressing and started magnesium medication through an IV to lower my blood pressure. They were also giving me Ibuprofen and Vicodin to kill the pain. In addition to itching, I felt dizzy and developed a very bad headache. I was still unable to fall asleep.

....

Oleg slept for only a couple of hours. In the morning the nurse asked if he wanted to go visit our baby again. He was excited for the chance and left with her. When Oleg returned, he brought me a precious gift: he had taken a picture of our baby, so I could see him for the first time.

I loved our son so much and felt so sorry when I saw him. I needed an explanation about all the wires and tubes around him. When the doctor came, she tried to answer my questions, but there was just too much to understand. I wanted to see our baby, but my medical condition prevented this.

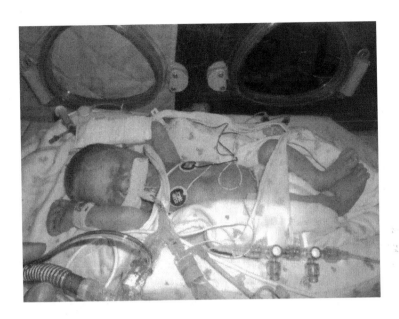

After the doctor left, Oleg and I realized how blessed we were to live in the United States with well-educated and skilled doctors, advanced medical equipment and medications. It is amazing how skilled and talented these individuals are, and how much they care. They do more than just their job. They are involved in our lives and work as fellow human beings, who care for other human beings with such strong convictions. They are special, and we are grateful for them.

Oleg and I understood that from then on, our lives would be different, since our baby would be staying at the hospital for a while. Oleg called his Mother in California.

"Mom, our baby has been born very early. Olga had a C-section. The school has started. Someone needs to be home to send David, Kristina and Michael to school and meet them after. Can you please come help us with the children?"

"Yes, of course, I will come," Oleg's Mother promised.

My parents continued to help with our children, while Oleg was with me at the hospital. That morning we realized how lucky we were to have parents near us during such critical time.

....

A nurse brought me an electric breast pump to pump the first colostrum for our baby. I sat up in my hospital bed and started pumping, but didn't know if my baby would ever drink it. I couldn't believe this was my new reality. My first three children were all healthy. They were with me in the room after birth and I breastfed them. I knew it was important for our baby to drink colostrum, but he couldn't yet; he was being fed through an IV. The nurse brought me more bottles and labels. I attached the label to the bottle and the nurse took my milk to NICU to be frozen.

The cardiologist ordered an echo cardiogram of our baby's heart. With hope, we patiently waited for the results. Soon the cardiologist came back and said, "Unfortunately, the echo cardiogram of your baby's heart showed that all the predicted problems are still there. Your baby may not survive." He gave us a list of our baby's diagnoses:

- *Right dominant unbalanced atrioventricular septal defect with large primum ASD;*
- *Second superior secundum ASD;*
- *Inlet VSD;*
- *Hypoplastic left ventricle;*
- *Severely hypoplastic aortic arch with severe coarctation;*
- *Large patent ductus arteriosus;*
- *Ex-30-week premature infant.*

We didn't understand all of the medical terms, but knew there were many problems with our son's heart. When the doctor left, we were quiet for a while.

66

"I feel like God doesn't hear us," Oleg finally spoke. "Why doesn't He help us? What about the prophecies that others had told us that God would heal our baby in the womb? Why had individuals prophesied that which is not true?"

Reality set in. Maybe God was stronger in Oleg, because he was still in a supportive role in his trust of God. I, on the other hand, questioned, "How can a loving God do this to my baby? Is it a God I still want to love and believe in?"

"Olga, we need to accept God's will," Oleg tried to answer my questions. "People can be wrong. They can tell us things that hurt us. They can prophecise what may not come true, but God is God. We have to believe in Him. He is there. He is alive. He will help us."

That day was difficult for both of us, but we ultimately decided to accept God's will and move forward with our lives. We now had a son who would require vast amounts of our attention and care, and somehow, we would have to make accommodations within our lives and within our children's lives.

....

6

You never realize how lucky you are with a healthy child, until you have an ill child.

Our friends and relatives called us, worrying about me and my baby. But that day, I asked for visitors not to come because I couldn't move, had lots of pain and needed rest. We appreciated our friends' and relatives' support. Even too many doctors and nurses kept coming in and out from my room.

When I had a moment, I called my Mother. "Our baby has been born, but he is very ill," I broke in tears while talking to Mom.

"Olga, please be strong. I feel your pain, my Daughter, and I wish I could help you, but what can I do? We will be praying. I know God has been healing other people. He will help. We will take care of your children. I will help you with meals. Tell Oleg to stop by any time. I will give him food to eat," my Mother cried on the other end of the phone, while trying to ease my concerns.

Because of our son's critical condition, I wasn't able to breastfeed him or do the skin-to-skin contact. I knew this was important because in my job at WIC that was what I taught new mothers. I knew the skin-to-skin contact would enhance our son's immune system. It would provide him better oxygenation, better heart rate and better temperature. He was all alone in an incubator, surrounded by wires, tubes and pumps with medications. I knew that the nurses were taking good care of him, but he was my baby and I was missing him. He and I were separated.

Surprisingly, I was at peace. Oleg also felt at peace. He stayed with me that whole day and the next night.

....

By the morning, the anesthesia was no longer affecting my body and the magnesium medication was stopped. The itching ended and, finally, I was able to sleep. I no longer felt dizzy and could walk with the nurse's help. I was beginning to feel better and thanked God!

I received a phone call from my former co-worker, Kathy, "Olga, I am coming to visit you!"

At the same time, Oleg received a phone call from his cousin, Eddie, "I am coming to visit you, brother."

Eddie and Kathy arrived at about the same time, so Oleg spent time with Eddie and I spent time with Kathy. Kathy brought me two cards, one from her and one from my former co-worker Marge. I started reading them and the words from one of the cards made me cry. It said, "*God knows everything you are going through and He will help you...*"

Kathy comforted me. It was wonderful to have such friends, who worried about me and brought me cards that showed hope.

"Olga, I would like to see your baby," Kathy said.

"I haven't seen my baby myself," I answered. "I felt so awful yesterday after the anesthesia and all medications, but I feel a lot better today. We can go see my baby together."

"Walking that far would be impossible for me."

I looked at Oleg.

"How will I get there? I am on the 14th floor and our baby is on the 12th. Is it far?"

"It is pretty far," Oleg answered. "You will need to take a wheelchair."

"No way. Wheelchairs are for disabled people. But now I have to use one?"

I wanted to see my baby so much, I complied with the rules and went to the NICU in a wheelchair. Kathy pushed it for me, while Oleg and his cousin walked behind us. We arrived at the NICU.

"Only three healthy visitors can see your baby at a time," the clerk explained. "No children are allowed, only siblings."

We signed in and washed our hands all the way up to the elbows. Then we went to the last room at the end of the hall, where the smallest babies were. Because there were four of us, Eddie waited in the hall and then came in after Kathy left. Four doctors were by our son's bed. The doctors greeted us and told the updates on the baby.

"The last two days we have been worried and didn't think that your baby would live. But he lives, so we are planning to meet with the surgeon and come up with a care plan for your son."

After the doctors left, I looked around the room. There were four other raised beds with tiny babies, covered with a glass lid and small blankets. I realized our family was not the only family with problems. There was a baby who was even smaller than our baby. Two nurses were taking care of babies in that room. Some parents sat in the rocking chairs by their baby's bed. Our son's bed had a sign on it: "Anischenko Baby" with tiny footprints on it and the baby's weight and length: 3lb 1 ounce and 14 inches.

With Oleg's help, I got out of the wheelchair and came closer to the incubator.

"Our baby is so tiny!" surprised, I told Oleg. "David, Kristina and Michael were all 8 pounds at birth. I never imagined that our fourth baby would be only 3 pounds."

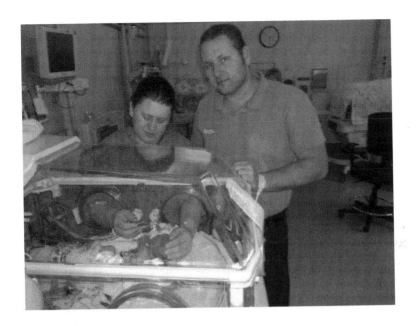

Two rounded windows were on each side of the incubator. The nurse and Kathy were staying next to us.

"Olga, you can open the round windows and put your hands through to your baby," the nurse explained. "But do not make any strokes. He may not like it. Your baby still needs to be in your womb for more than two months, not being touched."

I opened the round windows, put my hands on our baby's head and legs, and looked at his face. He was so beautiful with blond curly hair and looked so much like Oleg. The nurse told us more about his tubes and wires.

"An oxygen tube, taped to baby's mouth, is going down into his lungs to help him breathe. The sensors on his chest check his oxygen, pulse, heartbeat and body temperature. The umbilical intravenous line is inserted though his belly button, so we can draw blood for labs. The PICC line (a prolonged IV) is inserted in his hand, so we can send in nutrition and medications."

There was a tiny diaper on my baby and, luckily, his legs had nothing attached to them. Everything seemed beyond our control. Seeing our baby with the tubes scared me.

"It is real. What do we do now?" I asked my husband.

Oleg hugged me tight. I wanted to hold our newborn son and have some quiet time with him, but it wasn't possible. I felt a strange wave of emotion like he was mine, but at the same time not mine. I tried so hard to control my feelings and to not cry. "This is serious. We and our baby are in deep trouble," I thought.

"Your baby has jaundice, a medical condition with yellowing of the skin and whites of his eyes, arising from excess of the pigment bilirubin," the nurse said. "We need to turn on the special light that will help his jaundice go away. I need to cover your son's eyes with black glasses, close his incubator and keep him under the lights."

Oleg and I stepped aside. I didn't want to leave our son, but due to my pain, we returned to my room for more medications. I needed rest, and it was time for me to pump more milk. Tears rolled down my cheeks and I couldn't say a word to Oleg, who laid quietly on the couch with his own tears.

When I calmed down, I called my sister, Luda. One of her children was also born premature.

"Olga, I know what you are going through," she said. "I feel your pain."

We both talked and sobbed. It was easier to talk with someone who had had similar experience and understood. I was so grateful for my sister's support.

....

In the afternoon, Oleg brought David, Kristina and Michael to visit me and meet their baby brother.

"Mom, why did the doctor cut your stomach? How big is your cut?" Michael asked, scared.

72

"The baby would have died if the doctors had not cut my stomach," I answered. "The cut is about five inches long."

"Did it hurt, Mom?"

"No, it did not, because the doctors used numbing medications during the surgery," I answered. "But it hurt after the surgery and it hurts now."

"How long it will take to heal?" Kristina asked.

"About two weeks. I will need to be very careful when I come home. You guys will need to help me a lot."

"Mom, we will help you." Kristina laid by me on my hospital bed and hugged me.

"Why was the baby born early?" David asked.

"Because Mom's blood pressure raised very high," Oleg answered. "Mom has some health problems. We need to take good care of Mom."

"How soon will you and the baby come home?" David asked.

"I will come home after about four days, but the baby will stay at the hospital for a while. He needs a surgery on his heart."

The children were sad. Even children know that heart surgery is serious. They had no more questions. We were all quiet. After getting the information, they wanted and seeing that I was likely to be okay, they just turned the TV on and watched cartoons. How much could we expect from our children? David was the most concerned, but Kristina and Michael, because of their age, didn't understand much.

After spending a few minutes with me, the children wanted to see their baby brother. We thought they could handle it. Seeing the wires and tubes, attached to the baby, the children were scared because they didn't understand what was happening. They knew that their brother was in a trouble and that he was sick. They didn't want him to die.

73

This was the first time they ever experienced the possibility of death. Oleg explained the problems with the baby's heart and asked our children not to be scared, but to pray for God to help their baby brother.

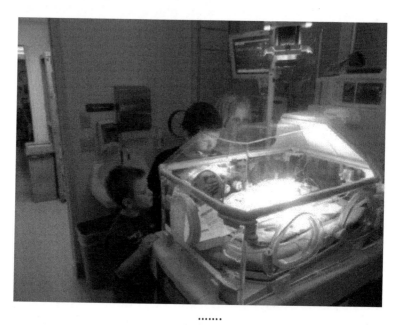

....

That afternoon, the doctor came and told us, "During the meeting of cardiologists, neonatologists, surgeons and medical students, we decided to delay your baby's open-heart surgery until he weighs at least five pounds. We think medications will enable his heart to keep working until he has grown larger and stronger, which will give him a better chance for success. We will feed him intravenously and let him grow, while keeping his heart duct open with medications. We will also continue providing oxygen to help him breathe. Your baby will stay at the hospital at least two months before the surgery and few more months after the surgery."

Hearing the doctors' long-term plan, Oleg and I understood that our son would not be coming home any time soon. We had to decide how our family would manage these changes for many weeks to come.

"Have you decided on a name for your son?" the doctor asked.

"Not yet," I answered. For a parent, whose baby is born healthy, the most important thing is to give him or her a name. But for us at that moment the most important thing was for our baby to live, not his name.

"During one of our meetings, one of the doctors called your son the "Russian Prince". While you are still deciding on his name, would it be okay for the doctors to use that name for now?"

I liked the doctors calling our son the Russian Prince. "Yes," I answered. "He deserves it."

"During this week, we will need to perform many blood tests on your three-pound son," the doctor continued. "He may become anemic and a blood transfusion may be necessary. Is that okay with you?"

We had no choice and signed the consent.

"Finally, some good news," the doctor said. "Your baby is stable, so he can start having breast milk through a feeding tube!"

Oleg and I were so relieved to hear the news and thanked God.

....

On Saturday, friends and family with beautiful flowers and gifts visited us. We couldn't walk everyone to see our baby. With some we just talked, prayed and hoped for the best.

Tanya was the first one of my siblings to see our son. When we came to the NICU, the lid of his incubator was raised, and the nurse was changing the dressing on his arm.

Our baby's eyes were covered with black glasses, but he was awake and moved his arms. We could not hear his voice due to the breathing tube in his mouth, but we could see it by the look on his face and by the way he was breathing that he was very upset. He cried without noise. Quietly, Tanya and I stood by his bed, trying to withhold our tears. My heart ached from not being able to help our son. Tanya didn't ask a lot of questions, but later I heard she cried after leaving the hospital, because she saw how fragile and ill our baby was.

A little later, my brother, Leo, came to visit us with his wife and children. They brought snacks and presents. While I was talking to Leo's wife, I heard my husband tell Leo, "Being home with the children without my wife has not been easy. I had to clean, cook, send children to school, figure out their school bus stop, read all their school papers, wash their clothes. It is hard to be home without my wife. She does so much. I realized how hard it is to be a single Dad."

Later I learned that Leo was calling everyone in our family, asking them to fast and pray for our fragile son.

....

Oleg met his Mom at the airport. His brother and sister helped her arrange the flight and paid for her ticket. Oleg's Mom was planning to stay with us for two weeks. We knew that she would take wonderful care of David, Kristina and Michael. Most importantly, she would give them lots of love. We were so thankful for our family's help. It amazed us how one event could impact the hearts and actions of so many people and they were all ready to help. We began to realize what was happening to us and our baby not only affected our immediate family, but impacted our extended family, friends, relatives, neighbors and co-workers. They all understood our pain.

....

Sunday, the third day after delivery, I woke up at 5 a.m. and pumped the milk. Since Oleg was still sleeping, I decided to take the milk to our baby. This was a big deal. I had never walked there by myself before. Holding onto the wheelchair, I slowly walked to the NICU.

"Good morning, Olga," the nurse greeted me. "You are here early today!"

"Good morning," I said, happy to be there.

"We have good news for you!" she continued. "Your son's milk dosage has increased from one to two milliliters! He is doing well!"

I was so happy to hear good news! Through the little incubator's windows, I could touch my baby's head, legs and hands. He seemed to be sleeping.

"Olga, have you decided on a name for your baby?" the nurse asked.

"We have not decided yet," I answered. "I am sorry. I need to talk to my husband about that."

I spent about an hour by my baby and returned back to my room. Oleg already woke up.

"I have great news for you, honey!" I said. "Our baby can tolerate more milk!"

"That's great!" Oleg exclaimed.

"We need to give him a name. The nurse asked me about it again."

"Okay. What names do you like?" Oleg asked me.

"I like Jacob, Elijah, Aaron and Nickolas, but I feel that Elijah would fit our baby the most. It is a Biblical name, which means "My God is Jehovah". What do you think?"

"I like Elijah," Oleg said.

"Our son has a very serious heart defect and his life will not be easy for him. I think the name Elijah would suit him the best," I said.

On his birth certificate, that day we wrote:
Elijah Joseph Anischenko
The baby of Oleg and Olga Anischenko,
Born on September 9, 2010.

Oleg visited Elijah and spoke with the doctors. Then he went home to spend some time with our children and his Mother. I had a lot to do: return phone calls, pump and take my milk to Elijah, take my medications and choose healthy foods to eat. My blood sugar and blood pressure were both elevated. Most importantly, I needed to rest and recover.

....

At about 1:00 P.M., I heard a knock at my door and saw the worried faces of my parents. They hugged me and kissed me.

"It all will be okay, my Daughter," Mom said.

"I love you so much," My Father added and hugged me.

It felt good to feel the love of my parents. I smiled through tears.

"We named our baby Elijah," I told my parents. "He is your 20th Grandchild."

"We would like to meet him," Mom said.

I got up, sat in a wheelchair and my Father pushed it with his left hand, his only hand. When we came to the NICU, my parents didn't say much, just asked some questions. Most of the time, they looked at the baby quietly and breathed in deeply. The nurse took a picture of us. Then, we returned to my room.

"Olga, it is very difficult for me to say this, but please, let God do His work," my Father spoke, "Elijah is very ill. It would be not easy for him if he was ill all his life. It would be better for him to be with God. If you had only called me when you were in labor, I would've told you not to save the baby. Please, don't ask God to leave him here with you. Ask

78

God to either heal him, so he would be healthy, or let God take him to Heaven."

When I heard my Father speak, words got stuck in my throat and I almost choked. I knew my Father was speaking the truth as he knew it, but we had already made a decision and the baby was already here.

When I was finally able to speak, I answered to my Father, "That is exactly how I am praying, Dad. For some reason, Elijah is still here, and God gives him life. I feel God has plans for him. It is God, who will decide if Elijah will live or not. But it is our choice to give Elijah every chance for life."

Mom and Dad spent a little more time with me, prayed for me and left to go home. It was hard for me to hear my Father speak at that time. Today I respect my Father even more for willing to express his honest opinion. Upon reflection, I understand now how difficult this must have been for my Father, who loves me dearly and whom I also love so much.

....

After about an hour, I heard another knock at my door. My sisters, Irena and Luda, came to visit me.

"Olga, our dear sister, we love you so much," Lyuda said and hugged me on my shoulder.

"We brought you flowers and freshly prepared, homemade food," Irena added and gave me a big hug.

"Thank you so much," I answered. "Would you like to go see Elijah?"

"Yes, of 'course!" my sisters answered.

I sat in a wheelchair and Irena pushed it for me. Those were special moments for me. I felt loved and well cared for by my family. They did for me what I could not do for myself and I appreciated that. My sisters were excited to see Elijah.

"Olga, he is so beautiful, but I can't believe how small he is," Irena said.

"I am so sorry, Olga," Lyuda said and hugged me tight.

My sisters looked at Elijah through tears. I stood next to Elijah's bed and was able to put my hands on his head and legs. Elijah was lying still. His eyes were covered with black glasses and we didn't know if he was asleep. My sisters asked me some questions and took pictures of us. Then it was time for them to go home. I took my hands off Elijah. He started crying, but could not make any noise, as he still had a breathing tube in his mouth. Immediately, I put my hands back on his head and his legs, and he settled down. Apparently, during pregnancy, babies can hear sounds from the womb. Elijah knew my voice and when I again removed my hands, he started to cry again. Eventually, my sisters and I had to leave.

"I will come back, my sweet little baby," I said through tears. "Mommy is in pain and needs to take her medications. I love you. You will be okay."

Elijah calmed down. It was heart-breaking for me to leave him all alone in his tiny incubator.

....

Soon, Oleg came with our children and his Mother. Oleg's Mom hugged me.

"How are you, Olga?" she asked.

"I am okay. Thank you for coming to help us," I answered with tears on my eyes.

After spending some time with me, Oleg took his Mom to see Elijah. When they came back, Oleg's Mom kept repeating, "Oh, God, please help my fragile Grandson."

Later Oleg told me that his Mom cried when she saw our tiny and very ill son, her ninth Grandchild. After about one hour, Oleg took his Mother and children home, and then returned to the hospital. Grandmother was taking good care of our children.

Later that evening, my Mother-in-law called me and read the poem that her friend wrote. The last verse was so promising:

The years will pass and take its course,
We will remember this day of course -
For Mom and Dad – a very hard decision,
For heaven and for earth – Elijah's day of birth!

Tears filled my eyes. "God, please make it a good ending," I prayed. "So many people already know about Elijah and are praying for him. Please make a miracle and heal Elijah. Show us Your glory!"

....

7

*Prayers of others provide comfort and strength,
and make you feel not alone.*

On the fourth day after Elijah's birth, Oleg returned to work. The doctors were planning to send me home and I was not sure if I was ready. For the last three days, I had no chance to let go of my emotions privately. I cried because I wanted to be with my baby. He needed my presence and my touch, and I needed him. The doctors were telling me I was going home, but my baby was going to stay. As I struggled with my situation, my former co-worker, Ruth, came to visit me.

"Good morning, Olga! Why are you crying?" surprised, she asked.

"Oh, Ruth. Thank you for visiting me. I am sorry you get to see me in tears. The doctors are planning to discharge me today, but I can't bring my baby home with me."

Tears rolled down my cheeks. Ruth handed me a tissue.

"Olga, please don't cry. It will all be okay. Your baby will come home soon. He needs to stay at the hospital just a little longer."

"I know, Ruth, but why does it have to be different with Elijah? My first three babies came home with me right after delivery. Why is Elijah's heart so ill?"

"We don't know, Olga, but God will help you. Please don't cry, or your blood pressure will rise so high."

Ruth held my hand and assured me that everything would be okay.

When Ruth left, I began to realize how many good friends I had and how much they loved me, and I cried even more. Soon, the nurse came in to check my vital signs.

"Olga, the doctors are planning to send you home today," she said.

"I know, but I don't want to go home without my baby," I cried. "And, my blood pressure is still very high. Can the doctor let me stay at the hospital just one more day? I would feel safer here."

"I will ask the doctor," the nurse said and left the room.

Unfortunately, the doctor came, increased the dose of my blood pressure medication, and discharged me to go home. In my heart I was mad, but I didn't show it to the doctor. He had to comply with hospital and insurance regulations.

As the doctor was discharging me, Tanya came to visit me. She was kind enough to give me a ride home. We collected all my items and went to say goodbye to Elijah. My heart was breaking apart. My children and my husband needed me at home, but Elijah needed me more.

I hadn't been home for eight days. Thanks to my sisters and Mother-in-law, our house was shiny clean. Flowers and a hot dinner were on the table.

"Mom, we are so happy you are home," Kristina gave me a big hug. "Can you please sign my school papers?"

"Mom, I have few papers for you to sign, too," Michael said, as he gave me papers and hugged me tight. "I missed you, Mom!"

David stood next to us, with a half-smile on his face. He was happy that I was home. I smiled at the kids and hugged them. Oleg, his Mom, our children and I ate dinner together. All attention was on me. The children forgot that Dad signed their papers yesterday. Today it was all back to Mom. They knew I had surgery, but they didn't know how much it hurt. I didn't feel like reading or signing my children's school papers, but patiently I did it, squeezing back tears due to pain and thinking about Elijah.

When I could sit no longer, I asked Oleg to help me walk upstairs to our bedroom. Each step was more painful than the last, and a flood of tears streaming down my cheeks. In the privacy of our room, Oleg hugged me tight and also broke down in tears. We both needed that hug. It was not the way we came home after delivering our first three children. With them we were happy, but with Elijah it was different. We were overjoyed Elijah was still alive, but at the same time, how we could be happy when he was so ill. It was like joy had been ripped from our hearts. We couldn't bring that joy to our kids, put Elijah in his crib, dress him in his new outfits, and use the gifts from our friends and family. Without him home, we felt like an incomplete family.

The insurance company already delivered an electric breast pump for me. Also, my friend gave me a beautiful rocking chair. Everything was ready for me to sit and pump the milk for my baby. I sat down. The pumping supplies were falling off my hands. "Why do I have to do this?" I asked myself as I tried to pump the milk for Elijah. "I wish my baby was home with me and I would just breastfeed him." When you breastfeed a healthy baby, it is exciting. But pumping milk for a baby, who may not be healthy enough to drink it, is unfulfilling.

When Oleg saw the large amount of milk I had pumped, he tried to cheer me up and said, "Olga, you could probably feed the whole hospital with that much milk!"

But it wasn't funny to me. I just smiled back at him, as I knew I had more milk than Elijah could drink.

....

My first morning at home without Elijah was quiet. Oleg was getting ready to go to work and asked, "Olga, would you like me to bring you anything before I go to work?"

"Can you please bring me hot chamomile tea and some cheese?" I asked. The cheese gave me energy and the chamomile tea kept me calm.

After we prayed together, Oleg left for work. Grandmother Olga sent the children off to school. When I had a moment, I checked my emails. Friends wanted updates on Elijah. I sent one email to all and thanked them for their support.

Oleg and I planned to visit Elijah in the evening, so all day I rested. Then I thought it would be a good idea to call our neighbors. I called. Sandie answered the phone.

"Olga, what has happened?" she asked. "It has been very quiet at your house. When I saw Oleg's truck in the driveway hadn't moved for couple of days, I called your house, but an unfamiliar voice answered saying that you were not home. How are you?"

I took a deep breath and told Sandie, "My blood pressure increased so high that I had to have an emergency C-Section. Our baby has been born very ill and I almost died, too..."

"Oh, Olga, last Friday, when I realized that something was wrong with your family, the Holy Spirit encouraged me to pray for you all day," Sandie said with compassion.

I felt the love of our neighbors and thanked Sandie for prayers.

I also called my neighbor Charlotte. She lived alone, and I frequently visited her, taking over a home-made meal. I knew she would want to know what had happened. Charlotte promised to pray for our family and add our names to her church prayer list.

After calls, I just laid in bed and thought of Elijah. I wondered how he was, so I called the nurse.

"Everything seems to be about the same," the nurse said. "But there is something that the cardiologist wanted to talk to you about. She will be calling you soon."

I could think of no reason the cardiologist would call me unless there was a problem. I worried and needed to rest to heal myself. Yet somehow, logically or not, it seemed that if I could be at the hospital, I could help.

An hour later the cardiologist called, "Olga, I would like to meet with you to talk about the procedure we need to do on Elijah. It is not something I can explain over the phone. Can you come tomorrow at 10 A.M.?"

"Yes, I can," I answered with a trembling voice.

Even though I knew it would not help, I began to worry even more. There must be a problem. That evening, Oleg and I visited Elijah together.

......

Oleg and I knew this would be an important conversation. But we also knew that the cardiologist's recommendation would not change just because Oleg was not there. Oleg had to work; we had no savings and we would have financial problems if he continued to miss work. Tanya, my oldest sister, drove my Mother-in-law and me to the hospital.

"Olga, our whole family is fasting for Elijah today," Tanya said. "We are planning to gather at our sister Irena's house in the evening to pray for him."

"I am so thankful," I replied to Tanya tearfully. The love from my family washed over me.

At the hospital, we came to Elijah's room. The nurse was changing his IV tubes.

"This is a sterile procedure," she said. "You cannot be near your baby or touch him until I finish."

86

Therefore, we stood back and watched from a distance. Elijah seemed content, yet I felt intensely separated from my baby. I ached to be close to him, touch him and comfort him. Soon, the cardiologist came and took us to a conference room.

"Olga, we are facing problems with Elijah," she said, while drawing a picture of Elijah's heart. "Too much blood is flowing to his lungs and not enough to his intestines and the rest of his body. Because of that, we can't increase Elijah's feedings, as his intestines would not digest the milk. To fix the problem, the surgeon needs to perform a risky procedure to tighten the tiny arteries in Elijah's heart. If he would tighten the arteries too much or too little, the surgery would fail."

I couldn't say a word. It was not what I ever wanted to hear.

"The surgeon is very skilled," the cardiologist continued. "He has done this procedure on small babies, but he has never done it on a baby as small as Elijah. There is a high risk that Elijah may not survive."

My heart started beating so fast. Stunned, my breathing became difficult and I could barely understand this turn of events, but I tried to control myself.

"Before this procedure, we plan to increase Elijah's oxygen from 19% to 21%, in the hope it will make a difference," the cardiologist continued. "If not, the open chest surgery for Elijah would be in four days, provided you agree. Do you have any questions?"

Unbelievably, within me were still enough tears to fill my eyes. I couldn't speak. Listening to her and seeing her drawings of where the surgeon would cut our baby's chest, made me sick to my stomach.

"I have no questions," I uttered. "What is there to ask?"

"I will step out for few minutes, Olga. You can stay and think," the cardiologist said and left the room.

Tanya and my Mother-in-law were speechless and said nothing; there was nothing they could do or say. This was a decision only Oleg and I could make. I wiped away my tears.

"Can we go back to see Elijah?" I asked.

We quietly left the conference room and went back to Elijah's room.

"I am finished changing the IV tubes," the nurse said. "You can now get closer to your son."

My hands quickly slid inside the incubator windows and I touched my baby's head, tiny hands and legs. What the doctor had told me set like a heavy stone in my stomach. This was an unexpected surgery on Elijah's heart, in addition to three we had already discussed. It seemed as if there was no hope left.

"God, either heal my baby today or take him," standing by Elijah's bed, I pleaded with God in my mind. No one but God heard me. Sobbing, in my mind, I was saying good bye to my baby, whom I had loved beyond comprehension. My Mother-in-law and Tanya tried to tell me calming words, but I couldn't stop crying.

Elijah's eyes were covered with the black glasses. He couldn't see me, but suddenly he smiled! He smiled again and again, and I could feel a smile spread across my face. How can you not smile at a baby, who is smiling at you? I stopped crying. "Thank you, my precious baby, for your beautiful smile! Is this a sign from God that everything would be okay?" I wondered.

Next, Elijah slipped his tiny foot out from under the blanket. I tried to cover it, but he kept kicking the blanket off, three times, and made us all laugh! It was like a game.

Tanya, Mother-in-law and I all smiled. Elijah was just so funny!

Still in pain from the surgery, I could not stand for long and had to leave. Quietly, we drove home. I laid in my bed, exhausted. Thoughts one after another passed through my mind. After a time, I called Oleg.

"The news is not good, honey," I said through tears. "Elijah needs an unexpected procedure. During this procedure he may die, but I want my baby to live."

"God will help us, Olga," my husband said. "Please don't worry."

That afternoon, while my husband was still at work, I just wanted to be alone. I didn't feel like talking to anyone else or answering other phone calls. At the same time, my entire family was fasting and praying for Elijah. In the evening, Oleg, I and the children prayed at home, crying out to God to help Elijah.

....

The next morning, when Tanya and I came back to the hospital, we met the same cardiologist in the hallway.

"Olga, actually..." the cardiologist paused.

"'Actually' sounds promising," I said, excited. I could sense that the news was good.

"Actually, we took Elijah's breathing tube out and provided a nasal cannula. It delivers extra air to his lungs. Elijah is now breathing 21% of oxygen instead of 19% and is doing so much better! More blood is still going to his lungs and less to his body, but Elijah is now able to tolerate more milk! His feedings have increased from 2 to 4 milliliters! The doctors plan to postpone Elijah's surgery, if he continues to make such good improvement."

I couldn't believe what I heard. The news was so good! If it were not for the pain of my C-section, I would probably be jumping, happy, in the hallway.

"Thank you for the good news, doctor!" I exclaimed. "Thank you, God, for hearing our prayers! Thank you for helping Elijah!"

I couldn't wait to see Elijah. When we came to his room, I couldn't see his eyes under his black glasses, but it seemed like his face was giving me a message, "Everything will be okay, mama!"

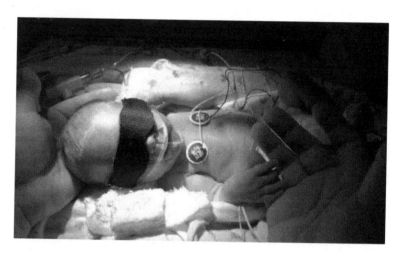

I put my hands inside to Elijah, held his hand and we "talked". I felt so relieved to hear the good news. Good news, even small amounts, creates hope. The nurse was happy about Elijah's progress.

"Elijah had gained 1.5 pounds in his first eight days of life and now weighs 4.5 pounds," she said. "The doctors are planning to take out the IV from Elijah's belly button later today. We will insert a PICC line into Elijah's left arm, to keep delivering medication to his heart. Then, Olga, you will be able to hold your baby."

I could hardly wait for that moment!

....

When I got home, Sandie brought us fresh vegetables from her garden and told us, "Elijah has been added to a prayer list at our church, in our relatives' church in Florida, and on a prayer list at one of the biggest churches in Vancouver, the Cornerstone."

"Thank you, my good neighbor," tears rolled down my cheeks, as I hugged Sandie. "I feel that God loves us so much. So many people know about Elijah and pray for us. I know that Elijah would be a miracle for lots of people!"

After a couple of days, I received an email from Katya, a girl I know, who attended Cornerstone. She wrote, "Hello, Olga. One of my friends has received an email from your neighbor. Our whole congregation is praying for your family. Let me know if you need any help."

Touched, I cried and thanked God for the love with which He surrounded us.

....

On the ninth day after Elijah's birth, my blood pressure was very high again. Oleg drove me to the hospital emergency room. That day it was his 35th birthday. We should be celebrating and giving him lots of love and attention. However, it was not going to happen. I felt sorry for Oleg, but there was nothing I could do.

"Olga, the eclampsia has come back," the doctor said. "It is necessary to hospitalize you again. Because Elijah is at OHSU in Portland, we will take you there by ambulance."

I was so thankful to the doctor for sending me back to Elijah. At OHSU, the same doctor, who had cared for me just four days earlier, came to see me in my room and said, "Olga, very rarely are mothers hospitalized again with postpartum eclampsia, and you are one of them. We will start a magnesium medication through an IV for 24 hours again. Hopefully, you will feel better by tomorrow."

By the next morning my blood pressure had dropped so much that it gave me a terrible headache. The doctors adjusted the medications, but the headache remained for a whole day. I was dizzy, scared and not sure what was happening to me. I called my parents, who were on their way to church.

"Mom and Dad, can you please ask the people at church to pray for me?" I cried. "I have developed a terrible headache and it is not going away. I am scared."

"Daughter, please don't cry," my Father said. "We will pray for you. You will get better. Please take care of yourself."

I laid in my hospital bed for a while and cried. I knew it would increase my headache, but I couldn't stop my tears. Even though I was at the same hospital as my baby, I couldn't be near him. When I calmed down, I called the NICU to check on Elijah.

"Elijah's IV had been taken out. Olga, you can start holding him!" the nurse said.

I broke into tears again and told the nurse, "I can't believe it. I had waited for this moment for so long and now, when my baby is ready to be held, I can't. I am hospitalized again with high blood pressure."

Disappointed, I cried the whole evening and my headache remained.

....

The next morning my headache and dizziness were gone. I was able to go see Elijah.

"Olga, would you like to hold him?" the nurse asked.

"Really? I can hold him? Yes, please! I would like to hold my baby! Thank you, God, for this opportunity!!!" I exclaimed!

For the second time, my incision kept me from jumping for joy!!! I could not believe it was actually happening!

"Olga, please sit in a rocking chair. I will put a pillow on your knees. Then I will put Elijah on a pillow," the nurse said.

Excited, I sat in the rocking chair and quietly exclaimed, "I can do skin-to-skin contact! I know this is very important for my baby!"

The nurse handed me my precious and fragile baby.

"We have to be very careful with his wires and tubes," she said. "When the oxygen poorly travels through Elijah's body, the alarm goes off."

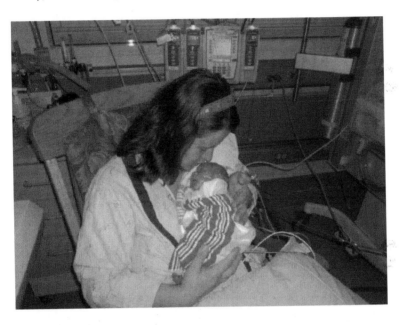

"I am afraid I might unintentionally do something that will hurt Elijah," I said, concerned. "What if a wire or a tube would get disconnected?"

"I am here, Olga, don't worry," the nurse assured me. "Cherish your time with your son."

I held my precious baby. Everything seemed to be okay and I became more comfortable. Then the nurse asked me, "Olga, would you like to breastfeed Elijah?"

"I would love to!" I said happily.

"Will you need help?" the nurse asked.

"Probably not. I breastfed three of my older children. I think I can do it."

The nurse put the screens around us for privacy.

"I will be here, behind the screens, charting. Let me know if you need any help," she said with a caring voice.

I tried to breastfeed Elijah and he actually latched on! That was a good sign! I was so excited. My baby had enough energy to breastfeed, but it wasn't for long. He was getting tired very quickly. Then, I just held him close to my chest. My baby was in my arms for the first time! Tears of joy filled my eyes. I was cherishing every second with my son and held him for about an hour and a half.

"Elijah is tired," the nurse said. "It is time to put him back into his warming bed. I will ask another nurse to help me situate Elijah because his tubes and wires required much attention."

The other nurse came. Together, very carefully, they put Elijah back into his warming bed. Elijah laid and looked at me like he knew who I was! This was the first time I saw his eyes wide open! I stood by his bed and held his hand.

"I love you so much, my precious baby!" I said with a smile. "You are so special! Everything will be okay. God will help you."

The nurse seemed to be happy for both of us.

"Olga, would you like to change Elijah's diaper?" she asked.

"Oh, I am more than happy to do that!" I was excited.

The nurse handed me a diaper, which was so very, very small. I opened Elijah's diaper and saw his tiny bottom for the first time.

"Wow! I can't believe how small it is! It is half the size of my other babies' bottoms, when they were born."

The nurse smiled, "Yes, Olga. Preemie babies are very tiny. They are a miracle from God here on earth."

Suddenly, I heard a noise.

"What is it?" I asked, confused.

"It is Elijah crying! His breathing tube is out, so he can now make a noise," the nurse smiled.

Oh, how dear those moments were for me. Having a severely ill child made me realize how lucky I was to have three healthy children. This was a special day for Elijah and me. It was a treasure I always will remember, when changing Elijah's diaper and hearing his voice for the first time was not a chore, but a joy!

Elijah fell asleep. The nurse put black glasses back on him, turned the special lights on and closed the lid of his incubator. Then she put a blanket over it. It was time for me to take the next dose of pain killing medications, so I returned to my room.

"The doctors are thinking of sending you home today," the nurse said.

I was devastated. The same feelings filled my heart as when they discharged me the first time.

"I don't want to leave Elijah," I told the nurse.

But I had to leave the hospital. Tanya drove me home again.

....

Later that evening, Oleg and I visited Elijah.

"Would you like to hold your son?" the nurse asked Oleg.

Like me, Oleg was concerned, "Are you sure? Will Elijah be okay? I don't want to do anything that would hurt my son."

"Elijah needs it," I assured Oleg. "I held him in the morning. Both Elijah and I loved it. You need it, too."

Oleg's eyes were full of excitement. He sat in the rocking chair and the nurse put Elijah in his arms. Tears filled Oleg's eyes.

"Thank you, my Heavenly Father, for this moment!" he kept repeating.

I sat next to Oleg and kissed Elijah on his head. Then, I took some pictures of Elijah and Oleg! Another special moment!

The next day, Tanya drove me to the hospital. She left to do some chores and I stayed with Elijah.

"Olga, would you like to hold Elijah again?" Elijah's nurse asked.

"Oh, I am happy to," I said, excited again.

"We will do a kangaroo care today," the nurse explained. "I will put Elijah on your chest, so you could do skin-to-skin contact. It is very good for Elijah. It will enhance his breathing and temperature. He and you will love it."

I sat in a rocking chair and the nurse put Elijah on my chest underneath my stretchy blouse. Elijah had no clothes on. It was skin-to-skin. Cherishing every second with my baby, I spent more than two hours holding Elijah and doing skin-to-skin contact. When Elijah's oxygenation started to decrease, the nurse and I put him back in his crib. I would hold him all day, if the nurse would let me.

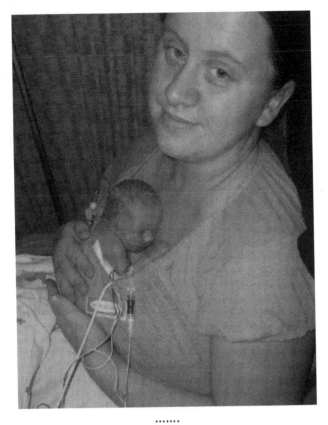

....

Two weeks after Elijah's birth, we received a phone bill of $352 instead of $150! Hospitalization and early delivery were unexpected emergencies and I had totally forgotten I had limited minutes on my cell phone. At that time, I didn't have text messaging. I called T-Mobile and explained our situation.

"Can you please lower our bill?" I inquired.

The representative put me on hold, to check with the manager. Then he came back and said, "Olga, my boss' family and mine have had premature babies. We understand how stressful it is. We will lower your bill by 50%."

"Thank you so much!" I said. "The world is full of good people! Thank you for helping us, when we are going through a difficult time in our life! Can I also change my plan to unlimited minutes and texts? I think I will need it."

The representative changed my plan, which was very helpful later. After I hung up the phone, I thanked God through tears. Even though we were going through a hard time, I felt like God was taking gentle care of us through good poeple.

....

8

Small things can give you great joy!

People were wonderful and helped us by providing comforting words, hugs and prayers. Oleg's employer amazed us. If Oleg suddenly needed to go to the hospital or take time off, it never was a problem. Somehow, as we received the love and kindness of others, the pain of the situation we were in seemed to be reduced. It was like they were taking a part of it, and we were not alone in the journey. I cannot express how much it meant to us.

Thus, we started a completely different lifestyle. Every morning, after Oleg left for work and the children left for school, I would drive thirty minutes to OHSU and care for Elijah from 9 A.M. until 2 P.M. Driving to the hospital was my personal time. I could cry, pray, ask God my questions, solve problems, and imagine what could be done. I would return home to see the children arrive from the school bus, feed them, cook, do the laundry, help with homework, and prepare dinner.

Each evening, either Oleg or I would visit Elijah again. Some evenings, Oleg was simply too tired to go. When Elijah felt better, Oleg or I held him. The nurses told us the minute Elijah heard our voices, his vital numbers would improve. He loved it when we came and held him. We tried to do all necessary things at home and also spend enough time at the hospital with Elijah. We didn't take any time for fun or vacation. Elijah came first --- everything else was background.

One of those evenings David asked Oleg, "Dad, what is your hobby now?"

"That is a good question, son," Oleg replied. "I used to go to the gym or work on antique cars. Those were my hobbies. But now I can't. I use that time to visit Elijah, therefore Elijah is my hobby now."

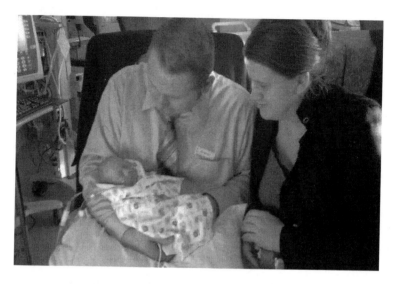

Our days were centered on Elijah; we could no longer imagine our life without him. We kept his pictures in the computer and started a baby album for him. In every situation, we thanked God and focused on the best. When I would come home from the hospital, I tried not to show my sadness to our children or Oleg. I spent time with them and gave them my attention, knowing that I had to be the same mom and the same wife, in addition to having ill baby 20 miles away. Sinking into depression was not an option, so I stayed positive and acknowledged the best in the worst situation.

On Sundays after church, we visited Elijah together as a family. Sometimes, the children could hold their baby-brother. They loved it when Elijah made funny faces and smiled. David seemed to understand more. Every day after school he asked about Elijah's progress.

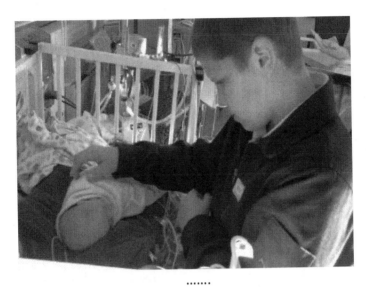

....

Not every mother at the NICU could spend as much time with her baby as I could. Some mothers lived up to four hours away. With some babies, there were no parents at all. Other parents were in jail, few gave their babies up for adoption. With some babies, there was a grandmother instead of a mother. Not many Fathers visited their babies. There were also babies, with whom both father and mother spent lots of time together.

One time, the doctor came to check on Elijah. She had time to sit down and we talked.

"Olga, Elijah is so lucky to be in your family," she said. "You are a very good Mom and know how to manage your time. You spend lots of time with Elijah and don't forget your older children or your husband."

"Thank you, Doctor, for telling me this," I responded. "You reminded me that I am doing my best and am a good Mother."

"We are so happy that you are Elijah's Mother. He is very ill and needs you. He is even doing better because he is loved, and you spend a lot of time with him," the doctor continued.

"Thank you. In our situation, I could have been unhappy and complain about everything, but I try to see the best and thank God that Elijah is alive, and we have precious moments with him. I am also so thankful to God that I have enough breast milk and can give it to Elijah. I am also so blessed that Oleg is such a big support and loves Elijah so much. My Mother and sisters help me with the meals and often watch our children. Even though our situation is hard, I feel that God is taking good care of us."

"I am so glad you can see and count your blessings," the doctor said. "You live not far, right?"

"Yes, 30 minutes away," I said.

"Many parents live three or four hours away. Not every city has such a well equipped hospital as OHSU. Some parents have to leave their fragile newborn here for weeks and spend only a little time with them. You are lucky to have a car. Your children are in school and you don't have to bring them here or take them to day care. There are many blessings to count," she smiled at me.

"Yes, I agree," I said. "We are also so happy to live in the United States of America. I can't imagine, if I lived in another country, what would have happened to us. It is possible that neither of us would have survived Elijah's birth. We see how dedicated the doctors and nurses are to find every possible way to help Elijah. Even the parking attendant is kind; he lets me park closer to the entrance door because I told him that I had surgery."

102

The doctor smiled. She liked talking to me. I believe she appreciated me, saying in my own way, they were doing a good job.

"I am also so thankful there is a wheelchair at the hospital. In the beginning, I was afraid to use it, but today I thank God it is available for people with physical limitations. I think in the process of all this, I am becoming braver."

"Yes, Olga. Hard situations change us forever. Even though it seems hard today, you will thank God for them later in life," she gave me a big hug. "Take care of yourself, Olga. I am going to check on other babies."

The doctor left. I sat in my chair for a while and thought about our conversation. I realized when we thank God, even if it was for only small things, the day went better. I knew I had to center my mind on things that I could control and leave the rest to God. I needed to deepen my trust in God.

....

Most mornings the doctors and I discussed the care plan for Elijah. One day I asked a cardiologist with a trembling voice, "Doctor, what percentage would you give Elijah if he survives the surgery?"

"I would give a full-term baby 75% chance to survive the surgery, but because Elijah was born premature, his chance would be lower."

"Thank you, doctor, for your opinion," I turned to Elijah, leaned in closer and talked to him, choking back more tears. I appreciated the doctor's honesty. It wasn't easy for me to hear his answer, yet, my heart understood he had the best intention for my child.

The doctors were always professional, caring and trying to do the right thing. Sometimes, it was hard to appreciate that in the moment, but now I know what wonderful people they are and how difficult their job really is each and every day.

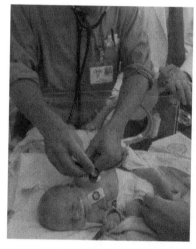

....

The next morning, when I came to visit Elijah, the nurse greeted me, "Good morning, Olga. I am getting ready to give Elijah a bath. Would you like to help me?

"Give Elijah a bath?" I asked. "How can you give him a bath with all the sensors, tubes and wires attached to him?"

"We will take the sensors off," the nurse explained. "I will cover Elijah's PICC line with plastic and hold his hand, while you will bathe him. Is that okay with you?"

"Sure!" I said excited. "I would love to do that!"

With the help of a nurse, I bathed Elijah in a tub with water. He loved it and I felt comfortable.

"I am so thankful to God that Elijah is not my first, but my fourth baby," I told the nurse. "When I was a first-time parent, I had many questions about how to bathe a baby, how to breastfeed him, change his diaper or give him medicine. But today I have more serious questions about Elijah's heart, his problems with breathing and his PICC line.

"Yes, Olga, you are right," the nurse answered. "If Elijah was your first baby, it would make your situation so much more complicated."

Bathing Elijah for the first time made it a great day. As he grew, the nurse and I bathed him often in water or with a sponge.

After being in the incubator for a month, Elijah was considered a big boy and was transferred to a small crib. That day the nurse dressed Elijah for the first time! I was so excited to see him dressed, but the next day he was undressed again. It was hard for the nurses to keep his clothes on due to his IVs. So, some days, he was with the clothes on, and some days without.

Elijah was growing well and gaining weight. From room five, where all the smallest babies were, he was transferred to room six, to be with the older babies. There were eight babies in that room. More mothers spent time with their newborns and more visitors came, so it was a little noisier. Elijah's bed was by the window with lots of sunshine coming into his room, which pleased me. A monitor by Elijah's bed displayed his vital signs and nearby pumps sent medications through his IVs. An oxygen tank was on the floor for the nurses to control the oxygen level to meet Elijah's breathing needs. A rocking chair was nearby, where I sat every day and held Elijah.

The nurses used a feeding tube to feed Elijah small portions of my breastmilk every three or four hours. That way he was able to digest the milk without problems. Sometimes Elijah would become hungry early and would scream. Feeling sorry for my son, I wanted to feed him, but I couldn't because of the doctor's orders. I understood the orders and had to exercise patience. Elijah had enough energy to be breastfed only once in two days. On days when Elijah had the energy to be breastfed, the nurses weighed him before and after, to see exactly how much he drank.

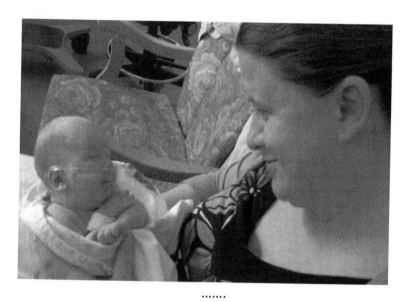

....

The nurses understood that Elijah would stay at the hospital for a while and became attached to him. One of the nurses, Patti, developed a special bond with Elijah. She began by checking on him daily, even though she was taking care of other children. Eventually, she became his primary care nurse. Patti loved her job. Whenever she was with Elijah, they had a good day, and everything seemed to be okay. I became friends with her and thanked God that there was someone I could ask questions about my baby and whom I could trust.

One day Patti shared her story with me, "Thirty years ago, one of my babies was born very ill and didn't survive. I went through a hard time. But, ten days later, I returned back to work and continued working with babies."

"Patti, was it hard for you to work with babies?" I asked.

"Yes, it was," Patti answered. "But I was helping other mothers."

Because Patti had experienced what I was now going through, I felt she understood me more than the other nurses. For as long as Elijah was at the hospital, Patti was a big support to me. Thank you, Patti!

....

At two months Elijah weighed six pounds. Adding weight gave him a greater chance of success for the surgery. An ECHO ultrasound of Elijah's heart indicated that the problems with Elijah's heart had not changed and the surgery was still necessary.

A week later, the doctors and the surgeon met together to review Elijah's growth. They scheduled his "Norwood" Procedure for November 9th, my 33rd birthday. I didn't say anything about my birthday -- it was unimportant relative to Elijah's situation. Thinking about the surgery brought me mixed feelings. Obviously, the sooner Elijah had his surgery, the sooner he would recover and go home. But if the surgery didn't go well, those might be our last days with our baby. I prayed for God to help us.

Together with our children we continued to pray every morning and every evening, and implore God to help Elijah. We wanted Elijah to be a part of our family and grow up happy and healthy. He was part of us. We already loved him so much. Every Wednesday, my family continued to gather together and pray for Elijah.

Four days before Elijah's surgery, the cardiologist met with me, and once again drew pictures of Elijah's heart. He told me where the surgeon would make the incision, what he would repair and how he would make the sutures.

"Elijah's chest would likely be left open for three to four days," he said. "The statistics show that 15% of babies don't make it through the surgery and 30% of babies don't make it through the first six months."

"I am happy the numbers seem more positive than I thought," I said. "But it doesn't matter if it is 70%, 80% or 90%, our son needs surgery. We have to move forward."

I listened, asked some questions and tried not to cry because I did not want my blood pressure to rise. After the cardiologist left and Elijah fell asleep, I left the hospital. Walking to my car, I felt sick to my stomach from what I had heard and seen. There would be more than just blood. It would be an open-heart surgery on our tiny, six-pound baby. Tears filled my eyes, as I drove home to meet our children at the school bus. "God, please help us," I sobbed.

At home, unable to stop crying, I sent a text message to my friends and family. "Please pray for me that God would give me strength," I pleaded, knowing that friends and family would definitely be praying for us.

Our faith teaches us that if we fast, pray, read the Bible, and concentrate on God, He will hear us and will answer quickly. We began to follow this teaching with greater intensity. I couldn't fast because I was still breastfeeding, but Oleg fasted often.

Learning how to trust God is hard, especially when you think that God is not doing what you are asking Him to do, and you don't understand why. Sometimes, we have to be patient with God, with ourselves, and with others. We have to remember that we are living in His world and on His schedule; and events happen according to His will.

....

A week before the surgery, Elijah was doing great. I breastfed him often and sometimes bottle-fed him. It seemed like he was doing what healthy babies do. We were all so happy for him! Three days before his surgery, when I came to the hospital, I met worried doctors standing by Elijah's bed.

"Elijah is very ill," one of the doctors said. "He has developed necro-colitis. We think he was drinking more milk than his body could digest. There was a lack of blood going to his intestines, which caused them to not function properly. Now, air is in his intestines and blood in his stool.

"And now what?" I questioned.

"We stopped his milk feedings and started nutrition through an IV. If Elijah doesn't get better on his own, an unplanned intestinal surgery may be required." For some unexplainable reason, I felt unusual peace. I just felt that Elijah would be okay.

....

On Sunday Oleg, the children and I visited Elijah with plans to take a family photo with him. It would be our first and might be our last family photo, depending on the outcome of his surgery. When we explained to the nurse what we wanted to do, she allowed us to violate the visitation rule, so everyone could be in the photo. As we prepared to take the picture, Elijah's oxygen saturation numbers dropped from 80 to 25. Suddenly something had changed, and his heart was unable to pump enough blood efficiently through his body.

"A baby with a healthy heart would have a saturation count of 100. For Elijah 80 is acceptable, but 25 is dangerous," the nurse explained. "I am very concerned. It may be better to let Elijah stay in the crib while taking the family photo." We took the photo. Fortunately, after few minutes, Elijah's saturation numbers went back up.

....

On Monday, our children and I woke up with stomach flu. I couldn't visit Elijah that day, even though his surgery was supposed to be the following day. I called the nurse to let her know that I wasn't coming that day.

"Olga, the doctors have cancelled Elijah's heart surgery that was scheduled for tomorrow," the nurse informed me. "They decided to finish Elijah's antibiotic course for the intestinal problems and make sure there is no infection. The new heart surgery date has not been set."

That evening only Oleg visited Elijah.

The next day was November 9th, my 33rd Birthday. Being sick with my children did not describe my ideal birthday. I couldn't visit Elijah, but my mind was focused on him and the upcoming surgery. The doctor called me that day and rescheduled the surgery for two days later. My children were playing downstairs, so I went up to my room. I quietly closed the door, fell on my knees, and implored God to help Elijah. After a good cry, I washed my face and came downstairs. I had no energy or interest in doing anything, except concentrating on Elijah.

A little later I received a very encouraging text messages. One of the messages from a girl I knew was very encouraging. She wrote, "OLGA, EVEN IF YOUR FAITH IS NOT BIG, YOUR GOD IS BIG!" This message reminded me that God is in control and all will be okay.

Around noon my sisters Irena and Luda came to see me. They brought flowers, presents and pizza to celebrate my birthday. Joy filled my heart at their kindness and loyal support. Luda told me that her co-worker heard our sister Tanya call our local Russian Radio 7 to request prayers for me and Elijah. The pastor prayed and asked all the radio listeners to pray for me. When I heard that so many people prayed for Elijah, it strengthened my faith and reminded me that we are not alone in our sorrow. I believed God will answer those prayers. He will provide a miracle and heal Elijah through the surgery or without it.

Later that day, Tanya stopped by with flowers and chocolate. Right after her, two of my younger sisters, Lily and Lana came. It was wonderful that my sisters remembered me on my birthday. Together they turned a heavy-hearted beginning into a very special birthday.

When Oleg came home from work, he seemed very tired, but I felt good enough to visit Elijah. Believing the evening would be heart-breaking, I did not want to go alone. I asked Tanya to go with me and she agreed. Tanya being there for me reminded me how small things can be really big things!

When we arrived, Elijah was so happy to see me; we had missed each other for the past two days. I held Elijah, kissed him and tried not to cry. Tanya took pictures of us.

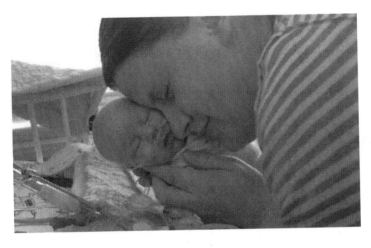

After, she took a card, which her daughter made and asked the nurse to make Elijah's hand print on that card. Then, Tanya gave it to me. Elijah's photo was on the front page of the card and his tiny hand print rested in the middle. It was so special to me. I looked at it and read through tears:

This little hand will never grow;
It will always stay just so.
When I am big or far away,
this little hand with you will stay.

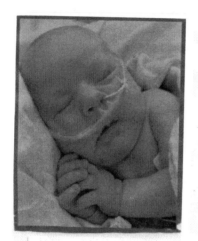

This little hand will never grow;
It will always stay just so.
When I am big or far away.
This little hand with you will stay.

♥ *I love you mommy very much* ♥

....

9

Through our grief we become aware and appreciate the miracles that doctors and nurses perform every day.

The next day Oleg and I met with the surgeon. He explained how he would perform the surgery, how he would connect Elijah's heart to a by-pass machine, make incisions, repair the damage, leave the chest open, and temporarily sew a special material on top of the open wound to protect it from infections.

"If everything goes well, then I would close Elijah's chest after three to four days," the surgeon said.

"Elijah's chest would be left open?" Oleg asked, confused.

"Yes. The swelling of Elijah's body needs to come down before the ribs can be closed," the surgeon explained. "There is also a possibility that Elijah can also die during this surgery. If his heart becomes weak, I can still attach it to ECMO machine, but that would be my last resort."

"What is an ECMO machine?" we asked.

"It is an Extracorporeal Membrane Oxygenation machine that circulates blood through an artificial lung back into the bloodstream. If needed, it would provide enough oxygen for Elijah, while allowing time for his lungs and heart to rest and heal. But that is the last thing I want to do because it requires lots of blood thinner medications and might cause internal bleeding. If Elijah's brain starts bleeding, it can lead to retardation and disability."

It was heart-breaking to hear about the surgery and the ECMO machine, but we needed to know everything. Tears filled my eyes and I had a hard time breathing. I didn't want my baby to go through this surgery and didn't want him to die either.

"I have completed many similar procedures," the surgeon continued with pain in his eyes. "I am capable and confident in my work, but I don't know if Elijah will survive the surgery. I have children of my own and understand how much Elijah means to you."

"We will be praying to God to bless your hands to do the surgery and for Elijah to survive the surgery. Our family, church, friends and co-workers are praying, too. God will help us," I said.

This was the hardest decision that Oleg and I had to make in our lives; it was the life of our son. Oleg had to leave for work, but I stayed. Jan, the social worker at the Pediatric Intensive Care Unit (PICU), was supposed to show me the room where Elijah would recover after his surgery. While waiting for Jan, I sat in a chair, not wanting to see anyone or talk to anyone. The emotions of possibly losing my baby and having him go through the surgery were overflowing.

"God, if Elijah is not going to survive this surgery, then take him today," I prayed in my mind. "God, please help us! Please, be with us."

"Olga!?" I heard someone call my name, while I was battling my emotions. It was Jan. "I will show you around the PICU. Elijah will be recovering there tomorrow after his surgery."

I went with Jan. From the hallway of the PICU, I saw many sick children. I also saw a woman I knew, whose twelve-year-old daughter's heart was failing. I couldn't even imagine what Elijah would look like after his surgery and didn't know what to think or ask.

"Thank you, Jan, for showing me where Elijah will be recovering tomorrow," I said.

"I will come and visit you, Olga, in few days," Jan assured me.

After meeting with Jan, I visited Elijah for an hour and then hurried home to meet our children getting off the school bus.

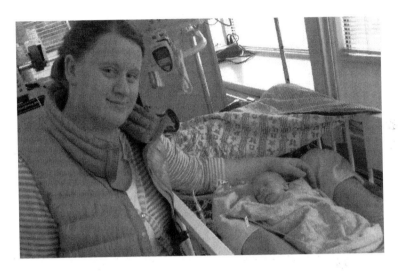

In the evening, Oleg and I visited Elijah again. We tried not to think about the surgery or what might happen. We held Elijah and cherished every second with him. Elijah seemed uncomfortable. We saw pain on his face and wondered why?

The nurse explained, "From a three-pound baby, Elijah had grown into a six-and-a-half-pound baby. His body is becoming too heavy for his ill heart to work."

That evening, as the nurses and doctors were going home, they hugged us and promised to pray for us. I saw how much they loved Elijah, who had become a part of their lives. Seeing that, I didn't feel alone in my sorrow. I knew there were so many people who loved our son and prayed for him.

....

The next morning, we arrived at the hospital at 6 A.M. We wanted to hold Elijah and be with him one more time before his surgery, the Norwood Procedure. We prayed that the surgery would go well and tried to have positive thoughts. By 7 A.M. the NICU nurses had prepared Elijah for the arrival of the special transport team. The special team arrived. As we began to leave, I could see the tears in the nurses' eyes, who had done so much for Elijah. We followed Elijah and the transport team through the halls of the hospital to the surgery area. There we met with the anesthesiologist and other staff, who would prepare Elijah for his surgery.

"Some parents take such babies home and don't do the surgery. They just let them die," the anesthesiologist said. "The surgery has a very hard recovery and is just too painful to see."

I didn't understand the anesthesiologist completely.

"Is it legal to take such babies home to die?" I asked.

"Yes," he said. "In a situation like this, it is."

Different thoughts went through my mind. "What are we doing? Are we making the right choice?" For a moment, I thought, "Could we really take Elijah home and just let him die?" But I knew instantaneously that we would not take such a path. The right choice was to go ahead with the surgery. He already has passed his 1% chance for life and has made it through to the surgery. We will give him all his chances for life! "Oh, God, please help Elijah!" I prayed in my mind. Oleg and I tried to make the best choice for Elijah, having no idea what we would see after his procedure.

Soon, it was time for Elijah to be taken to the operating room and we had to say goodbye. Separating from Elijah was like tearing my heart in two. I knew Elijah had to undergo the surgery, but I was so afraid he would not come out of the room alive. Oleg stood next to me with his own thoughts. With tears in his eyes, he embraced me tightly while the nurses rolled Elijah's bed out to the surgery room.

We were not given an option to be with Elijah during his surgery, which was probably a good thing. The surgeons are trained to handle such situations, but parents are not. No parent could forgive themselves if they were allowed to be in a surgery and would disturb a surgery in such a way to cause harm to their child. Sometimes, you simply have to trust and allow people, who are trained professionals, to do that which they do best.

"I will be calling you from the surgery room with updates," the nurse told us. "Please, remain at the hospital while the surgery is going on."

Oleg and I waited in the waiting room. Surprisingly, we were calm. Time passed slowly. It was like the hand of the clock never moved. We spent most of our day in the waiting room. Sometimes we walked out into the hall. It was a cold, sunny autumn day. Through the window, we could see beautiful Mt. Hood, covered with snow. The whole day, in our mind, we prayed for the surgeon and for our son. We knew that friends, relatives and our pastor were also praying. During the day, they called us and sent encouraging text messages. Oleg and I held no power over this day and this procedure. God and the skills of our surgeons were our only hope.

A nurse called us from the surgery room and said, "The surgery had finally started, after three hours of preparation."

We could not believe it took three hours to prep, but the doctors had told us about all the many complicated things that had to be done before the surgery could begin.

Two hours later the nurse called us again, "Half of the surgery is complete."

Finally, at 5 p.m., we received one more call from a nurse, "The surgery is almost over."

Two hours later, the surgeon came out and told us, "I am pleased with my work and have accomplished everything as I planned. Elijah's tissue is young, fragile and hard to sew, but I think I have been successful."

"Thank you!" Oleg said.

"Thank you, God, for such talented surgeons!" I added, relieved to hear the good news.

"Elijah's heart issues are so complicated," the surgeon continued. "Today, I basically have done four surgeries in one in Elijah's heart."

"What do you mean?" I asked.

"All people have two sides to their heart, but Elijah's heart only had the right side and a tiny undeveloped left side," the surgeon explained. "Between the two sides in Elijah's heart there was a wall with two holes in it. That's why Elijah's left side did not develop completely. I took the wall out and made a one-sided heart for Elijah. Also, the blood vessels are supposed to be on each side of the heart, but Elijah's were twisted on top of each other. The smaller vessel was bigger, and the bigger vessel was smaller, so I had to make one blood vessel out of two. To replace the second vessel, I had to insert a shunt and stitch it from each side to the heart and aorta.

"What kind of a shunt?" Oleg asked.

"I made it from a goat's tissue. That shunt will be taken out during Elijah's second surgery at six months," the surgeon explained. "I also patched Elijah's aorta to make it wider. There is one thing I am concerned about, thought. When I disconnected Elijah's heart from the bypass machine, it stopped working."

"It did?" I asked, worried.

"I am not sure why it happened, so I pumped Elijah's heart with my hand for two minutes. It started working again."

"So, Elijah has been without oxygen for two minutes?"

"Yes, but I don't think that any brain damage has occurred," the surgeon said. "The nurses need time to clean Elijah and prepare him to transport to his room at PICU. You will see him in about forty-five minutes."

We were so relieved to hear that the surgery was finally over and that our baby was alive.

"Doctor, we have not eaten all day and are exhausted. Do you think we have enough time to go quickly eat at the cafeteria, while waiting to see Elijah?" I asked the surgeon.

"Sure. It is not a bad idea," the surgeon said.

However, before eating, we wanted to thank God and needed a quiet place to do so. So, we went outside the hospital to our car, thanked God in a prayer and then made a few phone calls to let our family know that Elijah had survived the surgery. We also asked them to continue praying as Elijah was still in critical condition.

After praying, we went to eat at the cafeteria. Before we even had a chance to eat, Elijah's nurse ran into the cafeteria.

"Please leave your food," she quickly said. "You need to go back to the PICU immediately. We were paging for you to come back to the recovery area. You were not coming, so I ran to get you."

"We did not hear the page because we were in our car, thanking God that the surgery went well," I said. "Why do we have to go back to PICU immediately?"

"While we were transferring Elijah to his recovery room, his heart stopped working again," the nurse quickly explained. "The surgeon is trying to connect his heart to the ECMO machine. We don't know if Elijah will survive."

Oleg and I were shocked and speechless. When we came to the PICU, a social worker took us to a private room, brought us tissue, and asked, "Do you need help making phone calls?"

"What phone calls?" I asked, confused. "Elijah is still alive. Can we please have some time alone?"

She left the room. Oleg and I sat next to each other, not knowing what to do or what the next minute could bring us. We sat there for about thirty minutes, wondering what was happening to our child. It seemed like an eternity to us. Then I stopped crying.

"Why am I crying?" I told Oleg. "Elijah is still alive! Everything will be okay!"

Soon, the cardiologist came and told us, "The surgeon is finishing up connecting Elijah's heart to the ECMO machine. It will pump his blood and take the load off Elijah's tiny heart."

This cardiologist knew Elijah from day one. We saw pain in his eyes.

"With my wife and children at home we always pray for the hospitalized children," the cardiologist continued. "I have been at the hospital all day and will be staying with Elijah overnight, to make sure he is okay."

"Thank you, doctor. We appreciate you caring for our child," I said through tears.

Tears filled the cardiologist's eyes and he left the room. Soon we heard the knock at the door. It was Elijah's neonatologist from the NICU.

"I heard the announcement and understood that things were not going well. I came to check on you and Elijah. Is everything okay?" she asked.

She was the one, who knew Elijah and who named him the "Russian Prince".

"Elijah's heart had stopped working, so the surgeon is connecting it to the ECMO machine," I said tearfully. "We are facing a lot of unknowns,"

The doctor gave me a big hug.

"Do you have any questions? she asked.

"We don't know what to ask," Oleg replied. "We just have to wait and see. God is our only hope."

"Please take care of yourselves. I will go check on Elijah," she said and left the room with eyes full of tears.

Again, we were in a room alone. Death felt very close. I tried to send all my negative thoughts away and asked God to help me find something positive to concentrate on. I began to thank God for the good doctors and nurses, who were doing their best to save our baby's life. Positive thinking made me feel better. Oleg didn't say much. He just sat and looked at the ceilings with tears in his eyes. About 11 P.M., the surgeon came and explained what had happened.

"While being transported to his room, Elijah's heart stopped working again," he said. "I had to squeeze the heart for about two minutes. Luckily, it started working again. Time is critical, because when your heart doesn't pump blood, oxygen doesn't move through the body. I am unsure how much damage had been caused, but I think that Elijah is still okay. We are doing everything we can for Elijah to have a normal life. And, if we knew Elijah had no chance for a normal life, we would let him die."

"Will Elijah be okay?" I asked, worried.

"I don' know. Elijah's heart is too weak to work on his own, so we connected it to the ECMO machine. Elijah's heart will have time to rest and heal for two days and then we will make a determination."

"You said, the ECMO machine would be your last resort, and now you had to use it?" Oleg asked.

"Yes, it is our last resort, but it still gives us hope," the surgeon explained. "Because Elijah is attached to the ECMO machine, we have to use blood thinners, which could possibly cause bleeding in his brain and potential retardation. So, we are concerned. Hopefully, Elijah will be okay."

"When can we see Elijah?" I asked.

"The nurses are washing the blood off of Elijah's body, so it will not frighten you when you see him. As soon as they are done, you can go see your son."

The surgeon left. We remained in the room, not knowing what to expect or what was expected of us. I was scared and could not imagine what I would see.

....

After about ten minutes, the nurse came and said that we can go see Elijah. We followed her to his room. This was the room that Jan had previously shown me where our son would recover. Having been there before made me more comfortable. We paused by the door. Three nurses hovered over our baby. Elijah was lying high on the surgery bed in the room full of medical equipment.

"Hello, we are Elijah's nurses," one nurse calmly introduced themselves. "One of us adds medications to the pump machine. The other one is writing down in the computer everything we do. And the third one is watching the ECMO machine, to make sure it works correctly."

Not knowing what to do, we politely listened to the nurses and asked them questions. Oleg even took few pictures. All I wanted to do was to be with my baby and make sure he was okay. Medical equipment was everywhere. Several tubes were connected to Elijah's body.

"What is the purpose of all this equipment and tubes?" Oleg asked.

"The tubes drain blood and other fluids from Elijah's body into the buckets, which you see on the floor at the end of his bed," the second nurse explained. "The purpose is to remove fluids from Elijah's body, so the swelling will go down. It will allow the surgeon to ultimately close his open chest with stitches."

The nurse, who was watching the ECMO machine, added, "The ECMO machine, which you see in front of Elijah's bed, assists Elijah's tiny heart to pump the blood throughout his body. It will allow his heart to rest and recover from the surgery."

And the nurse, who was adding medications to those pumps, explained, "The pumps you see on each side of Elijah's bed, are programmed to administer different medications, blood transfusions and nutrition through IVs. Elijah is given 23 medications, including two narcotic pain medications, which we will slowly wean Elijah off over a period of several months."

All I wanted was to see my baby.

"Is there a way I can get to Elijah to see him up close?" I asked.

"Yes, you can go through the equipment, get on a step and be by Elijah," the nurse explained.

Scared of what I might see, I slowly worked myself through the medical equipment. There was a step beside his bed. I stood on it, so I could see Elijah better. Lying swollen and pale, Elijah didn't look like himself. It was heart wrenching to look at Elijah. I had always been scared of blood and would never choose to be in this situation, but it was my son. I had to be there with him and for him. I was afraid that I might faint.

"Honey, can you please stay close to me so I don't fall?" I asked Oleg.

My husband came and stood by me. Having a hard time breathing, I could not say a word. I had never seen anything quite like how Elijah looked after his Norwood procedure. It was something I never wanted to see and never imagined that I would see. Everything we experienced in the past, seemed like nothing compared to this. The first thing I thought of was Jesus' crucifixion on the cross. It wasn't like I was comparing Elijah to Jesus, I was connecting suffering with suffering. The nurse explained more of what we saw.

"The paralytic medications put Elijah into a deep sleep," she said. "His body is purposely kept cold so that his blood will not clot."

I looked at Elijah's body. There were six IVs attached to his arms, chest, leg and neck. A ventilator helped him breathe.

"What is on Elijah's forehead?" Oleg asked.

"Those are the sensors that monitor his brain," the nurse answered.

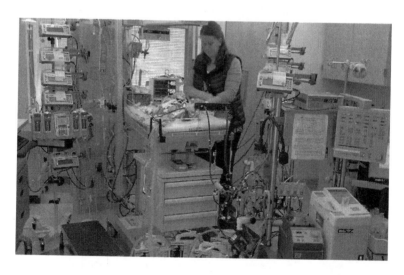

The big cut on Elijah's chest and few more under his ribs were covered with gauze. Dizzy and nauseated from what

I was seeing, I tried to hold onto Elijah's bed. I was so shocked I could not cry. I wondered how God could bring us through all these problems. They just seemed overwhelming, but deep down in my heart I knew that God could solve anything. That is what my faith had taught me.

"I was helping to save Elijah's life when he was born," the nurse, who was watching the ECMO machine, said, on the verge of tears. "This night, after his surgery, I am here for him again. No one knows what this night can bring."

After spending about an hour by Elijah, holding his hand and telling him that we loved him, we left the hospital at one o'clock in the morning. It had been a very long day; we had not eaten the entire day. I called my Mom.

"The children have already fallen asleep," she said. "Let them spend the night here."

Oleg and I went straight home. I am not sure if Oleg slept at all that night. I, frightened and shaky, laid in my bed and prayed to God about Elijah. Death seemed so close, but in the name of Jesus, I sent bad thoughts away. I implored God all night to save our son, if it was His will.

....

10

Life experiences make us stronger, wiser and patient. Be thankful, not angry.

Early in the morning, Oleg and I returned to the hospital. Everything was the same as last night, except it was so much more. Elijah was even more swollen than the day before.

"Why is Elijah so swollen?" I asked.

The nurse explained, "The amount of fluids entering his body through IVs are more than his body can excrete. His tubes drain the excess fluid created."

The gauze was removed. I could see where the doctors made the cuts in Elijah's chest and I could see the material stitched to the skin of his chest. The material moved with the beat of his heart. I became nauseated as I could visualize Elijah's tiny heart under the material in his open chest.

"Honey, please stay close by me. I am afraid I may faint," I told Oleg.

He came and stood by my side. I had never fainted in my life, but I knew I might, because it was more than I could handle. I tried desperately to compose myself. Elijah didn't look like my baby at all.

After a while, we realized there was nothing more we could do and needed rest. It was as if all the energy had drained out of our bodies. We had nothing left to offer, so we went home. We needed to be alone. As much as we loved our children, we were not able to give any attention to them that day, so they stayed at my Mom's again.

We didn't feel like seeing or talking to anyone. We did not even have any strength to pray. Earlier, I heard a preacher say, "Pray ahead of time. Because when the disaster comes, you will have no strength to pray." We just laid on our bed and looked at the ceiling, not knowing what would happen next. Time had stopped for us. The day after the surgery was even more difficult than the day of the surgery.

When we came back in the evening to visit Elijah, I just stood by his bed and looked at him. Elijah's bed was high and I couldn't even get near enough to kiss him, with all the tubes and wires around him. When we were ready to leave, the nurse, Louise, came and gave me a hug.

"Kiss him," she said.

"How?" I asked her. "I can't reach Elijah."

I didn't feel comfortable because I felt that the doctors and nurses were watching us through the glass door from the hall.

Louise lowered the side of Elijah's bed.

"Kiss him," she encouraged me. "He needs it and I know you need it, too."

There was barely a part on Elijah's body that wasn't filled with IVs or tubes, where I could touch him, hold his hand or kiss him. I leaned over and kissed Elijah on his forehead. Tears filled my eyes. In my heart, I thanked Louise and God for this moment.

Then, Louise hugged Oleg. "Can I pray for you, the Mom and Dad of Elijah?" she asked.

"Yes, please," Oleg said.

I started crying. Louise was full of love for Elijah and us, whom she had only known for a few hours. She was there with us and worried for Elijah, too. I felt better, leaving Elijah with her and knowing how much she cared.

....

After barely sleeping, the next morning we went to the hospital early. We wanted to be there when the team of doctors would be disconnecting Elijah's heart from the ECMO machine. We prayed it would be successful. After about thirty minutes, Louise came out to talk to us in the waiting room.

"Elijah's heart has been working without the ECMO machine for about fifteen minutes. He is doing well!" Louise said.

I almost fainted. Good news, like bad news, sometimes is just too much to hear.

"Thank you, God!" I whispered through tears.

Oleg was sitting next to me. He couldn't stop thanking God. Unfortunately, after an hour and fifteen minutes, Elijah's heart did not have the strength to continue on its own. The surgeon turned the ECMO machine back on and decided that Elijah's heart needed two more days of rest.

Time went by very slowly. Because Elijah was on the ECMO machine, the doctors were giving him blood thinner medications. Because the side effect was potentially bleeding on the brain, we were extremely hopeful that Elijah would be removed from the ECMO machine as soon as possible.

Finally, on Monday, November 15th, the fourth day after the surgery, Elijah was taken off the ECMO machine! His heart was working on its own again! It was hard for us to believe it, but it really happened. Elijah was quiet throughout the day and his blood pressure stabilized.

....

Although the hospital would allow visitors to come and see Elijah, I didn't want anyone there. Oleg and I had to be there, but I thought it would shock my parents and relatives. We weren't sure how they would react. It might be too much for them to see.

"The doctors don't allow any visitors for the first two weeks," I told my parents and relatives.

We had a right to make decisions about who could see our child. I loved my parents and didn't want to see them hurt. I hoped they would forgive me as it could have been the last time they would have seen Elijah.

Later, I regretted my decision. The very next morning, which was the fifth day after the surgery, Oleg returned to work. I had a choice to wait for him and visit Elijah in the evening or go to the hospital alone. No matter how scared I felt, waiting at home all day was not an option for me. My little deception was now backfiring on me. I wanted someone to be with me, but at the same time I didn't. Elijah's condition was extremely fragile---a crisis could develop in an instant. But I still didn't feel comfortable asking my Mother, sisters or friends to come with me. What I was dealing with was mine to bear, which terrified me.

Beyond my fears, I didn't want anyone to see what I saw or ask me questions I could not answer. Being in such an emotional state, even though they were trying to be helpful, some comments and questions could only result in me being hurt, or I could hurt them with a response they might not like. It was better for me to avoid such situations.

Even though I was scared, that morning I visited Elijah alone. He was doing better than expected. I was relieved and happy for every bit of good news. The surgeon came and checked on Elijah's tubes to see if there were any blood clots.

"The Norwood procedure, which we performed on Elijah, is much more complicated than doing a heart transplant."

"Why didn't you just do the heart transplant for Elijah then?" I asked, confused.

"Even though Elijah's heart is very ill, it is still better for him to keep his own heart. Also, it is almost impossible to get a new heart at his age" the surgeon explained.

129

At that moment, I understood what we were going through was a living hell, in which only bad choices were available.

....

By the next morning, Elijah's oxygenation and blood pressure had decreased significantly. The cardiologist came to talk o me.

"We need your permission to perform a CT scan to see if there is internal bleeding," he said.

Having no choice, we agreed and patiently waited for the outcome. We prayed for the best, but feared the worst. Soon the cardiologist came back.

"The CT scan showed a small amount of bleeding on Elijah's right front side of the brain. We believe there is no brain damage yet, and we hope it will not bleed more."

It was terrifying to hear such news. In the evening Elijah's oxygenation and blood pressure had decreased again. The CT scan was repeated twice. Luckily, the bleeding was not getting worse.

....

Jan, the social worker, came to visit me in Elijah's room.

"How are you Olga?" she asked.

I started crying.

"I have never seen anything like Elijah's surgery," I replied. "All I can do is to stand by Elijah's bed, look at him, pray and wonder what damage the bleeding in Elijah's head has caused."

Jan embraced me with her hands and said, **"Olga, forget about yesterday, be happy for today, and don't think about tomorrow. You can't change yesterday. If you worry about tomorrow, you will miss the precious moments of today. Tomorrow will take care of its own. Your baby is still alive, so be happy about that."**

Jan's words made me realize that she was right. Elijah was still alive, and I should be thankful for it.

Jan continued, **"Olga, I also read a legend that in heaven there are many healthy and ill babies and they each choose their mother. For some reason, Elijah chose you. He knew you would be able to take good care of him, and your family would love him and give him the best of everything. God also knew you would be strong and able to get through it."**

Jan's comforting words were a turning point for me. Instead of complaining to God that He gave me an ill baby, I started thanking God that He chose me to be Elijah's Mom. It gave me confidence that what appeared impossible, was possible; with God's help and our faith, as a family, we could do this. I started concentrating only on the positive and took life one day at a time. Elijah's life was in God's hands.

....

On the ninth day after the surgery, I brought Kristina for the first time to visit Elijah. I didn't want her to see Elijah's wounds, so I covered them with the blanket. Kristina took some pictures, while I held Elijah's hand. Then, the nurse Louise asked me, "Olga, would you like to hold Elijah?"

"I would love to, but how can I hold my baby with his chest still open?" I asked, confused.

"You can do it."

Louise raised my chair and moved it close to Elijah's bed.

"Sit on this chair," Louise told me.

Then, she carefully moved Elijah, so his head was on my arm. My baby, whom I had missed so much, was in my arms again! It was a very special moment to hold my son again! For the last nine days, I could only stand and look at him. I was learning to be thankful for things in my life we had taken for granted with our three other children.

"Thank you, Louise, for finding the way to bring me and Elijah together again," I said, half crying, half smiling.

Soon the doctor came in to check on Elijah's liver. When he pressed on it, the blood gushed out from Elijah's chest hole. I saw it and knew it must be something bad, but I was used to problems happening all the time, so it didn't surprise me. I was calm and didn't panic. What do you do? You can be thankful that he is still alive, or angry it just happened.

"Call the surgeon!" the doctor instructed.

"He just left for home," the nurse answered, as she picked up the phone to call the surgeon.

Surprisingly, eleven minutes later, the entire surgery team was ready to work.

"Olga, please wait in the waiting room, while the surgeon will open the material on Elijah's chest to see why so much blood gushed out from there," Louise told me.

"Mom, I am scared," Kristina said. "I want to go home."

I panicked, what do I do? I couldn't leave. But then Kristina saw the computer area and started playing games. I felt relieved and waited calmly, feeling that everything would be okay and God would give Elijah life. In my heart, I believed there was a reason that Elijah was surviving.

While waiting for the procedure to be completed, I met another couple, whose full-term baby had also had the Norwood procedure with lots of complications. He had to wait for 28 days to have his chest closed. These parents lived six hours away from Portland and had two older children, who stayed with their friends. They had already been in Portland more than a month, living in a hotel and visiting their baby daily.

When I heard their story, I thanked God that I lived close enough, could visit Elijah daily, and still be home with my husband and older children. When we think our problems are insurmountable, we can always find others, who have problems greater than our own. Even though you are in a terrible situation, you can always find things to be thankful for.

After two hours, the procedure was completed, and the surgeon came to talk with me.

"I found a small hole on the surface of Elijah's heart," he said with a sad tone of voice. "Small amounts of blood slowly leaked over a period of time and accumulated under Elijah's heart. I am pleased that I have discovered the problem and was able to correct it before the chest was closed. However, adding more medications and blood will delay the closing of Elijah's chest."

Every time, the closing of Elijah's chest was delayed, my heart sank. I knew that postponing closure would increase the risks of infection and lower the chance of Elijah's survival.

For two weeks after the surgery no one knew if Elijah would live or die. The doctors had predicted that he would have a challenging recovery, with only a 70% chance of survival. Some days, they were not sure why Elijah responded the way he did. Later, we found out that Elijah was the second 30-week-baby at OHSU, who went through the Norwood procedure. The first baby-girl, born at 30 weeks a year previously, didn't survive her surgery. There were still a lot of unknowns.

....

On the seventeenth day after the surgery, the doctors were finally able to close Elijah's chest! Thank God! Elijah's wound had been open for such a long time that Oleg and I wondered if it would ever be closed. We had the hardest time believing the procedure went so smoothly.

It was heartrending to see Elijah's freshly closed wound and stitches. I can't explain how emotional it is to see your child's body cut and bruised, in the manner Elijah's chest was. It evokes all the maternal feelings every mother has. You imagine all the pain, all the suffering your child is going through and you want to do something. And yet, you know the best thing you can do is to let the doctors do their job, and pray they are guided by God.

"Closing of Elijah's chest reduces the chance of infections," the surgeon explained. "The next step is to remove all the tubes."

"How soon do you think all the tubes will come out?" I asked.

"Over the next two weeks."

"Will Elijah be waking up soon?" I asked.

"We will start reducing the support of medications and a breathing machine today, so that Elijah can start waking up slowly."

I could hardly wait for Elijah to really wake up. He still slept most of that day, but started moving his hands and legs.

....

The next day, when I came to the hospital, I noticed six nurses in Elijah's room. It scared me to death because I knew it usually meant that something critical happened. One of the nurses noticed my pale face.

"We are taking out Elijah's breathing tube and will replace it with a nasal cannula," she said. "We hope in few days Elijah would breathe on his own."

The good news was so unexpected that I almost fainted. I could not believe it was happening. The nurse wrapped Elijah in a blanket.

"Olga, you might be able to hold Elijah tomorrow!" she said with a smile.

Soon the doctor came to check on Elijah and told me an excellent news, "We will stop the nutrition through an IV and will start giving Elijah your breast milk through a feeding tube again."

"I am overjoyed to hear that," I said. "I know how much better breast milk is for Elijah than formula. And I am excited that I will soon be breastfeeding my baby again!"

Unfortunately, by evening the cardiologist told me the opposite news, "Olga, we have discovered that Elijah's body is unable to properly digest the breast milk. We believe Elijah's lymph system has been injured during the surgery. So, we prescribed Elijah a low-fat formula to be administered through a feeding tube for the next six weeks."

"I am so disappointed," I said, utterly dejected, "but I understand..."

Patiently, I continued to pump the breast milk, but my supply was slowly decreasing due to stress. I froze the milk, hoping that at the end of six weeks I would be able to breastfeed Elijah. I was sad. Formula does not have the same nutritional and health benefits as the breast milk. And it cannot replace the bonding and the skin to skin contact which is created with the child, while breastfeeding. I wanted to be close to my child and be there for him, but I knew that the doctors had made the correct decision. To be truthful, it was as much for me as it would be for Elijah.

....

When I arrived at the hospital the next morning, the nurse greeted me with news, "Last evening Elijah needed to use a by-pap mask, so he could obtain more oxygen in his lungs. A by-pap mask allows an additional amount of oxygen over the nasal cannula to assist in breathing."

Every day brought good news, bad news, good news, bad news... My level of patience was being tried.

The nurse wrapped Elijah in the blanket, with all the tubes still connected to him, and asked me, "Olga, would you like to hold Elijah?"

"Really? I can hold my baby?" I asked, scared and excited. "How can I hold him with all the tubes and wires attached to him?"

"Don't worry. Elijah will be okay," the nurse assured me. "You just hold him carefully and the blanket will keep his tubes together."

The last time I had held my baby was nearly a month ago. Tears of joy spilled from my eyes as I prayed quietly, "Thank you, God, for this moment! Thank you for bringing my baby back to life!"

Elijah was smiling in his sleep as if he was having a good dream! I smiled with him, having a hard time believing that my baby was alive, and that I was holding him again.

Oleg was able to hold Elijah in the evening. We were scared to hold our baby with all the tubes, cuts and stitches, but I cannot explain the joy and how precious it was to hold our son, who seemed to be coming back to life. Through tears we both kept thanking God!

……..

The following day, as suggested by the nurse, I brought an outfit for Elijah.

"I can't imagine how we can put an outfit on Elijah with all the tubes and IVs attached to him," I said.

"We can do it. Believe me, Olga. The outfit will hold Elijah's tubes together," the nurse answered with a smile.

We did it and it was better. I was holding my precious baby again! His ability to breathe improved. The by-pap mask was taken off and replaced with the nasal cannula. Elijah started to wake up and cried with a weak voice! He was looking at me and it seemed like he was asking, "Mom, what had happened?"

I held him tight and kept repeating, "Elijah, everything will be okay. God has returned you back to life. From now on you will be getting better and I will be here with you and for you!"

Elijah wanted to be held constantly and I was willing. Holding him gave both of us what we needed most: contact bonding, which provided a human element that medicine cannot provide. My heart and my experience whispered, "Olga, you need to be here 24 hours a day. Your presence will help Elijah."

When I went home that afternoon, I told our children, "I need to stay with Elijah at the hospital from now on. Dad will take care of you. Elijah needs me."

Michael and David were scared and quiet, but Kristina started crying, "Mom, we need you home."

My heart was torn apart. How could I do both? There was only one of me. After about 30 minutes of talking to Kristina, she finally let me go.

When I returned to the hospital to spend the night with Elijah, I couldn't fall asleep. There was a very ill baby across the hallway, whose alarm was going off every ten seconds. Elijah was sleeping peacefully, but I was miserable. Turning from one side to another, I wished I could be home in my bed. The noises seemed to be constant. I couldn't stand it, so I drove back home at 2:00 A.M. Thank God, I didn't fall asleep behind the wheel.

While driving, I wondered how the hospitalized children and their parents slept in the intensive care unit every night with all the alarm sounds. When you are tired enough, I suppose you can sleep anywhere. I had met some parents who had slept here for several months.

Normally, we live at home with well children and our life is good. We have very few problems, even though we may think we do. As Oleg and I spent more and more time at OHSU, our perspective about life, people and illness began to change.

If you could take the roof off the hospital, where your loved one is receiving care, and look inside at every floor and every room, you would see all the pain and suffering that is occurring. Then if you look even closer, you will see the good works and miracles that doctors and nurses perform every day. Life is so precious and we, sometimes, forget that the problems, that we see others have today, can become our problems. It is so easy to have your normal life turn upside down, and the life or lives of your loved ones, that are so precious, lost in a moment.

....

The longer Elijah stayed in the hospital, Oleg and I realized that we had to face several growing challenges, which did not directly relate to Elijah. Watching our tiny son undergo procedure after procedure, one moment doing well and the next moment being on death's door step, kept

138

us on an emotional roller coaster. Sleep deprived and not always eating normally, we were perfect candidates for acute depression. It was difficult for us to stay away from depression, to stay connected to our children, and to maintain our family routines.

Our normal schedule was disrupted by fear, illness and separation. We ran to and from the hospital and never had enough quality time for our children or for each other. I understood that I couldn't be depressed and cry 24 hours a day; my children and husband still needed me, happy and healthy. Leaving Elijah's problems at the hospital, I tried to concentrate at home on our family. It wasn't easy. If the children asked about Elijah, I told them, but we didn't talk a lot about him because I didn't want them to feel like we only cared about Elijah. I tried to give the same amount of love and attention to each of our children, whose needs did not cease simply because one of our children had a complicated medical condition. Like all children, Michael, Kristina and David wanted a happy Mom and Dad.

....

11

Everyone needs joy in their lives. Take time to create it for yourself and others.

Over the next week, Elijah continued to recover. We brought the children to see him for the first time since his surgery. Excited to see Elijah's eyes open and happy that he felt better, we had a great family time together. Soon Elijah got tired and fell asleep.

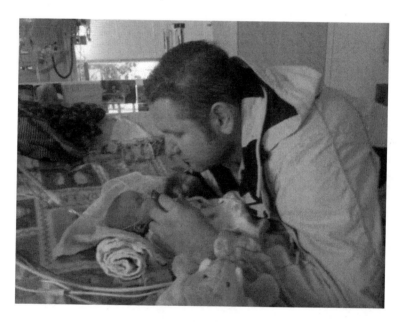

"While Elijah is sleeping, let's go have some fun!" Oleg said.

It was the first time in a while I saw my husband excited.

"The nurse gave me these free tickets for a TRAM in the air, which was built to ameliorate the hospital parking problems. We need to use these tickets!"

"Yes!" the kids jumped up, excited. "Let's go have fun!"

We had a very good time, seeing Portland from the air. That sense of joy had been missing in our lives.

....

A week later Oleg's employer was going to hold a Christmas party at the Oregon zoo. Usually, at the end of the party, the children receive presents and employees receive bonuses. I wanted to go to the party with my husband and children and then walk through the zoo, but at the same time I understood how important it was for me to be with Elijah. Not sure of what to do, I called Elijah's nurse, who happened to be Louise that day. I told her my worries.

"Olga, don't even come to the hospital today," Louise said. "Spend time with your family. They need you. I will take good care of Elijah."

Louise was very understanding. Her love for our family brought tears to my eyes. I was pulled between family and Elijah, wanting to do both, and that day she helped me to manage it. I felt that she loved Elijah and me, and that meant so much!

All excited, we drove to the party and then walked through the zoo. At the end, we stopped at the gift shop, bought soft toys for Elijah, and went to visit Elijah. Louise met us with a smile.

"I sat Elijah in an upright seat to help him breathe easier," she said. "And, I have an exciting news for you! Elijah has no more IVs attached to him! All his medications are going in through a feeding tube with his formula!"

We were so excited and wanted to take a family photo. Louise put Elijah in a chair in the middle, and we all stood behind Elijah. Louise took a photo of our family together.

"Thank you, Louise, for letting us have a normal family day," I told Louise, blinking back tears of joy! "Your thoughtfulness is such a blessing to our family."

It's amazing what nurses do! Sometimes, the most important gift we can give our family are the gifts of time and love.

That evening, my parents and sister came to visit Elijah. It was their first time seeing Elijah after his surgery. Luckily, Elijah had clothes on and looked a lot better.

....

Four weeks had passed since Elijah's surgery. His incisions were healing, and he was stable. The cardiologist came to talk to me, "Our plan is to transfer Elijah to a private room at the Pediatric unit," he said. "It would require you, Olga, to be with Elijah twenty-four hours a day. Are you ready for it?"

"I am prepared to stay, but at the same time I am concerned about all the problems of caring for our children at home," I said.

The cardiologist left. I prayed for God to make the best decision for our family. An hour later, the cardiologist came back with good news.

"Actually, we will be transferring Elijah back to NICU. Usually, only newborn babies are staying there, but Elijah was born premature. If he was born on time, he would be a newborn today. The nurses and doctors of NICU are letting Elijah come back!"

"That is a great news!" I exclaimed! "I can continue being with Elijah when I can and still be home with my family! Thank you, God, for hearing my prayer, for showing me a miracle and for taking good care of our family!" I thanked God through tears.

Caring for Elijah after his surgery was not a simple task for the NICU nurses. Together with doctors, they were still facing a lot of unknowns with Elijah, but were ready to love and help our baby. The NICU nurses knew Elijah very well and promised to take good care of him. Before Elijah was transferred back to NICU, the main cardiologist came to visit us one last time.

"We are glad to see Elijah do so well and hope to send him home after 10 to 14 days of recovery at the NICU," he said with a smile.

"Thank you, doctor, for all the great and complicated work you have done for our son! You are a beautiful vessel in God's help and I appreciate your hard work!" I said through tears of happiness.

....

Through the long halls of the hospital, the nurse pushed Elijah's bed and I followed her. Elijah was surrounded by pumps with medication, oxygen tank and other stuff. I was happy. It was like I was being given a gift to go back to NICU. I already knew those doctors and nurses. They knew how to care for our son and cared deeply about him. Nurses, like Patty, would go out of their way, doing extra things. They recognized there was more to caring for the patient than just attending to medical needs. Something as simple as asking how you are doing and offering words of comfort or a cup of water made our long hours there bearable.

When we came back to the NICU, one of the nurses asked, "Olga, how did you survive the time of Elijah's surgery?"

"I learned to forget about yesterday, be happy for today and not to worry about tomorrow," I answered. "My goal is to be positive. I wish Elijah could be home today, but it is not possible. So being back at NICU is better than being at the post-surgery unit of PICU."

The nurses hugged me and welcomed me back. Patti was taking care of Elijah that day. NICU was like a comfort zone because Elijah had already spent two months there.

....

The next morning Patti was with Elijah again. When I came, she told me, "Olga, I worry about Elijah. He had hard time breathing yesterday and required a by-pap mask. I hope he can outgrow this breathing problem."

Luckily, Elijah's breathing improved.

On the third day, while I was driving to the hospital to be with Elijah, I received a phone call from his neonatologist, "Olga, Elijah is not doing well at all. We need your permission to do more tests," she said.

"What is happening?" I asked, frightened.

"We don't know yet. We will find out more after the tests are completed."

"I give you permission. I will be there in 10 minutes," I said.

That day Elijah was close to death. His test showed he had an infection. The doctors worried and started him on antibiotics. Even the surgeon had to come to the meeting with the NICU doctors to help decide how to best care for Elijah. All of his medications were switched to IV again.

The nurses found it difficult to find a vein on Elijah's hands. They started looking for it on Elijah's scalp. It wasn't something I ever wanted to see, but I asked to stay with Elijah. While the nurses inserted the IV on Elijah's scalp, I held his tiny hand. Elijah did not even cry and just laid there, looking very pale. Those were the signs that he was close to death. A healthy baby would cry and scream, as the IV would be inserted.

Later, that evening, a female doctor came, kissed me on my head and said, "Olga, where does your strength come from? Elijah almost died. How can you be so calm?"

"I believe God gives me strength," I answered through tears, while holding my baby and treasuring every second with him.

Every moment could be our last moment together. It seemed like every day brought dramatic changes. I really had no choice, but to just go with the flow.

....

My Father's birthday was coming up in two days. My brother tried to organize our annual family trip to Sunriver Resort, four hours away from our home. He called and asked if we could go. I was exhausted.

"Olga, I have to work, but I think you should go and spend time with our older children," Oleg said.

"I feel bad leaving Elijah," I said. "But I also know that David, Kristina and Michael don't see me often and this would be good for our family. I need rest and my blood pressure is still high."

"Olga will go with our three children," Oleg told my

brother.

The next morning, I told the nurses I would be going, and they supported me in taking a break. They promised to take good care of Elijah. I appreciated their love and care.

"Volunteers came here often to hold babies. They can also hold Elijah," the nurse said. "When caring for others, a mother's own needs seem to come last. A mother has to learn to take care of herself to be able to care of others."

Most of my family, about thirty-five people, went to Sunriver for three days. We had a great time together, playing with our children in the snow and sitting with them in the hot tub. Each evening we would play games, drink tea, sing songs and pray together.

I was given a bedroom and a private bathroom all to myself. Everyone was so considerate of me. I continued to pump my breast milk, but it seemed so useless. My baby was dying. Yet, there was still hope, and I had to cling to that hope, for it was all that I had.

Each day Oleg would send pictures of Elijah and I was delighted to get them. Yet the pictures also told me I was not there and made me think maybe I should be.

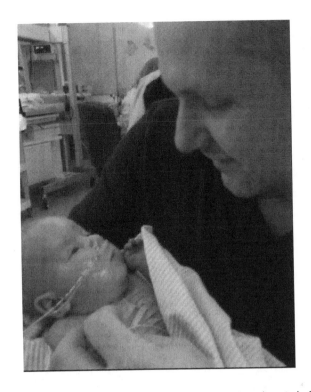

We returned to Vancouver. Impatiently, I left the children at my Mother's house and went directly back to the hospital to see Elijah. He was awake and smiled at me! I held him very close and he seemed to like it. It was like he had missed me. I noticed that his stitches had been taken out and small pieces of tape were on his wound! I kissed him and thanked God. To hold my baby again was a wonderful moment. Seeing him that day, knowing what he had been through, was such an amazing difference from when he first came out of the surgery! Being with Elijah, alive and awake again after such a scary surgery, was a blessing beyond belief for all of us and I thanked God!

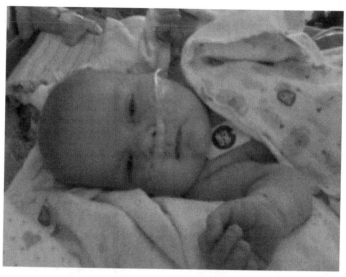

....

After being in the induced coma for a month, Elijah had forgotten how to drink milk from a bottle. The nurses had to retrain him. They were unsuccessful for a while and had to do an x-ray to see if there was an injury in his throat. Luckily, there was not. It just took Elijah longer to learn how to drink from the bottle. The amount of milk he could drink from the bottle was limited by his strength, thus he was still fed mostly through the feeding tube.

Over the next week, Elijah was weaned off the antibiotic, so all his medications were switched back to oral again. The last two drain tubes were taken out of his chest! Elijah had no IVs attached to him! He only had his breathing and feeding tubes attached to his face. What a big day! Our baby was doing better again!

....

Time passed, and Christmas arrived. On Christmas morning, before church, we drove to the hospital to take a family photo with Elijah in his first Christmas outfit. He was awake and Renelle was taking care of him. It was the day when Renelle needed to change Elijah's feeding tube, so

148

before we came there, I called Renelle.

"Hello, Renelle. Is it possible to take Elijah's feeding tube out before our family photo and then insert a new one after?" I asked.

"Sure," she said. "We can do that."

Elijah's face was clear of any tubes. It was a little red after the tape was taken off! After the photo, I changed Elijah's diaper. He had diarrhea and it was like a fountain exploded. It got on my hands and clothing. We all laughed. It was the first moment Elijah brought us joy. If this had happened at home with one of my other children, I would have been unhappy that I had gotten my church outfit dirty, but that was not the case that day. I was thankful and happy that my baby was alive and nothing else mattered.

That day I noticed Elijah was a little agitated. He seemed unhappy and kept crying. The nurse and I were not sure why. I wanted to stay with Elijah, but I also knew it was important for me to be with my family.

Christmas was a big deal in our family. Our traditions were to go to church and for our children to sing in the choir. After church, we would go to my Mother's house, open presents, have a large meal, celebrate the birth of Jesus and give the presents to our children. But Elijah couldn't come, and we were torn. I had to force myself to keep my heart as strong as steel, so that I could do these things with our family and older children, and leave Elijah. "It would only be a few hours," I kept reminding myself.

....

The next day, Renelle was on duty again. She told me, "Olga, for some reason, Elijah acted very agitated yesterday and would not stop crying. He and the other ill baby in the room kept me so busy."

I wondered why Elijah would be so agitated. Later, we discovered that every time the doctors changed his narcotic medications from oral to IV, it gave him withdrawal symptoms, which were difficult for Elijah's system to handle.

Early afternoon, I left to return home. Waiting for Oleg, I cooked red borsch, a Russian beet and cabbage soup. After we ate dinner, I went back to the hospital. I decided to bring dinner for Renelle, who that day had to work until 11 P.M.

"Okay, I will go eat it really quickly," Renelle said, happy that I brought her borsch.

Then she came back and checked to see if we were still okay.

"That borsch is so good; I will go eat a little more," she said and left.

When she came back she looked so satisfied.

"Oh, I ate all the borsch and bread," she patted her stomach.

"You ate it all?" I asked, surprised. "There was enough borsch for two people."

Renelle smiled.

"I was really hungry, Olga. Nurses work very hard."

Then Renelle became so happy and started singing Jewish songs. Another nurse in the room looked at her, wondering what had happened.

"Olga, did you add vodka to your borsch?" she jokingly asked.

"No," I said.

We had so much fun with Renelle that day.

....

150

12

A family that cares is a precious gift.

Four days after Christmas, the NICU doctors started talking about discharging Elijah. They planned on sending him home with a nasal cannula and oxygen, hoping that he could outgrow the problem of breathing. Elijah had no IVs attached to him, but I would still need to give him eleven medications with his formula. The idea more than scared the living hell out of me.

"What if something goes wrong," I thought. "Would I be able to handle it? What if I did something wrong, for example, give a double dose of medications or forget to give him medications? Would I be able to live with the consequences? I am not a nurse nor a doctor. How would I know what to do? How do I manage it 24 hours a day, 7 days a week, week after week?"

All these thoughts went through my head, but I did not have the answers. What I did know was that my baby had a chance to come home and I was excited!

That same evening, while at home, we received a phone call from the cardiologist with very bad news, "Elijah is having a hard time breathing. We need your permission to intubate him with the breathing machine. If we don't give him breathing help, he may die. We also need to do a cardiac catheterization."

"We give you permission," hopelessly Oleg said.

Both of us had a very hard evening wondering what the next minute could bring us. The doctors sedated and intubated Elijah, and switched all medications from oral to IV again. They performed a cardiac catheterization lab, which lasted three hours. The doctors wanted to know if it was Elijah's heart or his premature lungs that were causing the problem. Using the microscopic video camera, they went inside an artery to Elijah's heart to see if a shunt had gotten clogged. The day had started with such happy news of Elijah coming home soon. Now he might never come home...

The next day the cardiologist met me by Elijah's crib.

"Luckily, Elijah's shunt did not get clogged," he said. "But his aorta has gotten narrower. So, we had to insert a stint, which is also risky. If it moves, Elijah will die right away. The test also showed that the pressure in Elijah's heart is 14-15 instead of 4-5. His heart will not handle the second surgery, which is supposed to be in two months."

It seemed like Elijah's problems were continuing to multiply. I was losing strength, patience and hope. My eyes began to see the reality of what was happening. My mind slowly absorbed the message; Elijah's condition was not going in the direction we wanted. His chances of survival were diminishing, and my heart resisted the inevitable outcome. Driving home, I had no recourse but to implore God to help us.

．．．．．．．

Once home, I sent a text message to friends and family asking for prayers. We needed help. There were so many problems beyond my control and I was tired of trying.

In the evening I told Oleg, "I can't face these problems anymore and watch Elijah suffer. I need help. Can we please go away to get new strength? Today, I am the one who needs help."

Oleg knew from the tone of my voice, it was one of those moments when your wife says something, you have to do it. He called Skamania Lodge and made a reservation. We had paid little heed to the calendar and now tomorrow was New Year's Eve. There was only the most expensive room available. Oleg didn't question, he just reserved.

I called my sister and asked if we could leave our children with her for two days. But she said that she was going to a New Year's party and would not be able to watch them. I stopped calling. Who needs my children on New Year's? For people, it was a big holiday, but we didn't see the holiday in it. Our son was near death...

In the morning, together with our children, we visited Elijah, who slept and showed no signs of life, since he was sedated. Seeing their brother lifeless scared the children; to them, he looked dead. I told the nurses we were going away to Skamania Lodge for two nights and two days. They thought it was a good idea. The nurses were working so hard to save Elijah's life.

At Skamania Lodge, our family swam in the giant pool and enjoyed the Jacuzzi and sauna. We had a wonderful time together and then went to the buffet dinner at the lodge.

Late in the evening, the cardiologist called me and said, "Elijah is having a hard time breathing. We need your permission to take him to the cardiac catheterization lab again to check his lungs and heart."

"We give you permission," I sighed.

"Are you going to come here?" he asked.

"We are not," I said. "We are an hour away and I need help today. I won't be able to help Elijah or you. I will just sit there and cry. I can't make myself to be there today."

A few hours later the cardiologist called again and said, "We have placed Elijah on a full life support."

He was the same cardiologist who fought for Elijah's life right after his surgery and stayed with him overnight. And now he was with Elijah again, trying to help save his life. I appreciated all the hard work of our wonderful and skilled doctors.

That night I had the hardest time falling asleep, thinking about Elijah and his suffering. I realized when God left Jesus on the cross alone, it was hard for God Himself to see His Son suffer. I felt the same about my son. I couldn't watch Elijah suffer. I had to leave to gain strength.

This is a decision that everybody needs to make for themselves. You have to listen to your body and mind about what you need or should do. I knew that I would just sit by Elijah and cry. I would not be able to help anybody and would only do worse for my health. I couldn't face it. This experience taught me to be less judgmental. Sometimes, we are critical of others, when we see them doing something that we think is crazy. We make quick judgments about others and their behavior, when we fully do not understand their situation.

In the morning, we called the hospital.

"No big changes. Elijah is on full life support," the nurse informed us.

We knew subconsciously he was alive because otherwise they would have called us. We drove back to Portland and straight to the hospital.

Kristina and Michael were too scared to see Elijah.

"Mom, can we please stay in the waiting room?" they asked.

"Sure," I let them.

David made the choice to go with us. We respected our children's wishes.

When I saw all the equipment around Elijah again, my heart dropped. Elijah had taken ten steps back, which was so hard for me to accept. We always want the best for our children. This was a horrible step backwards. Oleg, David, and I stood quietly by Elijah. We felt devastated, seeing

Elijah like this. Totally helpless, we knew there was nothing we could do to help him. I could not believe that only a few days earlier our son was so much better.

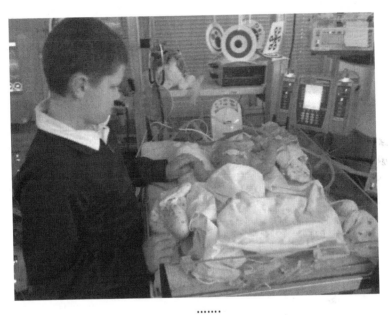

....

The next day, when I came to the hospital, the doctors were making their rounds and were by Elijah's bed.

"Do, you have any questions, Olga?" one of the doctors asked.

I started crying.

"I am out of questions and am losing my hope," I said, tearfully.

The doctors didn't say anything. They just stood quietly. What could they say? From that moment on, I no longer heard them say anything about discharging Elijah. Even though Elijah had an arterial line inserted into his artery, to obtain direct and continuous blood pressures and blood for labs, Patti still let me hold him on a pillow. When I sat on the chair and held Elijah, I could not stop crying. I knew I shouldn't cry, but I couldn't help myself. As I sat there, a young female doctor came and kissed me on my head.

"Olga, I thought it would be Elijah's last night yesterday," she said. "He scared us all, but he doesn't give up. He is such a fighter!"

....

On January 9th Elijah turned four months old and weighed about 10.5 pounds. He felt better again. After Elijah had been on the low-fat formula for six weeks, I was able to begin breastfeeding him again. This was exciting! However, for more than two weeks, Elijah would go through periods of good days and bad days. On the good days he would sit up, smile, play with his hands, and I would be able to breastfeed him. On the bad days, he would be close to death.

Elijah's heart was working hard, causing his heart muscle to become bigger and weaker. Sometimes Elijah's body retained fluids, which increased pressure in his veins, requiring his heart to work harder. Elijah was given diuretics to help correct this problem because it was important to keep his system in perfect balance. The nurses weighed Elijah's diaper every time they changed him, to have an accurate count of his output. By knowing the numbers, the doctors could adjust the diuretic medicine, to regulate how much he would urinate.

Additionally, the doctors started giving Elijah Milrinone, a strong medication to help his heart beat properly. It was given through an IV, but needed to be changed to oral as soon as possible. It was too risky for Elijah to stay on it for very long. The use of an IV meant that he was not getting better and he would not be able to go home. The doctors tried several times to convert Elijah to the oral medications, but each time Elijah had a hard time breathing and almost died. He also remained on the two narcotic medications, prescribed during his surgery, and any change of his dosage gave him withdrawals.

Three cardiac catheterization labs were already performed. Every time they brought a higher risk of his kidney's shutting down. Our hearts ached for Elijah, but the nurse, Patti, always reminded us to take one day at a time and we did. Some days we had to take one minute at a time.

The doctors started calling Elijah the "Puzzle Baby." He was their first premature baby, born at thirty-weeks, who had gone through a Norwood procedure and survived. The public often has the idea that if they go to a doctor, there will always be a perfect fix. Many know this is not true.

Doctors are skilled and highly trained professionals, yet sometimes, they are negotiating new medical territory. At some point, two good options can change to one good and one bad option. Next, it changes to the lesser of two bad options. And then, there is one bad option before the unknown. It is from the unknown that the doctors learn. Today I know that the doctors learned a great deal in caring for Elijah. This information they can use to help other babies with a similar diagnosis.

During this time one lady asked me, "Olga, don't you think that the doctors are just using Elijah to practice on?"

Her question hurt me. At the time I was not ready for it. Questions such as these made me angry and gave me a desire to avoid people. For if there were no people, there would be no questions or comments. But the question is valid. I knew that the doctors and nurses cared, and were doing everything in their power to help our son. They never did anything without our permission. All decisions were made by a team of doctors. If you think back in history and ask yourself, would you prefer the medical care of the 1700's or of today? Of course, you would choose today. And, hopefully, what the doctors learned in working with Elijah will help others in the future.

....

One day, I spoke with a mother of a child, whose bed was next to Elijah.

"My child has already undergone six surgeries," she said. "He has a permanent breathing tube attached to an opening in his neck and is paralyzed from the neck down. He is only living with the support of the machine."

When I was growing up, my Mother had always taught me, "Compare yourself to those who are in a worse situation. Then your life will be easier, and you will always find what to thank God for."

158

I did that, and it helped me live. I thanked God that Elijah had only one surgery, not six at that time.

....

The days passed, week after week. On January 19th, Elijah turned 4.5 months old. He was not doing well. The cardiologists, neonatologists and surgeons gathered to see if there were any ideas left on how to help Elijah. We worried the news would be bad. They were supposed to tell us their decision in couple of days.

The next day, on January 20th, David was turning twelve years old. Like all children, he wanted a birthday party. Did Oleg and I feel like celebrating? No, but we still did. David deserved it and we couldn't ignore him just because of Elijah's illness. So, we invited his cousins, ordered pizza, bought a cake and let the children have fun. During David's birthday party, Oleg was with Elijah at the hospital and I was at home. A smile was on my face, but my heart was crying.

....

Three days later, a cardiologist came and shared the committee's findings.

"Elijah's heart is failing," she said. "Our team of doctors had decided that Elijah has only two options left. The first option is a heart transplant at Stanford hospital in Palo Alto, California. The second option is to disconnect Elijah's medications and let him die. The doctors want to meet with you at 6 P.M. Will your husband be able to come?"

"Yes, my husband and I will come. We will be there." I said. "I have a question for you, doctor. You were the same cardiologist, who told me during delivery that our baby had less than a 1% chance for life. You asked if we wanted to let him die. And today you are telling me again that our baby won't live. How can you do that?"

159

"Olga, this is the hardest part of my job, but I have to tell parents the truth. At the same time, I don't want to take away their hope."

After Elijah was born, I was actually scared of this cardiologist. At first, there were days when I avoided her, because she always seemed to bring bad news. But later, I realized that she was very kind; she just had a very hard job. I cannot imagine myself doing what she does every day--- spending many hours caring for patients and telling people honestly what is happening, even when it is bad news. It must be difficult. Yet, she is able to do it with grace and dignity.

The doctor's news didn't surprise me. I knew this was going to be such an important decision. I called Oleg, told him what had happened, and asked, "Honey, can you please come to the hospital at 6 p.m.?"

"Yes, I will get off work early and be there," Oleg said.

By this time, it seemed that we were both immune to the ups and downs and to the tragedies that were occurring in our lives. It was like one more step in the process, which seemed to never end. A process, over which we had no choice, and yet must make the next decision.

I then called my Father, explained the situation with Elijah and asked, "Dad, we will have to make some serious decisions today. You don't have to come, but I want you and need you here. Can you please come and help us with the decision?"

"Sure," my Father answered. "I will be there. Please don't cry, my daughter. I love you so much. It will all be okay."

Since childhood I have had a special bond with my parents. I often ask for their advice, believing their answer would always be in my family's best interest. Even if I don't like the answer, I know it is what they honestly believe.

They have life experiences that I don't have. Even though in the very beginning Dad had told us that he would have made a different decision than we did, I still, like a little girl, needed my Father for support. I have always had great respect for him and trusted that he would give me his honest opinion.

That day there was a nurse with Elijah whom I didn't know.

"It may be a good idea to call Patti," she said. "Patti always wants to know the progress of Elijah."

Patti gave me a certain sense of comfort, which I desperately needed, so I called her.

"Yes, Olga, I will come," she said. "Please take care of yourself."

Wanting all the support we could muster, I sent a text to my brothers and sister, asking them for prayers. I remained at the hospital, waiting for Oleg's arrival. My emotional state only increased my stress level.

I motioned to a nurse, "Can you please place screens around Elijah and me for privacy? I don't want to see anyone or anyone to see me."

"Of course, I can do that," the nurse said, and quietly placed the privacy screens around us.

Sitting in a rocking chair, I held Elijah, looked at his pale face, and wept. I was saying goodbye to our son and asking God for strength. I cried, and cried, and cried. I felt that God's will was to take Elijah, so I struggled to accept it. That day I understood that I was clay in God's hands and could not tell Him what to do. What could I do? From our perspective, Elijah was suffering, Oleg and I were suffering, and our healthy children were suffering. How long were we to endure in this state?

I was ready to release our baby back to God. I could have been angry at God for failing Elijah, but for some reason I wasn't. I knew in my heart that God is real. He gives life and takes it away. He heals people, if it is His will. I wanted Him to let Elijah live, but was ready to accept His decision. When you truly accept God, you accept all of God, and all of his plans for your life. Some of those plans will be easy and you will be happy. Other times, your plan will be difficult beyond your capacity to believe what is happening to you. As you live through it, you will grow more than you ever imagined you could.

That day I didn't want to think about a heart transplant. Elijah had been through so much. I didn't want him to have to go through another surgery. I didn't know where the surgery would take place. One doctor had mentioned California; if we had to travel, who would take care of my family? Also, my blood pressure was too high, and I couldn't manage more stress. The nurse checked on me often, gave me tissues and comforted me, but there was nothing more she could do. That day she could not tell me that Elijah would be okay.

Arriving at the hospital, Oleg was quiet and just held pale Elijah, who slept most of the time. The nurse came and checked on us.

"All of Elijah's energy is going to his failing heart," she said. "That is why he has no energy to even open his eyes."

Every moment was hard for Elijah. Oleg and I didn't want to talk about the impending discussion with the doctor and the inevitable bad news. We could not hold Elijah enough, because we feared that we might never have a chance to hold him again.

"I am ready to give up," I told Oleg. "But somewhere deep down inside I still have that little hope."

"Me too," Oleg said and breathed in deeply.

"I also feel that Elijah has suffered enough," I continued. "The best decision would be to turn off his medications and let him go to God."

"Olga, I believe God can still help Elijah," Oleg said. "I also want to give Elijah all of his chances. If we don't take him to the Stanford hospital, he won't have that last chance to fight for his life and survive."

A little later my Father came. Before meeting with the team of doctors, we discussed the issues and he asked us some questions.

"Oleg and Olga. Please consider the impact on yourselves and your children," my Father said. "I believe it's better to disconnect Elijah's medications and stop his suffering. A heart transplant would be a long process with no guarantee as to outcomes."

Oleg was quiet. In my heart, I was agreeing with my Father.

"Are you prepared as parents for the reality of having to spend the rest of your lives with a disabled child?" my Father continued.

It was hard to hear my Father say that, because we already loved Elijah so much. We wanted Elijah to live. My Father loved his Grandson, too, and everything he was telling us was likely true. He was basically telling us the same thing he told us four months ago, when we had to make a life or death decision for Elijah right after his birth.

At 6 P.M., we gathered in a conference room and the doctors again told us our choices.

"Oleg and Olga, you can let nature take its course and let Elijah die, or you can go to California for a heart transplant and give Elijah his chance for life. Elijah and one of the parents would have to be in California for six to twelve months and wait for a healthy heart to become available for a transplant. This would require an organ donation from a baby, but babies don't die as often as adults. Therefore, it might take a long time. Other babies may have priorities over Elijah. It isn't a simple process of Elijah needing a new heart and one being available right away."

"Will Elijah have a normal life after the transplant?" I asked.

"It would not be a perfect cure and would likely result in changing one illness for other problems in the future," the cardiologist explained. "Elijah would likely, if he survived, spend a great deal of his time at the hospital. He could require additional medical attention for the rest of his life, including other organ transplants from donors."

"What do you think we should do?" I asked.

"Unfortunately, we cannot tell you what to do," the cardiologist said. "But we will respect and honor your decision."

After the doctors left, my Father had not changed his position.

"No one knows what kind of life Elijah will have after a heart transplant and how hard it will be for you to have a disabled child," he said.

"Dad, I agree with you," I told my Father. "But I also am willing to raise a disabled child, if it means that Elijah lives."

Patti was standing next to us and listening. Then she said, "Oleg and Olga, please wait and see if Elijah would qualify for a heart transplant."

"I, honestly, don't want to do that," I told Patti. "It is something new that I would have to deal with, but I feel I don't have any energy left for it."

It was as if I was being asked to go back to the beginning and travel down the same road a second time, only to end up in the same painful ending. If God was going to let Elijah die, why not let him die now? Overwhelm, grief and exhaustion washed over me. I just wanted the problem to go away, but all I was getting was more complications. It is terrible to think of one of your children as a problem, but Elijah was, as much as we loved him, creating conflicts within our family. He was making our normal life abnormal, and I wanted to return to normal.

Later that evening, my sisters with their husbands and my Mother came to say goodbye to Elijah. Some of them talked and some were quiet. Everyone had their own opinion, but no one could give us the solution. It was our decision to make.

Oleg and I left the hospital late and picked up our children at Tanya's house. At home, Oleg didn't say much, but I let out everything that was on my mind.

"I can't leave you with the children and go to California with Elijah," I told Oleg. "Having no more strength to see Elijah suffer, I am afraid I won't be able to handle the stress. I am done and don't want to deal with this anymore! I would choose to disconnect his medications."

Oleg didn't agree, but felt he had no choice but to agree with me. We decided to tell our decision to our children in the morning and take them to the hospital to say goodbye to Elijah.

The next morning was Saturday. When the children woke up, I went to talk to them, while Oleg was getting ready.

"Elijah is not doing well and will die soon," I said, while embracing my children with my arms. "Because we don't want Elijah to suffer any more, Dad and I have decided to disconnect Elijah's medications and just let him die."

The children started crying, "Why, Mom, why? We don't want Elijah to die! We love our baby-brother and want him to come home and be with us! Please don't disconnect the medications, please!"

The children sat on their beds and cried. I cried with them.

"Looks like this is God's plan," I said. "He hasn't healed Elijah's heart, which is very sick and can't work anymore."

It felt so weird to say that. Inside my heart, I thought, "God, do I have Your permission to do this? What is Your will?"

....

After breakfast, we were all ready to go to the hospital. Oleg and the children were waiting for me in the car. I decided to go upstairs to my room and choose an outfit for Elijah's burial. Somehow, I thought if we turned off the medications, he would immediately die. Then we would need an outfit and his blanket for his funeral. I sobbed over that outfit and his blanket and knew what it meant. I put the clothes gently into the bag and walked to the car.

We drove to the hospital quietly, all in tears. I don't know what Oleg and the children were thinking, but I wondered what would be next. As a child, I tried to avoid going to funerals. They had been a bad experience for me. If I had to attend a funeral, I would sit in the back row and not look at the casket. Now this was my own child, and I would be there in the very front row. I would need to stiffen my resolve and do that which I had not been able to handle before. We drove straight to the NICU.

"Can you please let us in all together to see Elijah?" I asked the clerk.

"No. Only three people at a time can go in," she said.

Frustrated, I dropped my head.

"Today is Elijah's last day," I said. "We have decided to turn off his medications. Can you please let our family be together for one last time?"

The confused clerk didn't know anything about the plan to disconnect the medications and left to check with Jen,

Elijah's nurse. Jen loved Elijah, took good care of him and, on hard days when I cried a lot, she comforted me. Jen let us all in.

"I need to call the cardiologist," she said. "If you would like, I can take you and Elijah to a private room, where you can say good bye."

I looked at so many of Elijah's IV tubes, wires and machines and said, "No, Jen. It's okay. We can stay here by Elijah's bed. Can you please put screens around us for privacy? We don't want the other parents to see us."

"Sure. Good idea," Jen said and moved the screens around us.

There were four other babies in that room, but luckily, their parents had not arrived yet.

Jen let Oleg hold Elijah. We all quietly cried over him, knowing that it was his last day. Soon, the cardiologist came.

"I wasn't at the last doctors' meeting about Elijah. What exactly did the doctors tell you?" he asked.

"They told us that our options are to either take Elijah to California for a heart transplant or disconnect his medications and let him die," Oleg explained. "We decided to disconnect Elijah's medications, so he won't suffer any more."

The cardiologist was not ready to hear that.

"Elijah's primary cardiologist is not at the hospital," he said. "It is her day off and I can't do anything without her permission. I will try calling her on the phone to see what she says."

The cardiologist left, and we stayed with Elijah. After a while, I left the hospital to take our children to my sister's house, as it was not necessary for them to be at the hospital. Oleg stayed with Elijah.

"If Elijah dies today, I want to be here, holding him," he said.

The children cried in the car.

"Mom, we don't want Elijah to die," they all said together.

"If you don't want Elijah to die, then I will probably have to go to California with Elijah for a long time, and you will have to stay home with Dad," I said.

"It's fine with us if you go. We will be okay. We are old enough. We want you to go to California, so Elijah will live!" the children cried.

I felt relieved, hearing that my children would be okay, if I had to leave. I left the children at my sister's house and came back to the hospital.

Oleg shared with me the good news, "The cardiologist came back. He couldn't get hold of Elijah's primary cardiologist and couldn't do any action on his own. He still thought that Elijah has a low chance to survive the second surgery and asked us not to hurry with disconnecting Elijah's medications."

"Really? Thank God!" I exclaimed. "So, okay, let's not disconnect the medications and give Elijah time. Hopefully, he will survive the second surgery."

We spent all that day with Elijah and went home late in the evening. Even though Elijah didn't feel good at all, at least we didn't have to plan a funeral. I felt that God tested us like He tested Abraham, asking him to bring Isaac as an offering to God. When Abraham was ready to do it, God told him not to. I felt like we had passed the test. We were ready to give Elijah back to God, if that was what He wanted. The whole day on Sunday, Oleg and I spent at the hospital by Elijah.

....

13

God is a personal experience. The more you search, the more you learn, and the more you understand about yourself and God.

Monday morning, when I came to be with Elijah, I felt as if no one in the unit knew that we had changed our mind and were NOT going to disconnect medications, but give God and Elijah more time. I saw sad faces of the nurses and could sense that no one approved of our decision. Elijah was sleeping, and Patti was taking care of him that day. She didn't seem so happy either.

"Olga, why didn't you call me to tell me of your decision?" Patti said with unhappy voice. "Why don't you want to check to see if Elijah qualifies for a heart transplant? If you don't give Elijah all his chances, your conscience will remind you of it all your life. You won't have peace. We will respect any decision that you make, and we will support you, but please don't hurry with your decision."

"Patti, we had changed our decision and we are not going to disconnect Elijah's medications, but it seems like no one knows about it in NICU," I said and started crying, as I already felt bad. "How could I even think about disconnecting Elijah's medications?" I asked. "I would never forgive myself."

Patti put her hand on my shoulder and said, "It is okay, Olga. It is a very hard decision. No one can tell you what to do, but Elijah is feeling better again!"

And he was. I could see it. Elijah acted like nothing was wrong. He was happy and smiling again.

"Would you and Oleg like me to ask the cardiologist to see if Elijah at least qualifies to go to California for a heart transplant?" Patti asked.

We agreed and thanked God that He didn't let us turn off Elijah's medications. If we did, we would have had to live with that guilt all our life. Only then I understood that the nurses loved Elijah and were attached to him more than to other babies. Normally, the babies spend a shorter time at NICU and either recover or are moved to another unit, but Elijah had spent the longest time there. He was one of the oldest babies in the unit. The nurses and doctors had developed a strong attachment to the care of our child. They would go out of their way to do special things, such as hold him, bring special toys to attach to his crib, all of which was beyond their "professional duty." I understood their attachment and appreciated it.

That day Elijah was so awake and seemed to feel better. He played with his toys and I even breastfed him. He was also looking at the nurses, trying to figure out if he knew them. Again, we began wondering if God had started the healing process.

....

The first four months Oleg visited Elijah two to three times per week. After we almost turned off Elijah's medications, he started visiting him every evening. He held Elijah, talked to him, read the Bible to him and prayed for him. Oleg's cousin Eddie and friend Johnny came often and supported my husband. They prayed with Oleg or just sat quietly with him by Elijah's bed.

Oleg, as the head of our house, felt responsible for everything. He worried about my blood pressure being high, about our finances, and about our child. What was happening to Elijah started to become overwhelming for Oleg. He was ready to do whatever it took to help Elijah.

Some evenings were especially hard for him. While lying in bed, he would cry out to God and wonder why Elijah had a defective heart.

"God, if we have sinned, punish us, not Elijah," Oleg would often say.

One evening Oleg's aunt called.

"I am so sorry, Oleg," she said. "So many times, I would pick up the phone to call you, but I didn't know what to say and would just hang up. I had no words of comfort for you that I knew would help."

This was the first time that someone from Oleg's side of the family, other than immediate family, had called. The call reduced Oleg, who is a strong man, to tears. It was important to know that his aunt would call and care enough to try, even though she did not know what to do. She promised to pray for us.

....

I have previously mentioned some of the important lessons we learned throughout our journey with Elijah. Most came from stressful situations and God lead us through them to teach us more about Him and His ways. However, that was not always the case.

In our church at that time, we followed the Biblical doctrine of the laying on of hands and the anointing with oil for the healing of the sick and afflicted. We had requested the ministers of our church to come to the hospital for the explicit reason of administering this ordinance to Elijah.

A few days later they came to the hospital. I was home at that time. Oleg welcomed them in and visited with them for a short while, and they occasionally looked at Elijah. He answered several of their questions and they prayed for Elijah. Then they said it was time for them to leave. Oleg responded that they could proceed with the anointing. One minister looked at the other minister and then turned to us to explain they would not be able to do the anointing for our baby because they had left the consecrated oil in the car. They muttered a quick good-by and left Elijah's room, leaving Oleg completely dumbfounded.

At first Oleg couldn't quite understand what had happened, or why. What he could see was that we had spiritual needs and we were not getting support from our ecclesiastical leaders. Seeing such an attitude towards us and our son left us questioning our church, the God it represented, and even our own lives. Months later we understood that this event was important to us and our spiritual growth.

One day our friends from church came to visit us at home. Several years before, their daughter was also born premature and stayed in the hospital for a long time.

"People who have not been in our situation will not understand me," this girl's father said. "But you, who are going through grief, will understand me. It may sound crazy, but we are very happy that God paid attention to your family. Through the illness of your son, God has come very close to you, and He will do a great job in your hearts. In difficult situations, we learn much and our lives are changing for the better."

Oleg and I felt God in our lives, but it was very difficult to walk our valley of tears! As each day passed, Oleg and I grew closer together. Our respect for each other grew. We knew what each of us was going through, how much pain we were experiencing, and that our hearts had scars on them. We needed each other's support as never before; I am grateful God blessed me with such a wonderful husband. So many times, when I would come home from the hospital after visiting Elijah, I would put my head on Oleg's shoulder, and we would cry together. He always hugged me tight and reminded me that we can do it as a team. God would help us and give us strength. Those days I needed Oleg's love and understanding as never before.

....

One Sunday evening, the leader of our young married couples' church group invited us to their house for dinner. Knowing the issues we were facing, they wanted to encourage us. Talking with them about life and God, Oleg asked questions about what he didn't understand from the Bible. Then he said, **"Only today I realize what is happening. I now remember my prayer from a few years ago when I was tired of being a lukewarm Christian. I** asked God to send a situation to my life, where I could meet Him, the real God. I really wanted to learn more about our God Almighty and have a personal relationship with Him, but I didn't expect His work to be so painful in my life. Now it all makes sense to me."

I also remembered that prayer. I could be angry at Oleg for praying that way, but I wasn't. Even though Elijah was born very ill, at the same time we had a lot of good changes happening in our life. We were learning how to be patient, how to see the pain of others, how to pray and study the Bible more, and how to search for our Heavenly Father and His wisdom. We started to see a different side of this life, which we might have never seen and experienced. It almost felt like the more difficult the time, the more God was opening up to us and we were becoming closer to Him. It seems strange because logically when things are not going right, we ought to be angry with God, but we were not. Through our pain, God was opening up a new life for us, in which we saw ourselves and others differently. We changed how we lived as we questioned and grew in our faith.

....

Every day Oleg read the Bible. As he learned something new, he shared it with the children and me. Excited, he would say, "This is what God showed me! This is what He revealed to me! I love my God!"

I usually listened to Oleg with my mouth open, having a hard time believing it was my husband. I was surprised that instead of growing apart from God, Oleg and I were growing closer to Him.

One day we stopped at the Russian book store, where Oleg saw the Torah. For some unknown reason, it meant a lot to him. With trembling hands, he bought it and read it daily. At that point, I didn't even know what the Torah was.

175

I didn't even know what a Rabbi was or that my ancestors were Jewish. I had read the Bible several times, but I had never explored it beyond the surface of my faith. I was far from it all, but for some reason, God was turning us that way.

Very often Oleg would go outside, raise his hands to Heaven and praise His Creator! In the evenings, Oleg was falling asleep with Jewish songs on his phone. Songs like "Raheim", "Shma Israel" and others gave him chills and reminded him that God is really alive, that Jesus is the King of Kings, and that God's Word has REAL power.

Oleg started talking to his friends, family, and our pastors about what he learned, but they didn't support him. They said, "Oleg, why do you want to dig in the Bible so deeply? It is easier just to accept God and not have any questions." But Oleg did not give up. He kept researching about the days of Moses, Jesus and His Apostles. Oleg also began talking about God's Festivals, kosher foods and the Sabbath day.

I realized Oleg had learned something very meaningful to him, but I still needed time to research, to understand and decide for myself. It was important for us not to offend our parents, yet it was important for us to do what we believed, even if it was different than what our parents believed. We began to seek a faith that we could support based upon the Bible. We wanted to know God and we became very serious about learning and finding answers to our questions.

....

Because of what was happening to Elijah and our family, I could see God working in our lives and the lives of our relatives and friends. Elijah reminded us to appreciate the good things in our lives. Through the power of a prayer and studying our faith, we began to learn and understand more about the meaning of love, hope, and charity. We were blessed with the love of the people who surrounded us.

During those days, my friends and relatives started saying to me, "Olga, you are such a strong person. You are still able to smile and be happy in your life, even though your baby is very ill. We don't think we could be as strong and positive as you are. We would never be able to go through it."

I must have been able to put on what appeared like a very good face. Inside, I felt I was struggling to survive the next moment or decision. I had no control of what was happening to me, my baby and the rest of the family. My world had turned upside down. I recognized my faith and trust in God had developed to the point I believed when I could not carry the load, He would do so for me. And He would not place me in any situation I could not handle. God was the place where I could find true peace because deep down inside I knew God was good and we could depend upon Him---He would carry us in His hands when we can no longer do it ourselves.

I wanted my baby to be healed and my family to be back together. At times, I would grasp at straws. A comment from a friend or a stranger on the radio, a comment on a card or a simple act of kindness would encourage me to believe that Elijah would be healed. For example, I heard a preacher talk on the radio about the power of Psalm 91 from the Bible. I thought, if that Psalm had power, it needed to be by Elijah. I made a copy of it, taped it to Elijah's crib next to our family picture and read it to Elijah daily. When we weren't there, Elijah often looked at our pictures and Psalm 91. We assume, if the words are in the Bible, God will do it. But we forget that God has a choice; it is His will and the outcome is in His hands. We do not get to design the world. God does.

Kathy, Elijah's night nurse, loved Elijah and took good care of him. Often, if Elijah didn't do well, Kathy would tear up, while telling us about his progress. One day she bought Elijah a beautiful mobile toy and attached it to his crib. It played music and Elijah liked it. With his eyes, he followed the monkeys that were attached to it and flew in a circle. Tears filled my eyes when I realized how much Kathy loved Elijah. I was so thankful to all the nurses. I felt like they were Elijah's second mothers, when I wasn't with him.

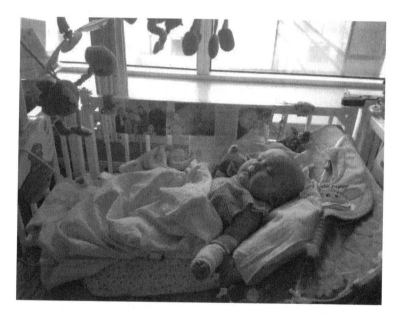

One evening Kathy told me, "Olga, when I was asked the first time to take care of Elijah, I was frightened! I knew his story was long, detailed and complex. But I fell in love with Elijah from the first day and signed up to become his primary night nurse. We have had some hard nights with Elijah. His medical status is constantly changing, and every night is very different from the previous one. Elijah is keeping me on my tippy toes. But we also have good nights. When Elijah feels good, he is such a charmer! When I hold him or read books to him, he holds onto my finger and looks into my eyes, sometimes with a half-smile, but more often with a deeply thoughtful glance. He listens very carefully! I know how difficult it is for you when Elijah feels bad, but you and Oleg are strong together. I'm glad you can spend so much time with Elijah. Watching your family at the hospital, I learned a lot from you. I feel more enlightened and more welcoming of religion and faith. I have seen how your faith has carried your family through this crisis. I may not be at a point of researching religion, but faith? Faith is what you have shown me, even if I reveal it in a different way.

....

14

Sometimes you have to respect your spouse's thoughts, decisions and rights, even if you totally disagree. No one can tell both of you what to do, except yourself.

We started the process for a heart transplant. Trying to learn more about it, I met with Jen from the billing office.

"Olga, your Kaiser medical insurance will cover Elijah's and your flight to California," Jen said. "It will also cover your housing expenses and give you $50 per day for personal needs and food. The heart transplant procedure would be covered at 80% and 20% would be covered by your secondary insurance."

"So, we would not have any out of pocket expenses?" I asked, relieved.

"No," said Jen. "Your two insurances will cover everything. But Kaiser contracts only with the Stanford hospital in Palo Alto, California. You will have to go there."

"So far? It is twelve hours drive there from our house. It will be so hard for our family to be apart and at such a long distance. Why do we have to go there?" I asked.

"The hospital in Seattle, which is only three hours away, also does heart transplants, but Kaiser can only cover the medical expenses, if the Stanford hospital in California will do it."

We had no choice but to agree to go to California. We wanted to help Elijah, who seemed to be improving and growing stronger. I continued visiting him each morning and Oleg visited Elijah each evening. Oleg and I worked as a team. We discussed the decisions and Oleg began working more with the hospital. The process to go to

California required lots of tests to determine if Elijah would qualify. Even though I agreed with Oleg to proceed with the heart transplant process, in my heart I had many concerns; I was scared and didn't want to leave my family. I wondered if it would do any good or just cause more pain. Mostly, I wanted to return to what used to be normal.

What I know today, in the normal course of events, normal slowly changes and becomes a new normal, but at times like these, the changes seem so great that they rock the foundation of your life. You are willing to sacrifice things, which you should value, to get back to a safe place. There is only so much the body can stand.

....

One day, when I arrived at the hospital, I saw a big machine standing next to Elijah's bed. The doctor was taping wires with a white paste onto Elijah's head. The nurse held Elijah's pacifier to keep him quiet. My heart dropped from not knowing what had happened.

"Since the surgery, due to the bleeding in his head, Elijah had been given medication to prevent seizures," the doctor explained. "Today we want to check if there is any seizure activity. If not, we will stop the seizure medications."

I breathed in deeply and thanked God that it wasn't anything bad again. After the wires were removed, Jen and I moved Elijah to the sink and washed his head. It was hard to get rid of that white paste. That day I realized that carrying Elijah ten feet to the sink was the farthest I had ever carried my son. He was always attached to his bed, wires and IVs. Thank God, the test showed no seizure activity and the medication was stopped! One less medication was a big deal for Elijah and me!

....

A week later, Elijah started to decline again. He required more oxygen to assist him in breathing. I was in tears again and began to have even more mixed feelings about the heart transplant.

I asked to schedule another conference with the doctors and asked them, "I feel that Elijah's heart is so ill. I wonder if the use of the machines is interfering with God's will?. If God wanted my child to live, He would want him to breathe on his own."

The cardiologist listened to me patiently and then said, "Olga, if we turned off medications, Elijah would still suffer for about three more weeks. I don't think it is fair to Elijah. I also think that Elijah has a low chance to survive the second surgery. If it was my son, I would give him time."

"I don't want Elijah to be on a breathing machine anymore," I said through tears. "If he has a hard time breathing or if his heart is stopping, can we just let him die so he doesn't suffer anymore?"

"Olga, you have a right to ask the doctors not to intubate and not to resuscitate Elijah when his heart is failing," the cardiologist explained.

"Given all the problems with Elijah, I have great concerns continuing with the heart transplant," I said. "In my heart, I just don't think Elijah is going to make it. Why inflict such pain on such a little person?"

"So, Olga, you no longer want to continue the preparation for a heart transplant process?" the cardiologist asked.

"Yes, that is how I feel," I said.

"Talk to your husband and let us know."

The meeting ended. I talked to Oleg in the evening.

"Honey, I can't watch Elijah suffer anymore. I don't want him to be on a breathing machine. And I don't want to leave you and the children. I had asked the doctors to stop the heart transplant process."

"Olga, I understand your feelings, but I am not ready to give up," Oleg said. "If we give up, Elijah will have no chance to live."

"I respect your feelings, thoughts, decisions and rights, honey, even if I totally disagree," I told Oleg. "But can we at least sign the documents not to intubate and not to resuscitate Elijah when his heart is failing?"

"Yes, I agree to that," Oleg said.

The next day we asked the doctors to continue the preparation for a heart transplant. We also signed the documents, asking not to resuscitate Elijah.

....

Oleg visited Elijah that evening. At 11 p.m, he called me.

"Olga, Elijah is having a hard time breathing and is retaining lots of fluids," he said. "He can die any second. The doctors are asking if they can intubate Elijah with a breathing machine?"

"Didn't we just a few hours ago signed papers not to do that?" I asked. "They can use a by-pap machine. This would give Elijah extra breathing support to his normal breathing process, whereas the breathing machine would breathe for Elijah. I want God to be in control, not the machine."

"Yes, Olga, I agree with you," Oleg said. "I will ask the doctors to use a by-pap mask."

I laid in bed scared, shaking and crying, with no strength to pray.

"God, please take Elijah. I can't see him suffer any more," I whispered, in tears.

For the next few hours, I could not fall asleep and wondered how Elijah was, but I was afraid to call Oleg. What if Elijah had died? The children were asleep, and I didn't want to receive such a call alone. At 1 a.m. Oleg came home and told me that the by-pap mask helped Elijah with his breathing.

....

In the morning, Elijah still had the by-pap mask on. I felt totally helpless. "Why can't God help us?" I thought to myself, while sitting with Elijah in a rocking chair with my back to the hall. Not wanting to see the faces of the nurses or visitors, I cried and continued to cry, while quietly praying to God.

In the afternoon, Elijah's saturation numbers normalized, so he was switched back to his nasal cannula. That day two other doctors came to check on Elijah.

"If it was your child, would you do a heart transplant?" I asked them both.

"We would never do it for our children," they answered. "We don't think Elijah would have a high quality of life after the heart transplant and he will always be tied to the hospital."

It was hard for me to hear what they were saying, but I appreciated their honesty. I knew we were in trouble.

"Olga, it is not our decision," one of the doctors said. "We will respect any decision that you will make."

Then I called Louise. I felt, as a nurse, her care for Elijah was extraordinary. Elijah was more than a patient for her and I had confidence that she would give me an honest opinion. She came and told me what she thought.

"Olga, I feel that you should do everything possible for Elijah that will not hurt him, but a heart transplant, in my opinion, is not a good option. I know it's not an easy decision, but whatever you decide, I will respect it."

Often with difficult decisions, we seek the advice of others, who should know what to do because they are experienced professionals. That is what I did that morning. What I learned, however, and Oleg later agreed, that the decision was ours and no one could tell us what to do. We had to find a peace inside ourselves, as to why we would do what we were doing. The role of anyone else, whether they agree or disagree with our decision, was to respect that decision and our right to make it. Not being sure about the heart transplant, I called Pastor Ivan again.

"Hello, Pastor Ivan," I said. "I need your advice. We are facing such a hard decision about the heart transplant for our five-month-old baby. Would you do it for your son? What should we do?"

Pastor Ivan was such a positive person.

"Olga, fight for life to the last minute," he said. "If a heart transplant can give him a chance to live, take your son there. What do you have to lose?"

"I praise God for such inspiring people, as you, Pastor Ivan!" I said. "Your words once again give me new strength to continue to fight for my son's life."

....

At five months Elijah weighed 11.5 pounds and was 22 inches long. Two days after he almost died, he had a good day again. Good days and bad days never seemed to end. At one point his stomach again was unable to properly digest the volume of milk that he was drinking. The doctors considered an intestinal surgery for Elijah. He was on antibiotics again. Luckily, no surgery was necessary.

After a few days, Elijah felt better again. During this period of time, on a good day, our children spent half a day with Elijah. They got to hold him and play with him for the first time. Kristina even videotaped him. We were a family. The children kept laughing at Elijah when he was making funny faces in his dream.

A week later, after the children had visited, Elijah started coughing and acting sick. The doctors decided to isolate Elijah because they were concerned he might have a virus that could be spread to other babies in the department. Everyone had to wear gloves, masks and gowns. Taking one day at a time, we moved forward. Luckily, Elijah felt better again, and the doctor transferred him back to the room with the other babies.

....

Elijah continued to receive many of his medications through his PICC line. One day, while I held him, I talked to him and he smiled at me. Suddenly, I felt something wet and noticed blood on my clothing. As I quickly looked for the source, I realized the PICC line had become disconnected. Blood spurted from the tubes. The nurse was gone to lunch and a different nurse from another room was keeping an eye on us. Just as I was ready to run and call for help, our nurse came back from lunch. I could see that she was frightened, but she was calm enough to tell me not to worry. She quickly fixed the PICC line. Elijah was calm through the whole event, and my sense of panic subsided.

....

The front desk clerk, Jeff, was very fond of Elijah. His office was across the hall, so he stopped to check on Elijah often. Sometimes, when I wasn't there, he held Elijah and sang him pirate songs. One day, Jeff brought Elijah a walker. We sat Elijah in it and he seemed to like it.

Elijah turned six months old! At that age, babies are usually at home, sitting up and starting to eat solid foods. But our "Precious Gift" was still at the hospital, with no plans to come home. He was having a difficult time sitting up and not eating solid food. He didn't even have energy to pick up a toy, chew on it, or play with it.

The doctors scheduled a phone conference with the Stanford hospital in California. Oleg, the doctors, nurses and I sat around the table and listened to Esther from Stanford talk on a speaker phone about the heart transplant, medications and the risks of it. The Ronald McDonald house could be available to help us. We had heard before of the potential negative outcomes, but the doctors had an obligation to tell us exactly what we were getting into. It was hard to hear what Esther was saying, but it was our son and we had a decision to make. After an hour, we were on information overload. I tried not to cry, had difficulty breathing and developed a massive headache.

After the conference, we asked our primary cardiologist to find us a local family, whose child had had a heart transplant. We wanted to talk to them. With permission of that family, the cardiologist gave us their number. Later that afternoon Oleg called them and spoke with that child's father.

"Our son's heart was transplanted at the age of eighteen months," the father said. "At the age of five years he is in Kindergarten, taking ten medications daily and is sick often. He means the world to our family. If our son will ever need another heart transplant, we will do it again."

Unable to fall asleep after that phone call, I decided to check online about heart transplants, about the Stanford hospital, about the Ronald McDonald house, and how children lived after the transplants. I read many positive stories. Many children survive heart transplants and live long after.

I was deeply touched to learn that Stanford University, one of the most prestigious institutions in the world, was founded in 1891 by the railroad magnate, US senator and former California governor, Leland Stanford, and his wife, Jane Stanford, in honor of their only son, Leland Stanford (Jr.), who died in 1884 at the age of 15. Stanford decided to dedicate the university, as a monument to his only son. Leland told his wife, "The children of California will be our children." Stanford University is rated very high as a school of academic excellence by several different publications. I thanked God that Elijah had this wonderful opportunity to become part of this university. I hoped they could help him.

The city Palo Alto was also established by Leland Stanford Sr. when he founded Stanford University. The city includes portions of Stanford University, and headquarters to a number of high-technology companies. It has a wonderful climate and is one of the most expensive cities in the United States.

I was also in tears, when I read the history of the Ronald McDonald House. It turned out that the owner was Philadelphia Eagle's football player, Fred Hill, whose young daughter in early 1970's was diagnosed with leukemia. After "living" countless hours by her bedside, trying to sleep endless nights without a bed, Hill recognized the need felt by all parents of a little one facing a serious illness - the need for a "home" where they could stay while their child received treatment. Hill's ambition, combined with support from the hospital and community, met with the generosity of McDonald's Owner/Operators, and in 1974 the first Ronald McDonald House opened. The House at Stanford is one of the largest of the 338 Ronald McDonald Houses in the world.

In the morning, while Oleg was getting ready to go to work, I told him, "Honey, I couldn't sleep last night and read a lot about heart transplants. Maybe, instead of waiting for Elijah's second surgery with a very low chance of survival, we should probably agree on a heart transplant?"

Oleg hugged me, looked into my eyes and said, "Olga, I was ready to do that a long time ago. I was just waiting for you to be ready. Having a disabled child doesn't scare me. Elijah would just be a special child. We would love him as much or even more than our other children. I am not embarrassed to have a sick child and am ready to do everything possible to help Elijah!"

"So, should I tell the cardiologist this morning that we are ready to go for a heart transplant?" I asked.

"Sure," Oleg agreed.

We loved our children equally, but because of Elijah's needs, we focused more on Elijah. Our love simply required it. I know that it might have been hard for our other three children to understand that. A mother or a father simply wants to do that which is best for all of their children.

After Oleg left for work and the children were on the school bus, I drove to OHSU and spoke with Elijah's main cardiologist.

"Instead of waiting for the second surgery with a low chance for survival, can we schedule a heart transplant as soon as possible?" I asked.

"Yes, but it will take about two more weeks to prepare. Elijah still needs to go through some tests," the cardiologist explained.

Elijah looked as if he was having a good day. Looking at how grown he already was, I believed he would get better. Even if our family had to be separated, I would be with Elijah.

The next day after the conference with the Stanford hospital, Oleg became very sick. Maybe this is how his body handled stress. Unfortunately, he missed a lot when he was not able to see Elijah for a week. It was like a real miracle occurred. Elijah became more like a normal baby. He began to breathe on his own without any help and started drinking from a bottle again. The feeding and the breathing tubes were taken out. His face was free of tubes! What the doctors thought might never happen, happened! Elijah was breathing and eating on his own, and smiling often. I was so happy, but Oleg missed it all.

....

It was so hard for me to even think about leaving my children, but I tried to stay positive. I talked to them about our decision to go to California with Elijah, but they didn't say much. They had already told me back in January that they would be okay if I were to go. Oleg also told me that they would be fine. He had already been helping me with everything around the house and with the children's homework. He even started cooking dinner on the weekends. (Today he is an excellent cook.) I was so thankful for my husband's help and knew they would be okay without me. I can always depend on Oleg to step up to solve problems and take care of our family's needs when a situation demands it. I also talked with my parents and sisters about our plans to go to California. They wished us the best and promised to help Oleg.

Before the decision to go to California, I was taking a small dose of blood pressure medication. After we agreed on Elijah's heart transplant, my blood pressure rose dramatically, and the doctor prescribed me a medication dose three times higher than before. I tried to do as much as possible, so when I left, Oleg and the children would be okay.

At night, I was losing sleep and kept thinking of what I needed to do the following day. During the day, I tried to remind our children what to do in my absence. While getting ready to go to California with Elijah, I found myself imagining what a dying mother felt when she knew that one day she would leave her children forever. The days went better, when I approached the events of the day with a positive attitude. Our own attitude makes such an amazing difference about how we look at our lives, our relationship, and what is happening in the world at large.

....

At that time, due to stress, my body quit producing breastmilk, which was very hard to accept. We still had lots of frozen breastmilk and I fed it to Elijah from the bottle. But I knew when this ran out, there would be no more for my baby. Breastmilk was extremely important for Elijah because it has many health benefits that formula doesn't have. And for me there was an emotional component as well. Knowing that I would no longer be able to nurse Elijah affected me emotionally. Illogical as it was, I felt inadequate because I could not feed my baby. That would deprive him of my milk and the skin to skin contact that babies need.

....

15

In the most difficult moments, try to find at least one thing to thank God for, and you will feel better.

After three days of drinking milk from the bottle and breathing without any help, Elijah started coughing and developed influenza and bronchitis. He had difficulty breathing and needed the support of a by-pap mask again. Elijah's kidneys seemed to be failing. He was urinating less and retaining fluid. Again, he was placed in an isolation room, so the other babies would not become infected. Gowns, gloves and masks became the fashion statement. The doctors came to talk to me while I was holding Elijah.

"Olga, the diuretic medications are no longer working," they said. "The only diuretic left is one that we use for adults. We are not sure if it would help Elijah. There is a good chance that Elijah can die within the next two days."

Immediately, tears flowed. After the doctor explained Elijah's condition, I ran to meet Ruth, my former co-worker from WIC. She now worked at OSHU and planned to visit me during lunch hour. I met her in tears and we rushed back to Elijah. He was screaming because he did not feel comfortable. The nurse was busy changing his IV tubes, so I picked him up. His face was swollen due to fluid retention and his weight had increased nearly two pounds.

Ruth brought me lunch, but I couldn't eat anything.

"My son is dying. Is it end of our fight for his life?" I cried out to Ruth.

"Olga, please don't cry," Ruth entreated me. "Things can still change for the better. Maybe these diuretics will work."

I appreciated Ruth's support, but at this point no words would console me; only the doctors and God could help. After two scary days, medications worked, Elijah improved dramatically, and we felt happy again.

....

Over the weekend Oleg, the children and I visited Elijah together. Afterwards, we planned to go to the Oregon Museum of Science and Industry (OMSI), to have our last family adventure, before Elijah and I left for California. Jen let us all in to see Elijah, so we could take a family photo. Elijah was awake, playing and excited to see us. I sat him up on the edge of his crib and held him. David, Kristina, and Michael held his hand, while talking and playing with him. It was so good to be together and feel like a complete family!

After a while, the children got tired and started asking to go to OMSI, but Elijah was wide awake and wanted to play. He was excited that his family came. I just couldn't leave Elijah like that.

"Honey, can you please take the children to the waiting room to watch a movie, while I put Elijah to sleep," I asked Oleg.

"Sure," Oleg said.

They said good bye to Elijah and left the room. Elijah didn't want to sleep; ten minutes later he was still playing. I wanted to stay with Elijah, but the children were eager to go to OMSI. I felt conflicted over my options: having only five days left to spend with my family or choosing to stay with Elijah. Oh, how I wished all our children could be together with us, yet, it wasn't one of my options

"Jen, I am sorry, but I have to leave," I told Jen tearfully. "I don't want to leave Elijah. Could you please take good care of him?"

"Olga, please don't worry," Jen answered. "Elijah is in good hands. I love him and will take good care of him. Please take care of yourself and your children. Go, have a good day with your family."

I appreciated Jen's love and support. As we left for OMSI, I hid my tears from the children. I was determined to have a good family afternoon.

The next day, Jen told me, "Olga, watching your family, how you cherish the time that you can spend together, and how much you love Elijah, I began to appreciate my family more. Your family reminds me to appreciate life more and every moment spent with friends and family. "

....

On Tuesday the doctors ordered a CT scan and a cardiac catheterization to see how Elijah's heart and lungs were working. They also waited to see if Elijah's influenza test came back negative. When everything was clear, he would be ready to go to California. The lab showed the pressures in Elijah's heart were already 18-19 instead of 4-5, which was good and bad news. Good news was that with such high pressures Elijah will be first on a waiting list for the heart transplant. Elijah's heart was so sick and might give up any minute.

The day after the lab Elijah was wide awake; he baby-talked, smiled and waved his hands. I held him and played with him. I kissed his eyes; he kept turning away and back to me, like playing peak-a-boo. Elijah acted like he wasn't sick at all. I was so excited, but the cardiologist mentioned, "Elijah's behavior is unusual. Usually, the children are very sick the day after a cardiac catheterization, but Elijah is such an unpredictable baby and may later act totally different."

That day I was so happy God had given us such precious moments.

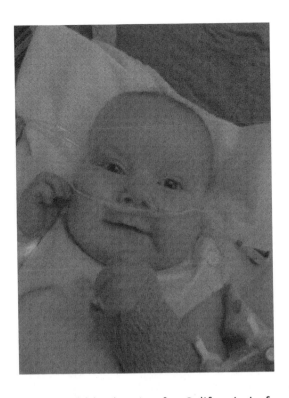

Because I would be leaving for California in few days, I turned in a boundary exception, which was approved by the school district. This changed the school which our children attended, therefore Oleg could drop them off at my Mother's house before work. From there, the children would take the bus to school; after school they would return to my Mom's house for care and meals. After work Oleg would pick them up and take them home. Once more the support of my Mother blessed our family. That day I was doing what I had to do, but every time I remembered I would be leaving my family in few days, my heart ached. Everyone in the entire family was putting themselves and their needs on the back burner. All thoughts and prayers centered on Elijah.

....

The next day Jen was taking care of Elijah again.

"Olga, Elijah doesn't look good to me. I wonder what is going on?" Jen said in a worried tone of voice.

I picked up Elijah to hold him.

"He doesn't look good to me, either," I said, scared.

Elijah's eyes were rolling up. I had never seen him like this before. It didn't look as if he had withdrawal symptoms due to the narcotic medication change. This was something else. He seemed very uncomfortable and cried weakly, like he needed help.

"It may be just a fluid overload after the cardiac catheterization lab," the cardiologist said and ordered an increase in Elijah's diuretics.

After an hour, a doctor came and said, "Olga, we are so happy for Elijah! His influenza test is negative, and he passed all the tests! California is waiting for him. You will probably fly out today instead of tomorrow!"

I was shocked. This created instant stress.

"I haven't even said good bye to my children, who are in school," I said, worried. "I need to go home, get ready and get the children from school, so they can say good-by to Elijah."

When Elijah fell asleep, I left the hospital and sent a text message to my brothers and sisters and said good-bye. On my way home, I stopped at my Mother's house. Tanya also came there to say good-bye. We hugged each other and just cried. Words could not change the situation.

A dozen details needed to be completed quickly. Soon I finished packing and was ready. The children had already arrived home from school and Oleg from work, but there was still no call from the doctor, notifying us that Elijah was ready to fly to California. I became worried and called Jen.

"Elijah is feeling worse," Jen said. "The doctors are trying to run more tests to see what is happening."

I worried.

Soon, the neonatologist called us and said, "The blood test showed that Elijah's kidneys have stopped working. That is one of the risks of the cardiac catheterization. Since 8:00 A.M. today Elijah hasn't urinated. This is a very bad sign."

"Is there anything you can do to help Elijah?" Oleg asked.

"There is no point in doing the kidney dialysis, because it would disqualify Elijah from a heart transplant. Elijah will probably die tonight."

After he hung up the phone, Oleg and I hugged each other tight and stood quietly for a while. "How can a good God do this to our baby?" I wanted an answer!

"We tried everything possible to help our son, but looks like it is the end," Oleg uttered and wept.

I struggled to regain control of myself and called my Mother. I told her nothing about Elijah not doing well at all as I didn't want her to worry.

"Mom, can you please watch our children, so Oleg and I can visit Elijah?" I asked her.

"Bring them over. I hope Elijah is okay. Kiss him for me," my Mom said.

On our way to the hospital I called Patti. She wasn't working that day, but she always wanted to know what was happening with Elijah.

"I will stop by to say good-by," Patti said.

When we arrived at the hospital, all three nurses, Kathy, Jen and Patti were there. Jen, the one caring for Elijah that day, had also called Kathy, Elijah's night nurse, to come early. We all stood quietly, stunned by this dramatic shift. It was so unexpected---hope was becoming no hope. My feelings froze. I didn't know what to do or say. Elijah was still alive, but I knew he could die any second and I had a real sense this might be the moment. We all felt helpless.

"Olga, please be strong," the nurses hugged me tight.

Earlier that day, I had given the doctors permission to sedate Elijah and provide him breathing help for the transfer only. It was so hard to see Elijah on full life support again.

As we stood there, the cardiologist came.

"I have never seen anything like this before!" he said. "The blood test just showed that Elijah's kidneys have started working again!"

He ordered another blood test, which showed again that Elijah's kidney function was getting better.

"Unbelievable!" he said. "Sometimes things occur that we have never seen before and can't explain. The Stanford hospital decided to give Elijah one more day to see if his kidney function will keep getting better. If so, then Elijah could go to Stanford tomorrow."

Uncertain what would happen, Oleg and I left the hospital and returned home.

......

The next morning, Oleg went to work, and I visited Elijah alone. No one from Oleg's or my family knew about Elijah being near death. I couldn't bring myself to explain what had happened. I also didn't feel comfortable asking anyone to come with me. "What if Elijah died? Could I deal with it alone?" I wondered as I was driving to the hospital.

Elijah was in a deep sleep and I was unable to hold him or talk to him. All I could do was look at him. Soon, the cardiologist came to talk to me.

"Olga, as soon as Elijah gets to California, he will have an open-heart procedure, called a "Berlin Heart", he said. "It is needed because Elijah's heart is not strong enough to wait until a replacement heart is available. He simply would not survive without this surgery."

"So, Elijah will have an extra open-heart procedure before his heart transplant?" I asked, confused.

"Yes, he will have his "Glen" procedure, which he was supposed to have at six months, and his "Berlin Heart" procedure at the same time. It will be two surgeries in one.

"Are these procedures going to be as complicated as Elijah's "Norwood" procedure was?" I asked.

"Unfortunately, yes," the cardiologist answered. "During this procedure, the surgeon will connect a mechanical device to Elijah's heart, to help his heart work until a donor is found. The sad news is that California doctors give Elijah only a 25% chance of survival, which is pretty low. They have installed about 70 of these devices on hearts with four working chambers, but not on a heart like Elijah's, with only two chambers."

I thought the 25% chance for success was very low and was ready to give up, but Oleg still wanted to give Elijah every chance possible.

"If we don't take Elijah to California, he won't have his chance," Oleg Said. "A 25% chance is a lot more than the 1% chance for life Elijah was born with."

"I have no more energy left in me to make any more decisions," I told Oleg. "So, even though I don't agree, I will just listen to you and do what you say."

Our situation was indescribably hard. Elijah was Oleg's child, too. We had to be in agreement. We found ourselves agreeing to continue as both of us could not agree to remove Elijah's life support.

....

The next day was Saturday. Because Elijah was in a deep sleep, our entire family stayed home, so we could spend our last few hours together. We waited for the doctors to call and tell us they were ready for us to fly out. I was packed and tried to have things ready for my absence, but how much could I prepare? I washed the laundry and the dishes, but they magically reappeared again! I wondered who would cook for the children and help them with homework. I knew they would be okay; it was me, I didn't want to be separated from my family. Regardless of how my kids and I felt, I knew I had to go.

A Kaiser travel agent arranged the hotel room in California for me until a room at the Ronald McDonald House became available. I believed I would be okay, but still worried, as I was facing many unknowns and would not have Oleg's help. Going to California made me realize how much I relied on Oleg. Before I had Elijah, I used to work full time. I would come home and have to cook dinner, wash laundry and dishes, help the children with their homework, go to their football practices, take them to Russian school and their piano classes, etc. Often, I complained to Oleg that he wasn't helping me enough, even though I understood that he worked very hard and was tired. When Elijah was ill, I realized that dirty dishes and an unclean house was not a problem anymore. If Oleg was there, lying tired on the couch after work, I would not complain. All I needed was his hug. It made everything better and gave me energy.

In the evening, Oleg and I visited Elijah again. He remained in a-deep sleep. At one point, when he heard our voices, he opened his eyes. When Oleg and I saw that, we shed tears of joy. Elijah recognized our voices. He knew we loved him and were there for him. Love is a powerful force.

Elijah didn't seem to be doing well, but the test showed that his kidney function kept getting better. Unfortunately, that evening the Stanford hospital in California didn't have a room for Elijah. They needed to discharge someone before they could take Elijah. Our flight would probably be the next day.

....

When Elijah was five months old, I stopped breastfeeding. My menstrual cycle began again as I had expected, but never ended. Due to stress, my hormones were affected, and I continued bleeding for a month. Because of all the problems with Elijah, I had not taken time to see the doctor. However, on the morning of our flight to California, it became apparent I needed medical attention. At 5:00 A. M. I drove myself to the E.R. The doctor said I would be okay if I took the medications as he prescribed. Five hours later I was at home. Obviously, my situation was abnormal, but was I supposed to worry about myself or about Elijah? I decided Elijah was more important.

....

At 12:00 P.M. the cardiologist from Stanford called. "Hello, Olga," she said. We have a room available for Elijah. You can come to California today. I also wanted to make sure you know where you are going and what you will be going through?"

"Yes, I do," I said, confused. "Why are you asking?"

"Separation is very hard on families. You could be in California from six months to a year. Soon after your arrival, we will do an open-heart-surgery for Elijah. Are you ready for it? The surgery is very hard to see."

"Yes, I understand it will be hard," I answered with a trembling voice. "I have a very good husband and he will take care of our older children. I think we will be okay. I believe God will take care of us."

A little later the surgeon called and talked to Oleg about the "Berlin Heart" procedure that Elijah would have.

After Oleg hung up the phone he called to the children, "David, Kristina and Michael. Please come here. Mom will be leaving soon for California. Let's pray together."

The children came and sat on the coach. They were silent.

"I will be flying to California today with Elijah," I said, looking at the three of them, unsuccessfully restraining my tears. "I love you so much and wish I didn't have to leave, but it is God's plan for me to go to the Stanford Hospital with Elijah. We need to help him. I will call you and you will be able to see me through Skype. If you are having a bad day and miss me, please thank God that I am still alive and will be back soon. Will you be okay?"

"Yes, we will be okay, Mom," David said. "Please go with Elijah and help him. We will be okay with Dad," tears filled his eyes.

Kristina and Michael were quiet, not sure what to answer. They all hugged me. We prayed together one last time. Then the children went outside to play. Reality sucked the breath out of me. I was leaving, and the children would have to be without me for an extended period of time.

Soon Jen called and told us that we needed to be at the hospital at 6:00 P.M. At that time, everything would be ready for the flight. I quietly went upstairs to my room, fell onto my bed and, sobbing, again questioned, "Why, God, You chose me and my child to go through this adversity? Why do You need to separate our family?"

When Oleg heard me crying, he came and comforted me, "Olga, please don't ask God why. It isn't right to accept only good from God. We should be able to accept all He gives us. Please don't worry. The children and I will be okay. I will try to come to California every two weeks. We will see each other often."

Oleg calmed me, and I stopped crying.

"I love you, honey and I am proud that you are so positive," I said. "You want to give our child all his chances for life. Thank you for your love and support."

"Olga, Elijah's life is the precious thing God gave us and we have to fight for it to the end," Oleg said. "It is important to me to give Elijah all his chances. I know I will have to continue to work and take on all the roles that you normally fulfill. It won't be easy, but the children and I will be fine.

"I know, honey, you will be fine. My Mom and sisters will also help you, but I will miss you and the children terribly."

I squeezed Oleg's hands and we sat quietly for a moment, each lost in our own thoughts about the future and our family.

After four hours of waiting, we took Michael and Kristina to my Mom's house. I chose to leave them there because they were coughing. Plus, I also knew that they might be scared to see Elijah, sedated and intubated. David, Oleg and I went to the hospital. The doctors and nurses were so supportive and wished all of us the best. Even those, not currently on duty, came to see Elijah off to California. We were so touched by such an expression of love; this dedicated staff had been partners with us very day throughout our experience.

Elijah was prepared for the transfer. He didn't fit into a baby bed, so he was buckled onto an adult stretcher. It was a strange sight to see his tiny body on an adult bed. At that time, Elijah was six and a half months old. If he had been born on time, he would be only four months old. From a three-pound baby he had grown into a twelve-pound baby! The IV pumps, the breathing machine and other equipment surrounded him. It looked like half the hospital was moving to California for our son.

I said good-by to Oleg, David, and the doctors and nurses. The driver of the ambulance asked me to sit in the front seat. The doctor and the transport team, who were flying with us to California, had to sit next to Elijah in the back of the ambulance. Knowing that Elijah's doctor was flying with us to California, made me feel more secure.

After thirty minutes, we arrived at the Hillsboro, Oregon airport. A small medical plane was waiting for us. We boarded, and I was, again, asked to sit in the front seat next to the pilot. This was a rare opportunity to see how the plane operated and see God's creation below, as we flew.

....

16

*We are the clay in God's hands. He
will mold us as He desires.*

On March 20th, after three hours of flight, we landed in San
Jose airport and were transported by ambulance to the
Lucille Packard Children's Hospital (LPCH) at Stanford, Palo
Alto. It was 10:15 P.M. when we entered the Cardiovascular
Intensive Care Unit (CVICU), where ten doctors and nurses
waited for Elijah.

They quickly transferred Elijah to his new bed and
reconnected his oxygen tubes and IV pumps. Suddenly,
Elijah woke up and started crying. His heart beat dropped
dramatically, which scared everyone. Doctors immediately
gave Elijah a dose of paralytic medication to put him to
sleep.

After the patient intake procedures were completed, I
realized how exhausted I was from the stress and the flight.
I stood in the hallway, where I could see everything, and
watched the staff situate Elijah. Two nurses taped local
labels to the bottles of my frozen breast milk from Oregon.
The California doctors talked to the Oregon doctor and took
a thorough report on Elijah. My baby fell asleep and the
nurses seemed to take good care of him.

It was getting late and I wondered, what is next? How
are Oleg and the children at home? Where is my hotel and
how will I get there?" Then I remembered that the
paramedics would be taking the Oregon medical team back
to the airport, so I asked them, "I was wondering if by any
chance, you will be going my way and could give me a ride
to the hotel?"

"Yes, of course," the driver of the ambulance nodded. "We will give you a ride."

"Thank you so much," It was such a relief. I was a welcomed stranger in a new town.

"Why did you come here on the ambulance?" the surprised hotel clerk asked.

"We just flew in from Oregon. Our six-month-old baby is at Stanford hospital, waiting for a heart transplant."

"I am sorry to hear that," she said. "Good luck in everything! Here is the key to your room. Are you hungry?"

"Yes, I am," I acknowledged.

"I have hot tea and muffins," she said. "In the morning there would be free coffee with pastries in the lobby."

"Thank you so much!" I gratefully replied. "Your generosity touches my heart."

"We also have a shuttle service," she said. "It is free and available every hour to take people to the hospital."

"That is great news because I don't have a car here in California," I said.

When I got to my room and saw how beautiful it was, I thanked God for our medical insurance, which paid for it, and for our safe trip here. Both required an expression of deep gratitude for His safe keeping. I dropped into bed at 1:00 A.M., desperate for sleep.

....

My first morning in California, I woke up at 10:00 A.M. and could not believe I had slept so late. For the first time in days, I felt rested. I called the front desk, ordered a shuttle for 11 a.m., dressed, and ate breakfast in the lounge. A shuttle driver drove an older couple and me to the hospital. The sun was shining brightly, and palm trees and blooming flowers lined both sides of the road. It was so different from rainy Oregon.

Fifteen minutes later we were at the hospital. Elijah had his own private room. He laid in an adult sized bed, near a big window, providing wonderful sunshine. A ventilator was helping him breathe and IV pumps on both sides of his bed provided him with medications. A nurse, named Jen, was with Elijah. I thought it was interesting that in Portland, Elijah's last nurse was Jen, too.

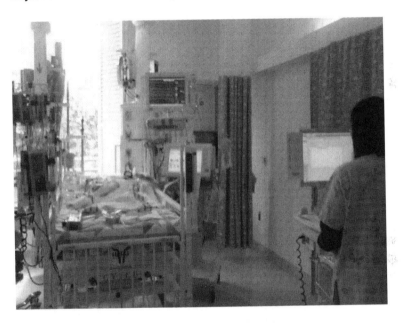

Soon the doctor came to talk to me. "The plan is to keep Elijah sedated until tomorrow," he said. "Then we will decrease his ventilator and let him breathe on his own. If he does okay, we will turn the breathing machine off and take the tube out of his throat. After that, Elijah may possibly start drinking your previously frozen breast milk and you may be able to hold him."

We had authorized the breathing machine for the transfer only, but Elijah was still on it. I had to rationalize that the doctors knew what they were doing and accept how badly I wanted this heart transplant, so my son would live, therefore, I said nothing.

Three hours later the doctor let me hold Elijah. As I stood by his bed holding him, I kissed him and talked to him.

"I love you so much, my baby," I told Elijah through tears. "I wish you were healthy and could go home with us. I want you to grow up as a healthy and happy child."

If Elijah was older, he would tell me what he needed and how he felt, but that day he simply laid in my arms and whimpered weakly. Often, I imagined what would have happened, if Elijah could talk. He might ask me questions that I would never be able to answer. For example, "Why God gave me an ill heart?" Later, I was glad Elijah was still so small and I didn't have to deal with such questions.

I knew that my crying and Elijah's crying were very bad for his failing heart. I tried desperately to be positive and not to cry. Soon, the doctor came and asked the nurse to give Elijah sedation medications to calm him down.

Because Elijah was stressed all day, his heart started working harder. The doctors needed to intubate him again with the ventilator and needed my permission. I was disappointed and sad, because in Oregon I signed the papers not to intubate Elijah, but then I gave permission to do it only for a transfer. I didn't want my baby to be intubated again and it wasn't the plan; but now Elijah was so close to that second surgery that I gave permission to intubate, to help him with his breathing.

When Elijah fell asleep, I took the shuttle back to the hotel. Exhausted, I needed some time to pray, to cry, and to pull my thoughts together. That evening I was very sad and called Oleg to tell him the news. Though still sick, he felt a little better.

"Olga, I know how hard it is for you to watch Elijah not do so well, but please be strong," Oleg encouraged me.

After speaking with my husband, I didn't feel like talking to anyone else and again cried myself to sleep.

....

On my third day in California, I woke up early and noticed the sun shining through the blinds. I decided to go for a walk, believing it would relieve some stress. For about an hour I walked around the hotel and adjacent neighborhood and enjoyed the beautifully landscaped grounds. After the walk, I got hot coffee and muffins in the lobby and went back to my room. As I walked up to the second floor, I noticed a table and a chair outside my window. I decided to sit there and read the Bible as I was enjoying the sunshine and tall palm trees.

I randomly opened the Bible and began to read the book of Jeremiah. My eyes stopped on Jeremiah 1:5 *"Before I formed you in the womb, I knew you..."* and Jeremiah 29:11 *"For I know the plans I have for you, declares the Lord, plans to prosper you and not to harm you, plans to give you hope and the future."* It was like God had provided those words just for me; I felt peace. I realized Elijah's first and last days were already written in God's book and I had no power to change anything. Our son would get a new heart and survive the surgery, if God willed it so.

Even though it was a good day, it was a day, when I felt like I was going through a process of "dying" and being born again. It was as if my body was drained of energy, questioning and complaining, and being replaced with a stronger faith in God, on whom I could rely.

Feeling rejuvenated, I readied myself to return to the hospital to sit with Elijah. I could not play, talk or hold him. He was so fragile. I sat in a chair by his bed and read about the heart transplants. It seemed like there was a lot of information and my brain was not working.

....

While I sat by Elijah's bed, the social worker, Mary, came to see me.

"Hello, Olga," she said with a big smile. "I brought you some information about the hospital."

"Thank you," I said and accepted the information packet.

"I reviewed Elijah's chart and noticed that he has been through more illness and procedures than many 70-year-old men have experienced in their whole life," Mary continued. "I feel sorry that Elijah had experienced all that, but I am extremely proud he isn't giving up."

Mary took me on a hospital tour and showed me the cafeteria, library, the computer area and an activity room for the older children. Then she showed me a room for parents and guests to sleep in.

"Olga, if you have guests, who need a place to sleep, just let me know. I will save this room for you," Mary said.

"Thank you, Mary," I answered, excited. "I am astounded at the facilities the hospital has to accommodate, not just the patient, but the families. It is so welcoming, like a huge expensive hotel with beautiful, colorful couches, where the families can visit. I am amazed they have such wonderful facilities, which Oleg and the children can use when they came to visit us during spring break."

Mary seemed happy to hear that.

"Mary, when my three active children come they will require more than just a room," I continued. "Are there any interesting places we can take our children?"

"Yes. There are many nice places around here. I will bring you the information," Mary said.

"Thank you, Mary."

"Olga, I am so happy to see you so positive in your situation," Mary continued. "Many mothers here with a sick child would not ask me questions like you ask. They only worry about their sick child and can't think of anything else. But you look at life realistically!"

Mary gave me a hug and left. Like everyone else at the hospital, she was happy, positive, kind, friendly and willing to help.

Next, I met with a psychiatrist. He asked many questions, wanting to understand all about our family and whether or not we would be able to care for Elijah after the surgery. His questioning covered the whole process of caring for Elijah for the rest of his life. The meeting went on for about two hours.

"Olga, how long have you been a Christian?" he asked me at the end.

"Since my birth," I said. "I grew up in a Christian family and it is part of me."

"Olga, I am so happy that you have such a strong family and faith in God," he concluded. "Working with many families who undergo major medical experiences with their children, I have seen many different situations. Many parents end up with broken marriages, mental stress and a rare suicide. What you and your family are going through is heart-breaking, but I am so happy to see how your faith in God carries you through this crisis."

I was happy to hear the positive comments from the social worker and the psychiatrist, who reminded me that Oleg and I were doing our best, and your best is all you can do.

Exhausted after so many questions and new information, I checked on Elijah and left the hospital. The shuttle driver was kind enough to allow me to stop at a local grocery store to buy some food. This is an example of how people associated with the hospital, would go out of their way to help. Even though these seem like small things, they really are big things, when you are dealing with major issues, and your accommodations are somewhat distanced from other businesses.

....

On the last day in Oregon, Elijah's doctors and nurses asked me to make a Facebook page, so they could get updated information about Elijah. That evening it took me a couple of hours, but I started the Facebook page and posted the first update. My friends and family could find out what was happening and could comment.

Facebook would allow me to put pictures, where friends and family could see what I couldn't explain in words. It was like my family and friends were there with me. This was important, not only because of the content, but because it saved time. It was also overwhelming how people, whom I hadn't contacted for many years, all of a sudden, were following Facebook and making comments. It was important to hear from them, a way of connecting. It helped to take the loneliness away.

....

That evening, Elijah's nurse from Oregon, Patti, called me.

"How are you, Olga?" she asked.

"The first three days I was okay," I said. "There are lots of new doctors and nurses that I have met, and I am trying to remember their names. Every day my family, friends and nurses call me, so I am not so lonely."

"Olga, I admire you," Patty said. "You are so positive and easy to talk to. I know you will find friends and will be okay in California."

Patti's comments made me feel better. It is amazing how words of encouragement can work wonders on one's perspective. Being positive creates a positive perspective.

"Patti, when I was in Portland, you always tried to cheer me up," I said, trying to hold back my tears. "And now you are not forgetting about me when I am so far from home. You have gone far beyond your professional responsibilities of caring for my child to caring about me. Thank you so much! It means a lot to me!"

After talking with Patti, I skyped Oleg and the children. We talked, but most importantly, we could see each other, and it felt like our family was together again. What a difference technology makes! It's amazing how important it is to be able to see the face and the smile of those you love, particularly when you are far away and would like to be so close.

"Mom, we miss you so much!" the children said, excited to see me. "We can't wait to come to California next Friday!"

We had good family time together. Finally, I called my Mother.

"Olga, I have tried not to call you the first couple of days because I thought you had limited minutes on your cell phone," Mom said. "I worried you would have to pay a lot for the long-distance calls."

"Mom, I don't have any extra charges," I answered. "You can call me any time."

My Mother started crying.

"I worry about you, my Daughter, and about Elijah. Are you okay there in California?"

"Yes, Mom. God is taking very good care of us. Please don't worry. If possible, help Oleg with the children."

After I hung up the phone, I broke into tears. I didn't want my Mother to worry, but I knew that she would. I was concerned that it could affect her health.

....

The next morning, nineteen medical professionals met to review Elijah's case and make a final determination about his eligibility for a heart transplant. When we were leaving Oregon, I thought Elijah had already qualified for a heart transplant. But in California the doctors still needed to run more tests and review the background of our family. Mary, the social worker, together with the psychiatrist, told the committee that Elijah had a good family, who would be able to take good care of him after the transplant. After a thorough review, Elijah was deemed qualified to be added to the heart transplant list as a first priority!

....

That day Elijah was not doing well at all, which caused me concern. I was afraid something would happen that would require Elijah to be removed from the heart transplant list. I would sit him up on his bed for about thirty minutes, but then his heart would start working hard again, the medications would be increased, and he would fall asleep again. Any movement or excitement increased the stress on his heart. We needed a donor heart to be available today. My heart was breaking; my son desperately needed a new heart and I was powerless to help him. This was so much different than our experience in Oregon, where I could spend hours with Elijah, holding and playing with him.

I was alone in California, except for Elijah, whose heart was becoming more fragile. This was a new experience. Before, it was as if I had so little time to do so many things. In California, I did not have the other members of my family and had a tremendous amount of time to be lonely and think.

....

17

God speaks to us through the wind and clouds, through flowers and trees, through a sun and a rainbow, and through our loved ones. These are beautiful gifts from God!

A room at the Ronald McDonald House became available for me. When I was checking in, the volunteer gave me an application to fill out. I knew it could be a year for me in California.

"My children will be staying with me during the spring break and, maybe, during the summer break," I said. "Will there be enough room for them in my room?"

"Olga, please wait a minute. I need to go check on something," the volunteer said.

Soon, she came back, excited and told me the great news, "Instead of just a bedroom that we were going to give you, we will give you a suite with your own kitchen, living room, TV and a couch, a huge bathroom and a bedroom with two beds, where four people can sleep. We will give it to you because we just found out that Elijah was added to a waiting list and will come to live with you after his heart transplant."

"Wow, I am so thankful!" I responded excitedly. "My children will have enough room to stay with me, when needed!"

The volunteer took me for a tour of the Ronald McDonald house.

"This place has 47 bedrooms, 10 suites and a small gym," she said. "It also has a special complex for the children with cancer and their families. Every morning the

House serves free pastries, milk, juice and coffee. Most of the evenings volunteers, families, groups from churches and from work bring dinners for the families, who live here."

"I feel God's gentle love towards me through your help," I said. "It touches my heart. I am so thankful because I am trying to save every penny. I know it will be expensive for my husband and the children to visit Elijah and me here. And I am so happy to see how much the Ronald McDonald House help the parents of ill children."

I settled into my room and loved it. I was now close to Elijah and could walk to and from the hospital. I knew walking would relieve my stress.

That evening the McDonald's restaurant brought sandwiches, salads and milkshakes to all the parents and their children at the Ronald McDonald house. Most of the families, who stayed in just one bedroom, ate together in a huge dining area. Because it was Friday, a family evening, I didn't want to have social conversations with other people and didn't want to tell anyone all my problems. I knew, if I start talking, I would be crying. So, I just got food and went to my room.

I called Oleg to tell him the good news about Elijah being listed for the heart surgery and about my beautiful new suite. Oleg was happy to hear the news. He was with the children; they were watching a movie and having a good evening. I was glad they were okay. I didn't want to share with Oleg that I was lonely, for fear of crying.

After our conversation, I let the tears flow as I worried about Elijah. I missed my family and felt all alone. I turned on my laptop and watched a slideshow of our family pictures. I didn't feel like talking to anyone and didn't want anyone to hear me cry.

When I calmed down, I remembered my retired neighbor, Charlotte, who was always home alone. I decided to call her.

"Olga, I am so happy to hear your voice. How are you?" Charlotte asked.

"You probably don't know, Charlotte, but I am in California now with Elijah, waiting for a donor heart to become available for him," I told her.

"Oh, I didn't know that," Charlotte said with a worried tone of voice. "Are you okay there?"

"I am trying to be okay," I said. "Today I am a little lonely. I remembered you and called you."

"Olga, I am lonely too," Charlotte said. "I had been thinking of a nice place to go for vacation and you called me just in time. Will it be okay for me to visit you in May?"

"Please come, Charlotte! I will be so happy to see you!"

I knew that Charlotte would come. After talking to her, I felt a lot better.

....

As I continued to learn, the Ronald McDonald House is an amazingly wonderful place! It is "home-away-from-home" for families to stay close by their hospitalized child at little or no cost. It is built on the simple idea that nothing else should matter when a family is focused on the health of their child. Families get their meals there and have a place to lay their head at night to rest.

The House believes when a child is hospitalized, the love and support of family is as powerful as the strongest medicine prescribed. They allow families to face the weight of illness together, by providing special suites for children with suppressed immune systems, accredited education programs, recreational activities, non-clinical support services, and sibling support services. In return, families either stay at no cost or are asked to make a donation up to

$25 per day, depending on the House. Their policy is that families are never turned away; if it's not possible to pay, the fee is waived.

The generosity of volunteers and donors make it all possible. I met a wonderful 70-year-old lady, Diana, who came to the Ronald McDonald House once a week and did massage for the parents of the hospitalized children. She got her license just to help the parents and did it in the name of Jesus.

I also met Wendy, who every Sunday drove parents to Walmart or Target. Wendy stayed at the House when her daughter had had three open-heart surgeries fifteen years prior. Wendy had been so grateful for her daughter's survival that she continued to volunteer at the Ronald McDonald House. Through people like Wendy and Diana, I saw God's never-ending love for me.

....

At the end of the first week, Oleg called me and said, "Olga, I have arranged to take time off work. The children and I are coming to California the following weekend! We would drive there, spend Saturday with you and Elijah, and drive back the next day."

"I am so excited you guys are coming! I can't wait to see you all!"

I was so happy they were coming, but I was also concerned. It was a twelve-hour trip one way. Driving for 24 hours back and forth in one weekend would be too much for Oleg. I was afraid he might get into a car accident. I also knew that our finances would not allow Oleg to miss any more work.

I had read earlier in a hospital letter that, somehow, we could buy discounted airplane tickets. I asked Mary, the social worker, if she knew anything about it.

"The plan is for Oleg to drive down, fly back the same weekend and fly back in two weeks to pick up the children," I explained to Mary. "The children will spend some time with me and some time with Oleg's Mother in Modesto."

"Let me go check," Mary said.

She returned shortly with two tickets.

"Olga, I just found out that Southwest Airlines provide free tickets to parents, whose children are hospitalized," she said with a big smile. "These two tickets are for Oleg."

"It is a miracle from God, Mary. Thank you so much!" I hugged Mary.

I called Oleg and told him the great news. This also meant that I would have a car for two weeks. The car would give me the freedom to drive to the hospital, shop for items or meet people, if needed. The use of the car would bring me more back to normal and I was grateful.

....

We started our second week in California. On Monday, when I came to the hospital, I didn't find Elijah in his room. My heart dropped as I wondered what could have happened. The nurse noticed me in the hallway. By the look on my face, she probably knew my question.

"Elijah is doing better," she said. "We have moved him to a big Cardiovascular Intensive Care room with other babies, because another very sick child needed a private room."

"Oh," I breathed out. "I am so relieved. I thought it was something bad."

In a big room with lots of babies, older children, parents and doctors, Elijah was wide awake and even smiled at me!

"Wow! Elijah, I can hardly believe that you recognize your mama and are so happy!"

I hugged him and kissed him on his forehead. I stayed like that for a moment, treasuring my precious time with my baby.

"Elijah, you seem to be getting used to the oxygen tube in your throat?" I asked.

Elijah just smiled. The first few days he moved his head, trying to get rid of that tube, but then he probably realized that it hurt to move his head and stopped doing that.

I kissed Elijah again. Then, holding him behind his back, I let him sit up a little. He liked it and we "talked". He seemed happy and alert. I cherished each moment with my baby. As I compare Elijah to five or seven-month-old babies today, I realize that Elijah did not have the strength to even keep his head up, to stand up on his feet, while I held him, to sit up or hold toys. He was a lot weaker. Even a simple smile required a lot of his energy. But that day Elijah smiled, and it meant the world to me!

It was very loud in that big room. Some children were recovering after surgeries and some were connected to the ECMO machines. Each child had a monitor by his or her bed and, if something went wrong, their sensors went off and made lots of noise. I looked at Elijah and didn't blame him for not sleeping. I was concerned that the additional excitement would cause his heart to work harder, but I also thanked God that Elijah was awake and happy. The doctors were surprised to see him alert. This was the first day they gave the nurses permission to start giving Elijah breast milk through a feeding tube, even though they were not sure if Elijah's stomach would be able to properly digest it.

I wanted to stay with Elijah for a while, but unfortunately it wasn't possible. In thirty minutes, there was going to be a procedure done on one of the children, so all the parents were asked to leave the room. I was disappointed, but had no choice. The nurse promised to call me when the procedure was over. Unfortunately, that procedure was replaced by another procedure, so the room was unavailable for the visitors until the next morning. While walking back to the Ronald McDonald house, I was surprised at how much more strength I had by putting everything in God's hands.

....

On Tuesday, the surgeon met with me to talk about Elijah's second open-heart surgery.

"Olga, Elijah is on the schedule for his procedure next week," he said. "I have performed about 70 such procedures on a normal heart, but not on a one sided-heart, like Elijah's. I don't know if I will be successful."

"I understand," I said.

"I will do two surgeries in one, a "Glenn" procedure, which Elijah was supposed to have at six months, and a "Berlin-Heart" procedure," the surgeon continued. "During this complicated procedure, I will divert half of the blood to the lungs, disconnect the artificial shunt, and connect the right pulmonary artery to the vein, which brings deoxygenated blood from the upper part of the body to the heart. Then, I will install a ventricular assist device, a "Berlin Heart", which will support the work of Elijah's failing heart in pumping blood effectively around his body. It will allow time for Elijah to reach transplant stage."

"It is complicated and hard for me to understand, but I know one thing: I have to trust you to do it," I told the surgeon. "May God bless your hands."

When I visited Elijah, he was asleep in the same noisy room.

"Can you please transfer Elijah back to his private room?" I asked the doctor. "I think it will be better for him. This room is too noisy for Elijah with his failing heart."

The doctor agreed. That afternoon, as the room became available, the nurses transferred Elijah.

....

On Wednesday, Elijah was wide awake again, which surprised me immensely! I sat Elijah up, held his back and he played. He reached for my nose and my eyes, and just played with the string of keys on my neck. Seeing Elijah feeling better, I really wished for a donor heart to become available that day and prayed for God to help. I did this, even though I understood that another child had to die, for his heart to become available for Elijah. I wished this wasn't the situation...

It was hard for me to imagine what my husband was experiencing at home, while Elijah and I were away. Financially, Oleg had to work full time; yet, he needed to be available for our children. During this time, half of his hair turned gray. He was a very good father to Elijah, David, Kristina and Michael, and a great husband to me. Looking back, I can't imagine what I would have done without Oleg and his support. He wanted to give Elijah every possible chance, and his love and determination kept us going. My husband supported me in every way and prayed for us.

The children seemed to be okay at my Mother's house or at home. My Mother was still doing day care and had other children at her house. She had no TV and no computers for children to watch and play. But she had lots of books to read, paper to color, shovels to dig, and cars and tractors to ride. I knew that my children would not be bored at her house.

....

On Thursday, Elijah was awake and hungry, but his stomach had enlarged by ten centimeters.

"Olga, we don't know why Elijah's stomach enlarged," the doctor said. "We have to stop giving him breast milk and start a water nutrition supplement though IV. We did an ultrasound and x-ray tests, but didn't see anything abnormal. We are not sure what is happening."

Elijah's heart rate started going up, so the doctor ordered him to be sedated. Later that evening, Elijah developed a fever. After a blood test was completed, the doctor came to talk to me.

"A blood test showed one of Elijah's PICC lines in his arms, which sends medications to his heart, had become infected," he said. "The good news is Elijah's PICC line will finally come out and Elijah will be able to move his hand freely, but the bad news is Elijah's veins are very hard to find. We are concerned we may have a hard time inserting a new PICC line."

After the PICC line was replaced, Elijah's fever still didn't go down. After the second test was performed, the blood test showed that Elijah's other PICC line and the arterial line were also infected and needed to be replaced. This was a very bad news.

Luckily, the doctors were able to find the new veins and replace it. I accepted what each day brought us. Elijah was hurting, and I hurt with and for him. It was as if I could feel his pain. Life is beautiful, but sometimes it can be so cruel.

....

Late in the evening, Oleg called me and said, "Olga, I was touched by the love of our neighbors, Sandie and Ross. They know that I am leaving for California early in the morning. When I came home from work, I saw a box by the door with goodies for our children to stay occupied during the long drive. Then later Sandie also brought me an envelope with money. I was touched by it and was refusing to take the money, but Sandie asked me to give it to you."

I called Sandie to thank her.

"Olga, buying goodies for the children was something I had never done before." Sandie said, "but I just happened to be at Target and thought of the idea."

"I am touched by your love, Sandie," I said, acknowledging her kindness. "I also know it is God, who helps our family through your hands."

....

Oleg and the children left Washington early Friday morning and drove to California. On their way Kristina took a picture of clouds in the sky. They thought the clouds represented two angels. When I saw the picture, I thought God was sending us a message.

Oleg and the children arrived at the Ronald McDonald House, and we were so happy to be together again. I showed Oleg and the children my suite and the game room, where the children could play. Across the street from the

Ronald McDonald house, there was Palo Alto mall with an open sky between the stores. I wanted Oleg and the children to see the blooming flowers, so we walked through the mall to the hospital.

Elijah was sedated. I was sad he wasn't awake to see the family. The children seemed unsure about how to react. After about ten minutes, they became bored and wanted to leave. It's fascinating how children, even in a critical situation as this, can quickly evaluate a situation and know there is nothing they can do, and nothing is expected of them. They have an ability to find another activity to entertain themselves. Maybe they do even better than adults, because adults worry about everything. While Oleg stayed by Elijah, I took the children to the Giant Cactus garden, not too far from the hospital.

We had never seen giant cacti before. Some had flowers, so we took several pictures. Then the children ran around and chased each other. After an hour, we walked back to the hospital, where we took a picture by a big red heart. We felt like it was a symbol of Elijah's ill heart, fighting every day to live and be with us.

The next morning, on Saturday, Oleg's Mother with her new husband, Sergey, and Oleg's older brother and his family, came from Modesto to visit us in Palo Alto. After we ate lunch, Oleg with his family walked to see Elijah. I stayed with the children at the Ronald McDonald house. Elijah slept most of the time, but when Grandma Olga came and started talking to him, he woke up and opened his eyes! It seemed like he remembered Grandma's voice from the time she was in Oregon. When Oleg's Mother saw that Elijah recognized her voice, she cried.

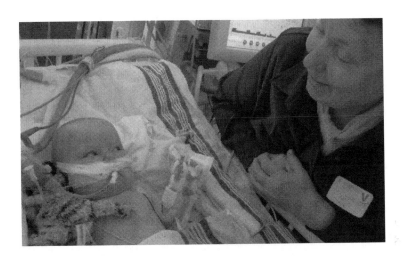

In the evening, Oleg's family drove back to Modesto and asked to take our children with them for a week. Our children were excited and couldn't wait to play with five other cousins in Modesto. They also wanted to swim in Grandma's pool. I wanted to be with my children, but I knew it was better for them to go with Oleg's family. Elijah's surgery would be in two days. I knew that I would be an emotional wreck. I reluctantly let them go to Grandma's house.

....

When Oleg and I visited Elijah the next morning, he slept most of the time. Tests showed that his heart was becoming weaker and weaker. It was a difficult day for Oleg, who had not seen his son for two weeks. That day he saw a child with a fever, fighting an infection and growing weaker. It seemed almost unfair. Two days before, Elijah had been not only awake, but smiled at me.

As Oleg and I sat by Elijah's bed, the doctor came to talk to us.

"Oleg and Olga, I wanted to ask if you want us to save Elijah, in case things turn for the worst. We need your permission to connect Elijah's heart to an ECMO machine, in case his heart stops working,"

Questions like these were difficult to hear and more difficult to answer.

"We know that the ECMO machine has possible negative outcomes," Oleg said. "Can you please do everything possible, as long as there is still hope that Elijah will have a normal life after it."

After consulting with other specialists, the doctor came back.

"We have decided not to connect Elijah's heart to an ECMO machine because it has a very high risk of internal bleeding. If Elijah's brain starts bleeding, he will not qualify for a heart transplant, so there is no point in connecting his heart to the machine."

The surgery was still planned for Tuesday. Oleg had to fly back home Sunday evening. I knew it would be difficult for him to get days off work and come back to stay with me during the surgery. Earlier, I had asked the surgeon if they could reschedule it for Monday, so my husband could stay with me, but they couldn't. I didn't want Oleg to lose his job, so I assured him that I would be okay.

What I saw after the first surgery in Oregon, was terrifying. There was blood, the cold body of Elijah, twenty-four medications in IV pumps around Elijah, and I knew that every second could bring death. I didn't want to see any of that again. Before, I had my husband for support. This time I would be alone, and I didn't have a choice. Even though I was not sure I could face the surgery alone, I told Oleg I would be okay. I drove him to the airport. His plan was to fly back to Palo Alto in two weeks.

....

18

*God will not give us a load more
than we can handle.*

Monday, April 5th Elijah and I entered our third week in
California. I woke up, knowing it would be a tear-filled day:
it was our 14th wedding anniversary. Oleg was at home in
Washington and our children were at Grandma's house in
Modesto. Elijah was at the hospital and I was at the Ronald
McDonald House all alone. Normally, Oleg gives me flowers
for our anniversary; but we did not even discuss our
anniversary when Oleg was in California. It wasn't even
important, compared to Elijah. There were no flowers and
no gifts. It was just a day we had to get through to the next
day, when our son would either live or die during his
surgery.

"God, why does our life have to be so harsh?" I prayed
and cried for a while. "Please consider our prayers."

When I arrived at the hospital later, Elijah no longer had
a fever. All his necessary tests were completed for the
surgery. But in the evening, Elijah's fever returned again, so
his surgery was postponed to Thursday.

....

On Tuesday, Elijah was wide awake and happy again. He
seemed to be excited and waved his hands, reaching for my
face. He looked at me with half a smile and wanted to play.
With the nurse's help, we raised the back of Elijah's bed and
sat him up very carefully, trying not to cause him pain with
his breathing tube. I knew the nurse preferred I not move
Elijah, but I wanted him to sit up, to play and to do what

healthy babies do. I set his toys around him: a monkey, an elephant, a sheep, a bear and a frog. He looked at them and tried to reach the monkey, his favorite toy. When Elijah got tired of playing, we laid him down and he fell asleep. That was the best day since coming to California – a day of play instead of a surgery!

At that time, Elijah's scar on his chest had healed and was barely visible. For a while, I stood by Elijah's bed and enjoyed watching him smile in his sleep. It was easy to believe he was having wonderful dreams. He had not smiled for a month and I was sorry Oleg was missing this time with Elijah. I wanted my husband to see a happy Elijah.

Posted near Elijah's bed was a string of beads; each bead represented a change in medication, a procedure, a test, x-ray, surgery, etc. A red heart bead represented a heart surgery. Elijah had undergone so many procedures, the necklace had many beads. To some it might seem a waste of time, a bead on a string, but it was so much more because it represented the struggles my son endured. It also represented the hard work and the special care the doctors were giving my son.

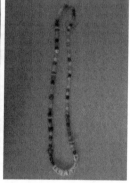

The next day, Elijah's heart had a more difficult time. It seemed when he had a good day, the next day would be difficult. Yesterday he had been so active. Today all he could do was sleep, and at moments, I wondered if he might not ever wake up. Since arriving in California, I had not changed his diaper, I had not bottle-fed him, and I had not held him. I so dearly desired to do all those things. In some respect, he was my child and I deeply loved him, and yet, it was like he was becoming a stranger.

....

Over the past few weeks my vision had become blurry. I was concerned it might be related to either my high blood pressure or to irritation from nearly constant crying. Since I had a car, I scheduled an eye appointment with a doctor at the Santa Barbara Hospital about 30 minutes away. Even though I felt fortunate to have a car, I was a little nervous driving in a strange city with only handwritten directions. In spite of stopping several times to ask for directions, I found myself terribly lost. What was supposed to be a 30-minute jaunt, turned into a 90-minute trip.

Arriving late, I explained the situation to the woman at the front desk.

"The doctor will see you in about an hour," she said.

The doctor eventually saw me, prescribed new glasses, and handed me a bill for $300. I was disappointed that our medical insurance covered only an eye exam, but not the glasses.

While seeing an eye doctor, I noticed I did not feel well. That day I had stopped taking anti-bleeding medications, as the doctor in Washington instructed, and I began bleeding heavily again. When I was ready to leave the clinic, I couldn't. The bleeding was becoming so heavy that I knew I had to see a gynecologist. Fortunately, there was a Women's Clinic at the Santa Barbara Hospital, the same place as the vision clinic. The OB unit was very close, so I walked there. The gynecologist determined I needed a D&C and scheduled a D&C procedure for me that night under a general anesthesia. Although I was not expecting to spend the evening at the hospital, I wanted to be healed and healthy again.

In the pre-op room, the nurse asked me, "Olga, who will give you a ride home?"

Tears filled my eyes as I said, "I have no one here. I am from Washington State and am staying at the Ronald McDonald House. My seven-month-old baby, Elijah, is at Stanford hospital, waiting for a heart transplant. I can't be hospitalized because I have to be by my son. His open-heart surgery is tomorrow."

"You will be well taken care of," the nurse assured me. "Because there is no one to drive you back to Palo Alto and you can't drive after the anesthesia, we will hospitalize you until the morning."

I felt relieved; this problem had to be fixed and I needed to be back by my baby.

"Olga, please sign the consent and give us permission for the procedure," the nurse continued.

I signed the consent.

"Do you have a will?" she asked.

"Is this procedure very serious?" I questioned the nurse, confused. "I am not planning to die here."

"There is a risk of excessive bleeding and infection, but you will probably be okay."

Trying to stay calm, I called Oleg.

"Honey, can you please pray for me. I am at the hospital, waiting for a procedure to be done..."

I tried so hard to hold back my tears.

"Olga, please don't cry," Oleg said with a worried voice. "I will pray for you and God will help us. I really wish I could be there with you..."

I knew Oleg could not come and I knew he would be worried. Yet, I wanted him by my side. Sometimes, reality does not allow what we want. After our conversation, I was in tears again. What could I do? I was afraid. Elijah was near death. His surgery was tomorrow, and I was hospitalized. Surely, God would not give us a load more than we could handle.

Soon, a nurse came to wheel me into an operating room. After anesthetic medications began working, I fell asleep and woke up after the procedure was done. I had no memories of what had happened. The doctors were still running tests, to determine why this condition had happened. They promised to have the results the next day. After an hour, I was transferred into a private room.

I had no complications, thank God, and was discharged at 5 A.M. It was a cold morning and I was in a light dress without a jacket. The nurse put me in a wheel chair and wheeled me around the outside of the hospital, because the other doors were locked. She covered me with two hospital sheets to keep me warm and let me keep the sheets, so I would not be cold in the car. I was so thankful for having health insurance, and for the doctors and nurses, who helped me.

....

Weak and in pain, I hurried back to Palo Alto because Elijah's surgery was planned for that morning. I had to be there. While driving, I called Elijah's nurse.

"Elijah's procedure has been canceled because he developed a fever again," the nurse said. "His heart has become worse, so he is sedated again."

I felt helpless. On the way to the Ronald McDonald house, I called Oleg to tell him I was okay, and that Elijah's surgery was canceled again. I can't imagine how difficult it was for Oleg to have a child at the hospital near death, have his wife at another hospital, undergoing surgery, and to be so far away and alone. Later he told me that while being home alone for those two weeks, he spent lots of time praying to God and reading the Bible. He also spoke a lot with our boxer, Jack, about his worries and wishes. So only God and Jack heard him. Surprisingly, besides my family and his family, not a lot of people called Oleg or visited him when he was home alone with his tears and worries.

I slept for half a day before the gynecologist called me.

"Olga, your lab results are back. We didn't find anything cancerous during your D&C procedure. Please don't worry," she said.

"I didn't even have time to worry about myself," I answered. "Elijah is my first priority."

In the afternoon, I visited Elijah and held his hand. Because of his huge bed, I couldn't even lean over to kiss him. All I could do was to kiss his hand. This made me cry, as I said, "Elijah, you have done so well and have come so far. You can't just give up. You just can't..."

Evening came, and I was alone in my room at the Ronald McDonald House. Lying in my bed, still weak after the surgery, I didn't know what to do or what to think. I didn't feel comfortable telling anyone about my surgery. I didn't even tell my Mom because I knew she would worry. Only Oleg knew. I am sure he was having a hard time, too. It always is hard for us to be apart. I wished he was near me, but he wasn't. I wished my Mom could visit me and bring me a hot homemade meal, but she couldn't. I struggled not to cry.

....

That evening, I received a call from Galina, who lived in Sacramento, two hours away from Palo Alto. I didn't know Galina, but I knew her sister. My friend from Washington had told Galina about me being all alone in Palo Alto with a critically ill baby.

"Olga, I wanted to invite you to come visit me and several prayer groups," Galina said.

"Thank you, Galina, for the invitation," I said, excited for that opportunity. "I have not been in a church since arriving in California. For me it is unheard of, the church is the foundation of my life. My relationship with God guides everything I do and choices I make. I want to come; I need to hear from God, who is providing me an opportunity to receive His message."

I did not tell Galina about my surgery because then she would start worrying about me and I would lose this opportunity. I also knew that Elijah would be sedated, and his surgery was not happening for the next two days.

The next day I felt a lot better. After visiting Elijah, I drove to Galina's home in Sacramento. She met me, fed her freshly cooked red borsch and seemed very nice to me. I ate borsch and tried to hide my tears. I missed it so much. I missed my Mom. I missed Mom's cooking. Galina reminded me of my Mom. She also showed me her daughter's room, where I will be spending the night. I really felt like a princess, being loved and taken good care of.

Galina, her husband, an older lady and I visited three different prayer groups, one that evening and two in the morning. With a group of people, we sang songs and prayed. I felt the presence of the Holy Spirit. Several individuals spoke words that were meaningful to me. I believed those words could only come from God. They didn't know who I was and, yet, they were right on point about what was happening to Elijah and my family.

One person said, **"The devil put his arrow straight into your heart, but I want to heal your heart."** The second person said, **"My daughter. I let it happen to your family, so you could be closer to Me."** And the third person saw a vision that a sick person laid in a bed. The doctors were around him, running out of ideas of how to help him. The angels stood around the doctors and the sick person. Then, he heard the voice of God, **"This was My plan. The doctor's plan will fall apart. My plan will take place."**

Hearing these messages from God, I understood that that our situation was just like Job's from the Bible. I knew we were being tested by God. I hoped the best for Elijah and for my family. While driving back to Palo Alto, I prayed for Elijah, for Oleg and our children, I prayed for my health, for our parents, siblings, and all the people who supported us. I thanked God for the new people from Sacramento, who would now pray for Elijah. Gratitude filled my heart for their faith and their friendship.

At the hospital, it was hard for me to see Elijah sedated. It seemed like the battle was being lost and, yet, something told me to have hope.

....

That afternoon Nina, who lived in Modesto, called me.

"Olga, I heard from your Mother-in-law that you are at the hospital with your baby," she said. "I am driving your way. Can my two daughters and I stop by and visit you?"

"Of 'course!" I said. "I would love to see you, Nina!"

I had never seen Nina, but I had spoken to her over the phone a year earlier about the Russian school in our church. When Nina was at the hospital, she called me. I met her by the elevators. I had no idea who she was, but the minute I saw her, I could feel it was her.

"Nina!?" I asked, not sure.

"Olga!?" she asked, also not sure.

238

We gave each other a big hug.

"Nina, only today I understand what it means to be united by the blood of Jesus. We have never seen each other, but we have hearts full of love and we know how to help others. Thank you for visiting me."

Tears filled my eyes as I experienced Nina's warmth. Nina wanted to know if I was okay and to provide comfort. Because of our common faith, and being directors of the Russian school in each of our churches, there was a common bond and a common understanding. Instead of being lonely and missing my family on that Saturday afternoon, Nina and I had a wonderful time visiting with each other.

Later that evening, back in my room, I knelt and wanted to pray, but I couldn't connect with God. So I opened the blinds, looked up towards blue sky and expressed everything I had in my heart. At the end, I added, "God, please speed up this process and send Elijah a new heart, so our family can be together again."

....

19

*Faith, hope and trust in God will provide
you strength and comfort.*

Sunday, April 11th started our fourth week in California. Elijah's fever was gone. He was on schedule again to have surgery on Tuesday. David, Kristina and Michael had already spent eight days in Modesto with their Grandparents. They had been on spring break for one week and would miss one week of school. I knew they would go back to Vancouver and I thought it would be important to spend time with them. Yet, I knew that I had to be with Elijah also. That afternoon, I drove to Modesto, spent the night at Oleg's Mother's house and early the next morning drove back to Palo Alto with David, Kristina and Michael. I needed my family to be near me. They could give me strength and make everything alright.

I signed the children in at the Ronald McDonald house and showed them around. Then, we visited Elijah, who just slept. It was like he wasn't alive. He had vaseline on his eye lids, a tube in his throat, a scar on his chest, a breathing machine, and IVs with medications around him. It was a place no one would want to be. The children stood quietly by his bed.

"I feel so sorry for Elijah," Kristina said with tears streaming down her cheeks.

"Mom, I am scared," Michael added.

"Please don't be scared," I embraced the children. "We need to pray to God to help Elijah. Hopefully, your baby brother will get better soon. The doctors are doing everything possible to help Elijah.

We left the hospital and returned to the more comfortable environment of the Ronald McDonald House. For the remainder of the day, the children played games, watched movies and I prepared dinner. We were waiting for the scheduled surgery tomorrow. I knew as a family, whatever happens, we would not be able to stop it, but, would have to get through it. Oleg would come, as scheduled, on Friday, and we would be a family again.

....

The next morning, I woke up at 6 A.M. I wanted to go to the hospital and pray for Elijah before his surgery, but there was a rule at the Ronald McDonald house, which meant I couldn't leave my children unattended. My children were still asleep, and I had no one to watch them. I wasn't sure what to do. David was twelve years old and a very responsible child. I knew my children would be safe. I felt I had no choice, therefore, I broke the rule and went to the hospital for an hour. I was hoping that God would perform a miracle during Elijah's surgery.

I was drawn to the hospital to pray for Elijah. You might ask why my prayer at the Ronald McDonald House would not be as good as the prayer at the hospital? I somehow felt the need to be near Elijah, put my hands on him and pray to God that He would heal Elijah. To me, that was important. In my faith, I would ask a pastor to pray and to anoint him with the holy oil, but there was no pastor and no oil. There was just me and I wanted this for Elijah. I didn't know if I had a right to do it, but there was no one else. I knew from my study of the Bible that the prayer of faith and anointing with the holy oil were customs that would help heal the sick.

When I came to Elijah's room, the nurse was preparing him for the surgery.

"Is it okay if I pray for Elijah?" I asked.

"Yes," the nurse said, kindly.

Nervously, I put my hands on Elijah's head and chest, and asked God to bless my son, bless the surgeon and the nurses, who would perform the surgery and assist in the care of Elijah.

Then I added, "God, I know it says in the Bible, *"If anyone amongst you is sick, call the pastor, anoint with the oil and God will heal the sick person.'* **There is not a pastor here and I don't have the oil, but in the name of Jesus, I anoint Elijah with my faith. May He be healed in the name of Jesus."** I had to have faith. It was the only tool I had left, besides hope.

After I finished praying, I sat by Elijah's bed and waited for the surgeon to come. While waiting, I sent a text message to my brothers and sisters and asked them to form a prayer chain and pray for Elijah every hour. Then, I called my Father and our pastor in Washington, and asked them to pray for Elijah's surgery to be successful.

A few minutes later, an older lady, Tessie, came from the Chaplain's office. She spoke to me. Then she reached into her purse and took out some holy oil. **I was shocked. She said the same verse that I had just used in prayer, and she brought me the holy oil! I could not believe what I saw! When I prayed, I prayed in Russian, so no one, except God could hear me. For me it was a real miracle.**

"Tessie, it is the same verse I just used in a prayer and hoped there would be someone to anoint Elijah with the holy oil," I said through tears.

Tessie embraced me in a hug. Then she poured oil onto my hands and prayed for me first. **It was as if God had given me some special power that flowed from Him through me to my son.**

"Olga, put your hands on Elijah and pray for him," she said.

"Tessie, I don't really know how to pray in this situation," I answered. "Can you please pray and I will repeat after you?"

We anointed Elijah and both prayed for him.

"Tessie, I also want to pray for the surgeon," I said, unsure how I would do that.

At the same time, the surgeon walked into the room. I asked the surgeon if we can pray for his hands to do the surgery successfully. He agreed and said that he believes in a power of a prayer. Tessie and I put our hands on the surgeon's hands, and we prayed for God's power to work through the surgeon.

Tessie left. I felt God's warmth and comforting in my heart that seemed to stay with me and allowed me to be calm, as I faced challenges and dealt with heart wrenching situations over the next three weeks. It was like God was holding my hand, guiding me, and giving me the confidence I could do it. I knew it was the presence of the Holy Spirit.

I called Oleg, then my Father, then our pastor and told them what had happened. At the end, I said, **"I have such grief, but God is with me, showing me His miracles!"** It was so powerful to feel God's presence and see His work. Somehow, I knew that Elijah would be okay in the surgery that day.

....

When I got back to the Ronald McDonald house, my children were still asleep. They knew nothing about me being gone. When they woke up, we ate breakfast. The doctors did not ask me to stay at the hospital, and I knew that my three children would not do well, sitting in a waiting room during surgery. I wanted to make it a positive day for them, so I told them that we would go to an Art museum. After that, we went to McDonald's restaurant at the Palo Alto mall. My mind was on none of this, but I tried to pay attention to my children. While the surgery was going on, I was calm and the children kept me busy. That day I didn't even think about the 25% chance survival for Elijah.

Early that afternoon we returned to the hospital, as we knew that the surgery would be completed shortly. The children read books at the hospital children's library. The library had staff monitor the children, while I checked on Elijah. I waited in the waiting area, as I thought that the doctors would be coming out with Elijah shortly. While waiting, I received several calls from Elijah's nurses in Oregon, checking to see how the surgery went.

Suddenly, I saw the elevator door open and there was Elijah, in his bed, surrounded by six doctors, IV pumps and an oxygen pump. His heart was working! I thanked God! His chest was already closed, whereas in Oregon it was open for seventeen days! I could not believe my eyes! The surgery was only *seven* hours, whereas his first open-heart surgery in Oregon was fifteen hours. It was a miracle. Everything went so smoothly. I called Oleg and told him the good news. He was excited, too. God had given us a special gift, one that I don't know how to explain, how wonderful it was! Even though our baby could die any minute, we were so happy that he was still breathing!

Thirty minutes later I visited Elijah in his room. He wasn't as swollen as after his first surgery. Elijah's chest was closed, and his body was covered with a cloth. The nurse explained more about the "Berlin Heart" mechanism.

"This mechanism is connected to Elijah's heart," she said. "We laid it on the mirror, situated on Elijah's stomach. The mirror helps us see if blood clots develop."

Seeing blood in the mechanism nauseated me. It was a normal process to the nurses and doctors, but to me it was my son's blood, running through those tubes.

"If it clots, Elijah can have a stroke any second," the nurse said explained.

Soon the surgeon came.

"Olga, the surgery has gone well," he said. "Now, we will slowly decrease the breathing machine, so that on the third day Elijah will wake up and breathe on his own."

"Thank you so much, Doctor," I said. "I appreciate your hard work."

The nurses were busy working around Elijah. I felt I was in their way and there was nothing to do to help my son. I knew the best thing I could do, even though I didn't like it, was to get out of their way, so that the nurses and doctors could do what they were professionally trained to do. I left the hospital, not knowing what may happen the next minute, or that night, or the next day. I hoped and prayed that Elijah would be okay.

Trying hard not to cry, I picked up the children at the hospital library. We returned to the Ronald McDonald House, where the children played in the game room. No one wanted to talk about the surgery. What was there to say? To pass time I did laundry. I tried to stay positive for both myself and my children, trying hard not to show my concerns. The children distracted me and we were okay, but not for long...

....

The rules at the Ronald McDonald House stated that no more than four people could sleep or stay in my room. All visitors could only go to the common room in the building. These were good rules. They protected the privacy and safety of all concern, including the fragile children, recovering in the building. And there were only two beds in my room. The problem was that Oleg was coming and there would be five of us. I called Oleg and asked, "Honey, what should we do?"

"Even though we will be spending extra money, lets book the hotel for two days. We need for our family to be together," Oleg said.

There was also another rule that you couldn't leave your room for more than 24 hours, or you would lose your room. I went down to the Ronald McDonald office and asked, "Can you please help us book a hotel with your discount?"

"Yes, we can. I will do it right now," the volunteer in the front office said.

While she was booking, I couldn't hold my tears anymore and started crying. The director saw me crying and came out from her office to talk to me. She embraced me with her hands and comforted me.

"Olga, why are you crying?" she asked.

"My husband is coming from Washington; I haven't seen him for two weeks," I said through tears. "And our three children are already staying with me. I know your rule says that only four people can stay in my room. Also, you have a rule that I can't be gone for 24 hours because you may give my room away. We need to book a hotel, so our family can be together. But I will be coming back here tomorrow."

"Olga, please don't worry. It's okay if you will be gone for 48 hours. We won't give your room away," the director said.

"Thank you so much," I couldn't stop crying.

"Come here, Olga. Sit down," she said and took me to another room.

"I am sorry I am crying," I said. "It's not just the hotel and five people problem. My baby had an open-heart surgery today and no one knows his future. I just can't be strong any longer."

The director hugged me, sat next to me and just listened. It took me a while to calm down. I didn't want to go back to my room and have my children see me cry. It is amazing what a good cry can do for you. Somehow, my strength returned, and I could return to my children and move forward. It is amazing how strong is the power of caring enough to listen.

....

The next morning, I took the children to the hospital kids' room while I visited Elijah. When I came to Elijah's room, I couldn't see him. Frightened, my heart dropped.

"What had happened to my child?" I asked.

"Oh, Elijah is there. We covered him with this silver foil blanket to warm him up," the nurse said. "Elijah's body was too cold. We need the temperature to come back to normal, so we can start waking him up."

I opened Elijah's blanket and touched his hand. It was freezing cold. Elijah was still sedated and did not move. My heart broke. As a mother, I wanted to protect my children in every way that I could, but I had no control in this matter. It seemed like I was a disinterested observer and, yet, it was my child. As I stood by the bed watching Elijah, I felt so detached from his lifeless body. My baby should be wide wake, reaching up for me to lift him from his crib at home.

....

In the evening, Oleg called me.

"Olga, maybe we should cancel the hotel. We don't have the extra money. Could you please take the children back to my Mom's house in Modesto?"

"Yes, I can," I said. "Driving there and back is still cheaper than the hotel."

The children were excited to go back to Modesto in two days and I canceled the hotel.

On Thursday, before leaving for Modesto, we stopped at the hospital. The children chose to stay in the activity room, while I went to check on Elijah.

"Olga, I just received the bad news that Elijah's blood test showed an infection in his breathing tube," the nurse said. "Everyone, who enters Elijah's room, needs to put on a yellow gown, a mask and gloves," she handed them to me.

I was so disappointed and hated it when we had to do this in Portland. But I knew this was routine, so I did it without saying a word. Shortly, a social worker came.

"Olga, your children can no longer be in the activity room because their brother is contagious with an infection."

"I can't leave this minute because the doctor had asked me to wait so she could talk to me," I said, not sure what to do. "I can't be in two places at the same time"

"I can take them out, if you give me permission," the social worker said.

"Yes, please," I answered, feeling relieved, but worried about the children.

"We will wait for you in the hall, Olga," she said. "I will ask the children if they have any questions about their ill brother."

Soon, the doctor came and said, "Olga, Elijah seems to be doing well. His numbers look good, but I want him to wake up so I know for sure that he is there."

"What do you mean?" I was confused.

"The breathing machine is breathing for him and the Berlin Heart is pumping his heart, so we won't actually know if Elijah is alive until he wakes up."

I was shocked. I had always assumed he was alive and had taken it for granted.

"I don't understand how this could be," I said. "Elijah has to be alive."

"The sedation medications suppress the brain's ability to remember to breathe," the doctor continued. "If Elijah is alive, he would be able to breathe on his own, therefore, the breathing machine would be slowed down and eventually turned off. Only then we would know for sure if Elijah is alive."

"I know, Elijah is there, and he is alive!" upset, I told the doctor.

How could he not be? He has gone through so much and I didn't want to think about death. I couldn't accept the thought of death.

....

From Stanford, we went to pick up my new glasses. They reduced the stress on my eyes, even though the doctor said it would take a couple of days to adjust. The Grandparents were happy to see us, even though I knew they were tired from a previous week with the Grandkids at their house. Our children took lots of their energy. The Grandparents played games with our children, sat in a hot tub with them, showed them their bunnies, and invited all our relatives to play with our children. I thanked the Grandparents for taking good care of our children.

After breakfast the next morning, I said goodbye to everyone. I knew that I would not see my children until summer, as Oleg would drive from Palo Alto to Modesto, and then back to Vancouver. It is hard to leave your children, knowing you will not see them for two months. I hugged them, kissed them and left in tears. While driving for an hour and a half, I kept praying to God that Oleg would have strength to watch over our children and that we would be reunited soon as a family. I knew that God had already blessed us. We were a loving family, who had health insurance and were financially surviving.

....

I drove straight to the hospital. It was the third day after the surgery and Elijah was slowly waking up. His body temperature was better, and the warming blanket was turned off. My eyes had not fully adjusted to my new glasses and Elijah's right cheek seemed a little swollen. When I began to ask the nurse questions, it seemed Elijah had heard my voice. He opened his eyes! I was so excited! I always knew my baby was alive and now I had proof! It was like he was trying to realize who is this lady with the glasses that has a voice I recognize? He started crying. I held his hand and talked to him.

"Elijah, my baby, I am so happy!" Elijah had survived the second most difficult heart surgery in the world," my tears flowed freely. "I love you so much and can't wait for you to recover, so I can hold you and play with you."

But Elijah kept crying and looked at me like something was hurting. I wished I could help him, but I couldn't.

"Elijah, your dad is coming in the evening and you will see him soon," I continued. "Also, you nurse, Patti, is coming from Oregon to visit her friend in San Francisco. She is planning to visit you tomorrow."

But Elijah continued crying, like something was hurting. His heart rate slowly climbed.

"For some reason, his saturation numbers are low," the doctor said. "We need to give him sedation medications and let him fall asleep again.

Throughout the day we are planning to decrease the breathing machine and, maybe, tomorrow Elijah will breathe on his own. Then you will be able to hold him carefully, cuddle with him and love him, while he recovers." I could hardly wait for that moment!

....

When Elijah fell asleep, I decided to go back to the Ronald McDonald house. I needed to clean up after the children. It was the last day I had a car, because Oleg with the children would drive it back to Washington. I didn't know how long I would stay in Palo Alto, but I knew it would not be easy without a car. It was a very hot day. My hair was just too long, so before going back to the Ronald McDonald House I decided to get a haircut. Two places quoted me $65 for a haircut, but I couldn't afford it.

I went back to the Ronald McDonald house and asked where I could go for a cheaper haircut. Again, I was surprised. They gave me a coupon for a free haircut at a very nice salon. A hairdresser shampooed my hair, cut it and even blow-dried it. I told her about Elijah. She thought it was the most unusual story she had heard, and promised to pray for us. I left, feeling like a princess. How good it felt to receive love from people, when I needed it, and when I was alone.

....

20

*You still believe in miracles until the
end, even if it is a small chance.*

I cleaned my room at the Ronald McDonald house and did
the laundry. At 7 P.M., I planned to return to the hospital
to be with Elijah. Then, at 11 P.M., I planned to drive to San
Jose and meet Oleg at the airport. In the early evening,
Elijah's doctor called me.

"Olga, Elijah's saturation numbers keep decreasing as
we slow down his breathing machine," he said with a
worried tone of voice. "This means that he can't breathe
on his own and oxygen isn't going to every part of his body.
If Elijah was a healthy baby, his saturation number would be
at one hundred. Eighty is acceptable for Elijah, considering
his condition. When his numbers drop below sixty, it is
dangerous. Elijah's numbers are in the twenties', which
means that if we turned off the breathing machine, he
would die."

I didn't know what to answer.

"We need to take Elijah to the cardiac catheterization
lab as soon as possible to see if the blood vessels, valves and
chambers are functioning properly," the doctor continued.
"It will also show why the oxygenation is very low. During
this procedure, we will need to use the dye, but are
concerned that Elijah's kidneys may shut down. Olga, we
need you to come to the hospital as soon as possible, to sign
papers and give us permission."

"I will be there in 10 minutes," I said.

Surprisingly, I was calm. Three days after the surgery
was just too long for the doctors not to call me with bad

252

news. I drove to the hospital and signed the papers. In Elijah's room, seven doctors and nurses were preparing him for the cardiac catheterization lab. I was standing in the hallway. It was like no one cared about me or my feelings. Everyone was concentrating on Elijah. I didn't even have a chance to come up to my son, kiss him or say goodbye.

"What about me?" I thought. I know the doctors had concern for me, but at that moment time was critical. This could be the last time I would see my child alive. The team of doctors with Elijah in his bed, hurried towards the lab.

"Olga, the lab will take about three hours," the nurse informed me. "You can stay here in Elijah's room and wait, or you can be wherever you would like in the hospital."

I wanted to be in a private area and went to the computer lab. I wanted to pray, but didn't know what to tell God. I just asked God to give me strength, to help Elijah and to give Oleg a safe flight to California.

When you want to know what is happening to your child, time moves so slowly. You can't just sit and wait. Because the computer was there, I checked my emails. Then I met a young couple, whose seven-month old baby was hospitalized. I told them about Elijah and they told me about their child. Sharing Elijah's story gave me new energy. I thanked God for all of His care.

....

At 10:30 P.M., I went back to Elijah's room. For some reason, he wasn't back from the lab yet.

"It is time for me to drive to the airport to pick up my husband," I told the nurse. "We will come back in an hour."

At the airport, Oleg was excited to see me. I didn't want to tell him the bad news, but I had to. Oleg was calm. It was not like it was something unexpected. We knew every day went either way. There was no pattern. And just because it was a really bad day today, it didn't mean that tomorrow couldn't be a better day. This may seem strange, but after all the months we experienced, one thing we had learned was, you never know where tomorrow could take you. We knew this was extremely serious and, yet, we took it as a normal event. We came to the hospital at 11:30 P.M.

"Elijah is still at the cardiac catheterization lab," the nurse said. "I don't have much information and don't know why it is taking so long."

Oleg and I sat on couches in the hospital hall and waited. Finally, one of Elijah's doctors came out to talk to us.

"After the surgery Elijah's left lung has shut down," she said. "The doctors could possibly do another surgery to try and fix it, but they have never done it before and will not be making a decision until the morning. The surgeon will come out soon to tell you more," she said and left to go home.

Oleg and I understood the news was bad, but we did not understand fully what it meant. One hour passed after another, but the surgeon wasn't coming out. For seven hours Elijah was at the cardiac catheterization lab and finally was brought back to his room. As we were told later, at the end of the cardiac catheterization, when the catheter was taken out, Elijah's artery ruptured, and blood started pouring out from the artery into his abdomen. Elijah's blood pressure was very low, and his saturation numbers decreased to 28. Normal should be at 100. The nurses had to add a lot of blood to Elijah to stabilize his blood pressure. When it stabilized a little, they transported him back to his room.

The nurses and the doctors were around Elijah all the time. Oleg and I could not be close to Elijah and sat in the hall, observing through the wide-open door how the nurses added blood and blood clotting medications to Elijah, one syringe after another. The blood pressure was stabilizing for a while, but then decreasing again.

"Does Elijah still have chances for life?" I asked the doctor.

"I think so," he said. "As long as we have hope, we will try everything possible to help Elijah."

Exhausted and in tears, I just kept quietly repeating, "God, thank you, for everything. Thank you. Please take Elijah. Don't let him suffer anymore." I knew that Elijah was a millimeter from death. Oleg held my hand and quietly prayed to God. We didn't know what to ask for. We just wanted God to be in control.

....

At about 6 A.M., Elijah's blood pressure stabilized. "Oleg and Olga, it may be a good time for you to go back to the Ronald McDonald House and get some rest," the doctor said.

We left, relieved. But as soon as we came to the Ronald McDonald House, my phone rang. I was afraid that the doctor was calling to tell us Elijah was going to die, because the normal people don't call that early. It had to be a doctor and news had to be bad. I just knew it.

"Honey, I am scared," I told Oleg. "Can you please answer the phone?"

I knew Oleg would have the strength to do what I couldn't do. Oleg answered the phone.

"Oleg and Olga, please come back to the hospital," Elijah's doctor said. "Elijah's blood test show that there is too much acid in his blood, which means that Elijah will not survive."

In tears, we went back to the hospital. The surgeon came to talk to us.

"I am sorry," he said. "I have done everything possible for Elijah. There is nothing more I can do."

"We understand," Oleg answered. "Thank you for all your hard work."

Then we met with a chaplain.

"Do you have any questions?" she asked, kindly.

Surprisingly, we were okay and had no questions. I had always been afraid of death, but that minute I was calm.

"I still believe God can heal Elijah," I said through tears. "I just don't think He would let Elijah die."

Oleg told me later that he felt the same. You still believe in miracles until the end, even if it is a small chance.

"Can I pray for you?" the chaplain asked.

"Yes, please," Oleg said.

She prayed. We cried. Then, together we went to Elijah's room. Elijah laid on his bed and did not move. His body was reddish and swollen from all the blood transfusions. As I bent over to kiss Elijah, I noticed his first curls on the sides of his head. I kissed him and cried. Oleg cried too. I am sure, when Oleg was flying to California, he did not expect to see what he saw.

In tears, but calm, we said goodbye to Elijah. Knowing that we did everything possible for him. Relieved, that Elijah would not have to suffer any more, we knew he would be with God, and one day we would see him again. When we were saying goodbye to Elijah and tears were flowing from our eyes, the chaplain just stood quietly with closed eyes and prayed for us. Her presence touched my heart. She was there to support us and I thanked God for her.

About fifteen minutes later, the doctor came and asked, "Is it okay for me to disconnect all of Elijah's life-support system?"

"Yes," Oleg said through tears.

I was scared, but tried to be okay.

"Would you like to hold your son while I do it?" the doctor asked Oleg.

I was afraid to hold Elijah and was glad that the doctor didn't ask me. Back in January, when we agreed to disconnect Elijah's medications, but then changed our minds, Oleg wanted to hold Elijah and now his wish was coming true! God waited for Oleg. Not only did He let Oleg hold Elijah and let him off to Heaven, but God saved me from the panic of being alone.

Oleg and I watched as the doctor turned off Elijah's medications and the breathing machine. I cried. After about five minutes, Elijah's pulse was no longer there, and he died in Oleg's arms. Elijah left us at 9:20 A.M., on Saturday, April 16th, on his 220th day of life and hospitalization.

While sitting next to Oleg and Elijah, I realized that he lived exactly SEVEN months and SEVEN days! It brought me chills and tears again, as I felt God's presence so real. SEVEN – is recognized as God's number of completion, repeated in the Bible again and again. I also realized that it was Saturday, the seventh's day of the week. In the Bible, Sabbath is the day of completion and rest. It brought me chills and tears again. God took Elijah on the Sabbath day – the SEVENTH's day, the day of God's rest!

I had never experienced God's presence so close. In my chest, I felt it as a burning fire and had peace. I knew it was the presence of the Holy Spirit. I had no fear and thanked God for "PUTTING THE PUZZLES FOR US TOGETHER". **I realized the surgery was rescheduled three times to wait for Oleg. Then, the miracle happened with the holy oil. Also, Oleg was able to come on time and the children were with Grandma, when Elijah passed away. Then the miracle happened with the number SEVEN and the Sabbath.** Those were the miracles that I realized that week. But when I looked back, there were more and more signs that God was present with us and did His work.

....

Oleg and I spent about one more hour with Elijah. Then, it was time for us to leave. The nurses cut off a curl of Elijah's hair and placed it in a small bag for our memory. They also made his foot print, collected all of his belongings and placed them all in a bag. We walked out from the hospital with the bag, but without Elijah. Our baby wasn't going home with us and there was nothing we could do. We wanted our baby to live and didn't like the outcome. God was in charge. For some reason, that was Elijah's last day in God's plan.

....

Oleg and I had not slept for more than twenty-four hours, but it was no longer important to us. We could have gone to the Ronald McDonald House and gotten a few hours of sleep, but for some reason, I didn't want to spend another minute there. I didn't want to see anyone or to tell anyone that Elijah had passed away. I needed to see and hug David, Kristina and Michael. I didn't want to tell them about Elijah, but I knew I had to. We also had to make arrangements for Elijah's transfer back to Washington.

I called the Ronald McDonald house and told the volunteer at the front desk what had happened and that we would be leaving.

"I just can't handle facing other people and having to explain to them what had happened to our baby," I said.

"We understand," the volunteer answered. "Olga, you can just come in through the back door, get your stuff and leave the key in your room when you leave."

"Thank you for being so gracious and understanding," I said through tears. "Thank you for the wonderful help and hospitality that the Ronald McDonald House has provided for our family."

We parked in the underground garage of the Ronald McDonald House, came in through the back door, collected all my personal belongings and left Palo Alto at about 11 A.M. It was like we were on auto pilot. We drove to the mortuary at the neighbor city, Santa Barbara and arranged Elijah's transfer to Vancouver. Oleg did all the paperwork. I just sat there numb and thanked God that I wasn't left alone on that very difficult day. It was Saturday. Elijah would be transported to Vancouver on Wednesday, four days later.

We decided to drive back to Washington the next morning, so we drove to Modesto to pick up our children. They did not expect to see me, and I wasn't sure how to explain my being with Oleg, because only he was supposed to pick them up.

"Oleg and Olga. Please don't tell the children about Elijah yet," Grandpa Sergey asked us as he met us by the gate. "Your children are having a good time with their cousins and I don't want to ruin their evening."

Our children were swimming with their cousins at the swimming pool. We went inside the house. Everyone from Oleg's family gathered together. They were comforting us and saying the words of condolence. Then our oldest son, David, came and sat by us on the couch. "How is Elijah?" he asked. That was David's question every day. He loved Elijah and always worried about him. We had no choice, but to tell David the truth.

"Elijah went to God," Oleg said with a said tone of voice, embracing David.

David sat quietly on the couch with tears in his eyes.

"David, please don't be scared," I told David. "Elijah was very nice and let me go back to Washington to be home with you, Kristina and Michael."

We had a quiet dinner and spent the night at Oleg's parents' house. The next morning, we woke up at 5 A.M., and were ready to leave for Washington.

"Oleg, please take these baby bunnies to keep the children occupied during the twelve-hour drive."

Grandpa Sergey gave Oleg eight little bunnies in the box. I don't know if Grandpa Serge would normally do that. And I don't know if Oleg would normally agree to take so many bunnies, but he did. Grandpa Serge wanted to do something to ease our children's pain and we were thankful for it.

"Thank you for taking wonderful care of our children," I thanked Oleg's parents and hugged them as we were leaving. "It is wonderful to have parents, who care for us and our children so much."

Oleg hugged his Mother and cried for a while. We settled into the car and left California to go back to Washington State.

....

It was still very early, so the children fell asleep in the car. After about two hours they woke up.

"Mom, why are you coming home with us?" Kristina asked, confused.

"Why do you think?" I asked her.

She thought for a minute, "Did something happen to Elijah?"

"Yes..."

The children had tears in their eyes. Oleg and I could not hold back our tears. We all had a quiet moment.

"Please, don't be scared," I said to my children. "Elijah was very nice to you, his siblings, and let me come back home to be with you. Elijah is now with God in Heaven and probably is sitting on Jesus's lap, listening to His stories. His Grandpa Sergey, your Dad's Father, is probably taking care of him in Heaven. Elijah will have no more pain. We will miss him, but it was God's will to take Elijah and we must accept it," I said, trying to be as calm and positive as I could.

God's peace was in our hearts. On our way to Washington, I took a few pictures of the scenery and a picture of our family in the car. As I looked at the picture, I looked happy in it. It seemed like I should be crying because I had just lost a child, but I was happy to be going back home. We would become a normal family again.

When we were getting closer to Washington, Oleg told me what had happened, "On Thursday evening, when I mopped the floor, our family picture frame, that hung on the wall in our kitchen, fell. Only the left side, with the picture of Elijah and his handprint, broke off into pieces. Now it makes sense to me."

When I heard that, it brought me chills and tears again.

"I feel that God tested us to the end," I remarked. "He planned everything. This picture frame fell for a reason. I feel that God is so real and is doing it all."

We were finally in Vancouver. It was good to be home, but someone was really missing. It was Elijah. When I walked into our kitchen and saw the broken picture frame, it brought me chills and tears again.

"I will nicely cut off these broken pieces and you can still hang this picture frame on the wall," Oleg said nicely.

"No," I said. "I want to keep Elijah's pictures in our family's picture frame. I will just buy a new frame."

I was crying and, surprisingly, I wasn't angry at God. That day, I wasn't sure why it all was happening to us, but I no longer had energy to ask my questions. I realized that God planned Elijah's life exactly that way. I knew one day I would understand why.

……….

That evening, my Mother invited us and all my siblings to her house for dinner. When my sisters and brothers came, hugged me and said their words of condolence, I said little and had no tears. I felt numb. My Father blessed the food and thanked God for our family being together again. It was wonderful to be with my family. Every time, I am with them, I always feel warmth and love. I am so proud of the way that my Mother and Father taught us to care and love one another. It is such a blessing and a special gift that many families simply do not have. When we ate dinner. After finishing one of my brothers spoke.

"Olga, I am so disappointed," he said. "I believed till the end that God would heal Elijah, but now I am losing my faith in God".

That moment I understood that the pain of losing Elijah was not only in our family's heart, but in my brothers' and sisters', our parents' and our close friends'. Everyone questioned why it happened.

"You are talking like a non-believer," I said. "It was God's will to take Elijah and we can't fight with it. We must trust God that what happened is for the best. Look how much He did through Elijah. He changed our family. We all started praying more and became closer to God. He touched the hearts of the doctors, nurses, neighbors and our co-workers through Elijah. We had never talked about God as much as we have in the last *seven* months. Elijah is my Hero and he will never be forgotten. If God left Elijah alive, this life would probably be very hard for him. I believe that through Elijah, God revealed Himself to us and tested us. Last week I experienced His presence so real that I have no more questions left. God let Elijah complete his mission and took him back. We should not be scared of His trials. Through them we get closer to God." Everyone in the family were quiet for a moment.

....

Later that evening, the ministers, who told us God was punishing us with an ill baby, came to my Mother's house to discuss the plans for Elijah's funeral. They looked at us so mournfully and one of them said with a sad tone of voice,

"We are so sorry for your loss. May God give you strength. You probably have so many questions today?"

"Surprisingly, Oleg and I have no more questions for God," I said, being a little agitated inside. "But we have questions for you."

"What are your questions?" he asked.

"I want to know why you were not coming to answer our questions earlier? We found other people to answer our questions. Because of them we are okay."

The ministers didn't feel comfortable hearing that. As they continued to console us, it made me even angrier. I didn't want to hear that.

"I know Elijah is alive with God and we are okay," I said. "When we asked you to go pray for Elijah at the hospital, you were not even willing to bring the holy oil."

"We forgot the holy oil," the minister said. "And we just knew that Elijah would not live."

I could not believe what I heard. Even though we tried to be polite, our conversation just didn't go well. I didn't have questions about Elijah's passing. I knew that he was on Jesus's lap and was listening to His stories. Or, maybe he was still asleep, waiting to be resurrected when Jesus comes to earth. I was still not sure of that, but I knew that it was God's will for Elijah to leave us. That evening we were questioning our ministers' ability to act as shepherds of our church. Again and again, Oleg and I wondered if the church and the leadership were what we wanted for our family. We knew we needed to make some changes. The life of Elijah has ended, but for us it was a beginning of a new life.

....

21

Life is precious, but everyone will experience death. It is only a question of time.

We scheduled an appointment at Evergreen Memorial Gardens, to choose a spot for Elijah and to set a date for his burial. I prepared a blanket, a hat and an outfit for Elijah to be changed into when he arrived. I did not cry as much as I cried over those same clothes back in January, when we were ready to disconnect Elijah's medications. It was not as hard for me anymore and I thanked God that He gave me strength and time to prepare. I believed I wanted to leave the monkey toy and the pictures of our family in Elijah's casket.

We chose a quiet place for Elijah in the Garden of Apostles, close to the statue of Jesus. I thanked God that Oleg and I were together. While waiting for the paperwork to be processed, I told Oleg, "How lucky we are to be together. It would be a lot harder if it was you or me alone, planning the funeral for one of us."

....

The next day I bought a collage frame and put ten pictures of Elijah from birth to seven months in it. I planned to use it at Elijah's funeral and then keep it for us as a memory. Lots of people had not seen Elijah and I wanted them to meet him. I also bought a ten-page baby album, inserted pictures of Elijah, wrote his story in it, to take it to the funeral and share more about our baby.

Every day before the funeral, our friends and relatives visited us. They brought us platters with sandwiches, fruits, cakes, snacks, flowers, teddy bears, cards with money, groceries and homemade food. They surrounded us with love and care. My sisters did all the flower arrangements for Elijah and we appreciated that kind gesture. During those days we realized again how lucky we were to have family and friends around us, people who did not leave us alone in our day of sorrow. Touched by their support, we thanked them and God.

....

On Thursday, we received a phone call from the funeral home.

"Elijah is already in Vancouver. You can come visit him," they said.

When we arrived, Elijah was in a private room, and looked different with makeup on to hide his redness, an after effect of the many blood transfusions. I knew the individual who prepared him for the funeral had done their best, but Elijah didn't look like himself. It was like he wasn't my son, and yet he was. I knew that the real Elijah wasn't there. He had already gone to God. Because Elijah looked different, he was no longer the baby I knew when he was alive, and it was easier for me to let him go.

Oleg touched Elijah's hand.

"It feels like plastic," he said tearfully.

"Is it okay if I don't touch Elijah's hands?" I asked Oleg. "I want to remember Elijah alive."

"Olga. It's ok. You don't have to touch Elijah's hand," Oleg said.

I cried, and it was so hard for me to see my husband cry. I tried to stay positive. In the name of Jesus, I sent all the negative thoughts away. Feeling numb, I tried not to think about anything. Our family pictures were on the inside wall of the casket. The monkey toy laid next to Elijah. I loved watching Elijah play with his monkey toy. I realized the toy meant little, just laying beside his cast off, earthly body, so

I gently reached into the casket and retrieved the stuffed animal, which was precious to me. Later, I was glad I saved it; it was the one item Elijah and I shared together for those several, sacred months.

....

Friday, April 22nd, 2011 was the day of Elijah's funeral, and more than 200 people came. My entire family attended the funeral. Oleg's brother and sister flew from California, but his Mother, very sick at home, could not come. Most of Oleg's and my co-workers, other relatives, friends and members from our church came. Grown-ups brought flowers and cards for us, and the children brought teddy bears. Many of Elijah's younger cousins had never seen him because they were not allowed at the hospital. They asked their parents why they had never had a chance to play with Elijah and why he was with God. I have no idea how my siblings explained Elijah's passing to their children. Later, I heard that one of Elijah's little cousins let his balloons go in the air, for Elijah.

During the service Oleg, David, Michael and I sat together, close to Elijah. Kristina was scared. She asked to sit by her cousins and I let her. If she didn't feel comfortable, she didn't have to sit with us. I did not want our children to be traumatized by their first funeral.

The service was conducted in Russian. We invited an interpreter to translate into English, as I knew many people would attend who did not speak Russian. Our pastor spoke first, then my Father, and then I was really surprised to see Oleg speak.

"We accepted Elijah and his illness as from the hand of God, and today we thank God He took Elijah when He did," with tears, Oleg said.

The pastor came to me.

"Olga, would you like to say anything?" he asked.

"No," I said.

Because we had only scheduled an hour of time, I felt our time was up. Later that evening, I regretted that I did not say anything. I had so much to tell the world about Elijah. Instead of me, a deacon spoke and said, "This baby had done nothing good or bad yet..." I knew it wasn't true. Elijah had probably done more in seven months of life than most people accomplish in a life time. In the deacon's defense, I knew that he was just simply trying to say that the baby was holy and in seven months what do normal babies accomplish? Unfortunately, words spoken by one person can impact others quite differently. But I knew that it was not so. If this minister called us at least or visited, while Elijah was ill, he would never have said these words. He just did not know what we were going through. I believed that in seven months of Elijah's illness, God did a lot of work in our family and in many other people whose hearts were touched by our son's short, but difficult life.

Five doctors and four nurses from OHSU came to give Elijah their last respects! One of them was the doctor who told me twice the bad news about Elijah. Touched to see the doctors, I hugged them and cried with them. Elijah was part of them also. We all loved Elijah and were all going to miss him. One of the doctors even spoke at the funeral.

"Elijah gave us all lots of love and received lots of love back," through tears she said.

Those words meant a lot to me. The doctors were not just medical robots. They did their best to help our son and were deeply touched by his strength and determination. They loved Elijah. Today I can say the doctors and nurses were a beautiful vessel in God's hands!

At the end of Elijah's service, the pastor announced for people to open their hearts and help us financially. Oleg leaned to me and said, "I won't take it". But he had no choice, when later he was given an envelope with money. It was a tradition at our church to help one another, and we were thankful for it.

After the service our pastor announced that the people could come and say their last goodbye to Elijah. I took the microphone and thanked all our friends, doctors and our family members. I thanked the nurses for being Elijah's second mothers, when I wasn't with him. Then, I thanked the doctors for helping Elijah fight for his life and for coming to the funeral, to pay their last respects. Our family and friends were by Elijah and the nurses and co-workers were by us.

From the mortuary we all went to the grave site. My two brothers and two brothers-in-law carried Elijah's casket. Oleg, Michael, my Aunt Lana and I walked behind them. David and Kristina, with their cousins, carried beautiful flowers. The rest of the people followed behind us. My heart was dropping just from the thought that Elijah would no longer be with us. **While walking to the grave yard, I realized, it was the Friday before Easter. That was the day of Jesus' funeral also! It brought me chills and tears again, and I thought, "God, just because of these small miracles, I know that You are with us!"**

At the grave site we sat next to Elijah, while our friends and family were saying goodbye to him. Then Oleg and I knelt, put our heads on Elijah and cried, saying our last goodbye. When we saw him it the casket at his arrival at the funeral home, I knew that as a mother, who loved her child, I should touch him and yet, I chose not to do so. Before they lowered Elijah down I finally reached out to touch him through the blanket. That was the best I could do. I wanted to tell him goodbye, say I loved him, and I would be okay.

I put three pictures by Elijah's face, a picture of him and Oleg, a picture of Elijah and me, and our family picture. Then, somehow, we closed the casket. That was the last time we saw our baby.

....

After the funeral, we invited our relatives for lunch. When Oleg and I walked into the restaurant, about 100 people were there already. I had no energy to cry, no energy to eat, and no energy to talk. I sat at our table and waited for Oleg, who stopped to talk to his uncle. Soon, my friends surrounded me, comforting me and didn't let me cry or think sad thoughts.

A day earlier, my brother called me and asked how much was the funeral cost. At the restaurant he came up and gave us an envelope with money to cover the funeral expenses. I was stunned.

"We cannot take it," Oleg told my brother.

"Forget that it was me who gave it to you. It is for you from God!" my brother answered.

We thanked my brother and said that since we no longer had to pray for Elijah, we would pray for my brother's family and his business. My brother's act touched our hearts so much and taught us a meaningful lesson about caring for people and helping those in need. Later my brother told us that he felt our prayers. He received a miraculous blessing from God in his business that week. And once again, we thanked God for such good people, and how often He had heard our prayers.

Once the luncheon was over, there was nothing left to do, except go home and sit down after the sheer exhaustion of the day and wait for restless sleep to come at nightfall. Two of our nephews stayed at our house and played with our children. This act of kindness helped our children be comforted by family, as they played together. Two of Oleg's cousins also stopped by with their families and we sat and talked. We had no energy left to cry in this day...but we understood tears would surely find us all again at daybreak.

....

22

You have to choose to heal as an individual and as a family.

The first week after Elijah's funeral was very difficult for our family. I tried not to think much and not to cry, but to stay neutral so my blood pressure would not rise. Elijah's plush monkey was in my office. It was something I could touch which represented Elijah. From time to time, I held it tight and hid my tears from the children. I did not want them to see me crying.

We hung Elijah's photos in our office and his portrait in the living room, next to the portraits of David, Kristina, and Michael. On the portrait of Elijah, we wrote the same words as on his headstone,

Elijah was so small,
But his influence was so great!
Elijah's life was short,
But the memory of him is long!

While our children were busy playing with their cousins, Oleg and I read all the cards from our family, friends, nurses, and doctors. The comments from the cards inspired us and helped us to see the best in the worst situation. They had a lot of meaning and made a positive difference in our life.

....

We were living in a state of shock. Some days we were okay, some days we grieved, and some days we prayed to find our peace. When I had a hard day, Oleg encouraged me to stay positive and continue living for our three

272

beautiful children. When Oleg grieved, I reminded him to stay strong. And when our children cried and asked questions about Elijah's passing, we tried to give them the best answers, even though we still had lots of questions ourselves.

I didn't want to imagine what would happen to Elijah's body in a grave, or start feeling sorry for myself because I was a lonely mother without her baby. I also felt like a guest in my house because I had been gone for so long. There were so many things that needed to be done: organize Elijah's pictures, finish his baby album, and decide what to do with his clothes. Then there were times I simply needed to free my mind from all these necessities, so I could give my attention to my children. Some days I felt guilty, like I was not a good mother. I also knew I couldn't close myself in my bedroom and cry for hours. Life doesn't stop to wait for you to cry.

Grieving affected each of us in a different way. David and Kristina broke into tears when they saw Elijah's pictures, when we talked about him, or when they saw someone else's baby. Our youngest son, Michael, seemed to have the most difficult time. He would cry even though it wasn't related to Elijah, then he would say, "I miss Elijah. I want to be his older brother." It would take us a while to talk to him, explain why Elijah was no longer with us, and calm him down. Michael was no longer a baby in the house, yet he was now deprived of the opportunity to be an older brother. He felt something was wrong, but at his young age it was difficult for him to comprehend death and the permanent separation.

....

During the second week, our children returned to school. Oleg was never able to take any time off from work while Elijah was ill, it was financially impossible. After the

273

funeral, Oleg was able to take a six week leave because of the help we received from family, friends and church, and we were able to continue living while grieving. Oleg had never told me he needed to work in the backyard, but for the first two weeks he was there morning till evening. I didn't see his tears, or hear the questions he asked God about Elijah's death, or any expression of anger, if it happened. Only God heard his questions, and his anger was probably left on those bushes. Sometimes he would come in and comfort me, other times he would come in and tell me: "Olga, you have to stop crying." It was like we were operating in two different worlds. Each of us needing our own space, and yet we were making sure each other was okay.

I saved Elijah's photos on the CD and finished his baby album. After I organized Elijah's photos, I chose the best photos and decided to make a book in memory of Elijah. When I had been in California, Mary, a social worker, showed me a similar book of a little girl, whose heart was transplanted and who was growing well. Her book was giving me hope. But when our situation turned out to be totally opposite from this little girl's, I understood that there are many parents like us, and some of them might be left without any hope. That little girl's book was positive. But I knew, even though Elijah's ending was not so positive, I still had to share it with other parents, who were going through a similar journey.

I wrote a short story about Elijah, added his photos and wrote my words of encouragement. I wanted people to understand they were not alone in their journey. Regardless of the outcome, they would face similar issues, would have to make decisions, and trust their judgement, their values, and their faith. What I really wanted to say was: I have been here. You can do it. You are not alone.

There are many talented and caring people who can help you even if the outcome is not good. When finished, I sent several copies of the book to the Ronald McDonald House, and the two hospitals where Elijah had been hospitalized.

Cover of the book I made for the hospitals.

......

I sorted Elijah's clothes, mourned over them and decided to donate the smallest outfits to OHSU hospital for the NICU. When Oleg and I took Elijah's outfits there, we wanted to walk through the area again, to see one more time where Elijah had been. We could walk through only two rooms before such sadness overcame us, we left. It was too painful to see the doctors and nurses, who fought for Elijah's life, and the small beds, where he used to lay. It was different – Elijah was no longer there. He wasn't at home either. Elijah was gone. Oh, how much pain it was. Would it ever go away?

I set aside a few of Elijah's outfits as keepsakes and gave the rest of his clothes to a friend, who was expecting a baby boy. Those days, my heart felt frozen. Like a robot, I walked through the days, doing only the things I felt were absolutely necessary. In my heart I believed my health would prevent me from having more children. The doctors didn't recommend it. That fact made it all the more difficult to let Elijah go. In reality, I was mourning two significant losses.

....

One day, shortly after Elijah's death, while the children were in school, Oleg and I got into an argument. Before this, Oleg and I almost never argued. I don't remember how it started. The issues don't really matter. What matters is that we allowed the raw emotions of dealing with Elijah to explode into an argument. For some reason, we simply could not contain our emotions. Oleg's conclusion was to move out, live separately for a while to give us time to think. When I heard that, I said, "Honey, I know that you love me, and you know that I love you too. You understand that we both have gone through tremendous stress and need time to cope. This is not the solution and we can't add more stress and pain to what we already have. We just can't separate." We hugged each other and broke out in tears.

Thank God, we did not allow our grief to destroy our marriage. But our argument that day taught us a lesson; the intense stress brought about by an ill child or a loss of a child can destroy a marriage in a brief moment, if you allow it. The statistics show that 65% of marriages in families who have severely ill children result in divorce. It is important to have an extra amount of patience, love and kindness that you extend to your spouse in stressful situations. The wound from losing your child is so deep that you may do or say things you don't mean.

....

We decided to visit Oleg's cousin, who was ill with cancer. I used to be afraid of people with cancer, but now I wanted to see her. I was surprised when I recognized my change of heart. When we visited her and talked to her, I realized we had a lot in common. Even though she probably knew she would die, she was so positive. We bought groceries for their family and helped them financially. While Elijah was ill, we learned a lesson of giving, helping and caring for others.

While driving back home, I tried to analyze our journey with Elijah and wrote a poem. While writing, I felt like God was speaking to me, giving me answers to my questions.

Why sorrows come to us?

Am I the biggest sinner? That's my question.
What's happening? Why God You chose me?
You gave me baggage that is so heavy,
Groans and moans, sorrow and grief.

Where did I sin? Are You condemning
Me for it? Or did I commit offense?
Is it possible, My God, you are forgetting
Everything good, what I did here on Earth?

All my good deeds and all my givings,
My prayers and my love for You.
My tears and my repentance,
And reading Bible, always loving You?

My God, remind me where I stumbled?
Where did I sin, did I condemn someone?
Or maybe I forgot to say: "I am sorry"?

Or maybe did not pay someone enough?

There is a sorrow at my house, it's my baby,
He's very ill and I can't find my peace.
I cherish every moment with my baby,
I look into his eyes and look with tears.

He has been born too early with heart problems
Still at the hospital, he can't come home, can't.
He is too sick, my God, my heart is crying,
Why did You leave us God? We can't

See You where You have been before. We lost You.
We cry and no energy to pray.
We don't see You God, You don't come to help us.
God, o my God, please come our way...

And I received an answer: "Oh my Daughter,
I am there with you and you are in My arms.
I forgave you all your sins and don't question
What wrong you did. It was My plan.

Because your son is Mine. I have the power
To give him life, take back, or glorify.
In happiness, in grief, or during bad days
I want to see if you will still love Me.

I want to know what's your foundation,
I want to test your love for Me.
Will you be able during hard days praise Me
Or will forget Me, turn away from Me?

I want to have good followers, who always
Will pass the test, as my friend Abraham.

And I will never leave them, but will show
God's glory. I will show it through them.

I want to test you and to change you,
As I have tested Job on this big Earth.
I want to see you singing and you praising
During bad days and good days, all.

After I test you, I will glorify you,
And you will understand, your life is Mine.
You will be helping people, who are crying,
And you will testify to them, you are Mine.

Through you I will be seen to others,
In days of sorrow I will be there with you.
I will be glorified and praised by people.
Because you are my child and I tested you.

I don't usually just test my people.
I saw your heart that you were seeking Me.
I saw you spiritually strong, I liked it,
And I decided, child, to harden you.

Don't crush, my child, because through sorrows
You become better, closer to Me.
I will accept your child in My heaven
And you will be best friends with Me.

May 2011

While still driving, I read it to Oleg and he was surprised how good it was. At home, I called my friend, Katya, and asked if I could read her my poem. I didn't usually write poems and just wanted to hear her opinion. When she heard it, she said, "Olga, Someone was telling you what to write." I answered, "No." Then she continued, "The Holy Spirit was telling you what to write..." I felt God close and knew that even though our journey with Elijah was over, our journey with God would continue.

....

Three weeks after the funeral, Oleg and I decided to go to Hawaii. It wasn't a vacation. Oleg didn't feel it was the right time, but I felt the need to escape from all the stress, to be away and get a chance to clear my head and get a new start on this new life. We left the three children with my Mom for a week and went to Hawaii. In reflection, this may not have been our best decision, but at the moment I felt we needed to heal ourselves as a couple, before we could heal our family.

The first two days we were fine, but on the third day, even in Hawaii, the emotions of Elijah's loss caught up with us. No matter where we were, the pain followed us. Almost the entire day we fought back tears. In the end, we thanked God for everything. We understood that we were clay in the hands of God and that God owed us nothing. The fact that He gave us life was already God's miracle. Our health was not our merit. We began to appreciate every moment of our lives and thank God for what we have.

Even in Hawaii, Oleg continued to study the Bible. He wanted to know more about our Creator and find answers to his questions. It was interesting for me to listen to Oleg and I learned from him. While swimming in the ocean and then just lying on the grass, we thought about God, looked at heaven and talked about Him. We seemed to be connected with God 24 hours a day and He gave us strength and peace. Despite the fact that we had difficult moments, we felt God much closer than ever before! We felt like we lived with God and breathed in Heaven.

On the last day in Hawaii, Lyubov, the teacher of the class "The Wisdom for Mothers", which I previously attended, called me. A group of women in her class always prayed for Elijah while he was ill. Lyubov wanted to know how I was doing. I told her I was okay and shared the little miracles which happened during the last week of Elijah's life. Lyubov was surprised to hear my positive voice. She believed my story could help many mothers of sick children and asked if I could share my testimony at the women's conference she was planning to hold in a month. I was afraid because I had never spoken to such a large group of people, but I had so much to tell, I agreed.

....

When we came back, I talked to our neighbor, Ross, who shared his understanding of life. He thought that everyone can live in the "Kingdom of Heaven" on earth or in "Hell" on Earth. He was right. Oleg and I realized that we had to make that decision. Would we blame everyone and everything about our life which has not gone the way we wanted, or would we accept our life and live positively? We decided to live positively, to concentrate on our family, and cherish every moment of our life.

Ross also encouraged me to start writing a book about our journey with Elijah. He said, "Olga, your family has experienced so much. You had a true journey of faith. You have to tell the world about it to help other people in similar situations." All I needed to hear were Ross's words to start writing Elijah's story. Ross encouraged me to start doing something I had never done before, and I agreed with him. While Elijah was ill, I had written down some notes, and promised God I would tell the whole world if He healed Elijah. Although our son was not healed in the manner we had hoped, I already had thoughts of writing a book.

Since Ross and Sandy spoke English and promised to help me, I started writing my book in English. Many times, I had to use a dictionary to find the proper word. Frequently I wanted to quit, but deep down I felt God wanted me to continue writing. Oleg supported me in this. Sometimes I asked if Oleg wanted to write a chapter or two, or to read what I wrote, but he could not. It was too difficult for him. Like many couples we grieved and coped with the loss of Elijah in different ways.

While writing, I tried to settle Elijah in my heart. Tears covered every page of this book. The plush monkey of Elijah's was next to me in the office. When tears filled my eyes, I hugged it tight and cried. I missed Elijah, and I did not want him to be forgotten. Telling his story would be a way to keep his memory alive for our children. Even though Elijah was no longer a part of our earthly life, I envisioned his life having a continuing meaning to others, through this book and through my help to others!

In seven months of Elijah's illness I felt like I learned more about life than during my previous 33 years. I began to appreciate life more with my family. I started to look at people as the creation of God and admired them when I met them. I also began to understand how difficult it is to have a disabled child: the difficulty in sorting out priorities between your special needs child and other children; the difficulty in maintaining a healthy relationship with your spouse while you struggle with varying degrees of stress, depression, anger, anxiety and pain.

I began to see God from a different perspective. He was so real and so close to us while Elijah was ill. Through this experience, I realized I had become a completely different person. I was a young woman who endured trials by God. I learned when God kept silent, He always hovered nearby. I drew nearer to God and magnified my belief in Him as He led us by the hand. Knowing our experience with Elijah was profound, I trembled at the very thought of even one moment with him being erased from our life.

....

23

Helping others can be self-healing.

Time came for the women's conference, to which Lyubov had invited me when I was in Hawaii. It was the first time I was going to share my story. I was so afraid to talk to a large group of people. There were about 300 women. Many, I noticed, were my previous clients from the WIC program, and I began to doubt if I wanted to speak. My child was no longer with me, what should I tell them? But God gave me courage. I stepped forward, shared about our journey with God and Elijah, and how in the most difficult moments of our lives, God carried us in His hands.

I encouraged women to be strong, to appreciate their lives and to cherish every second with their loved ones, since no one knows what the next day may bring us. When I spoke, I remembered the words of Pastor Ivan, who inspired me during Elijah's illness. He assured me that God did not punish us with an ill child, but most likely, through our difficult situation with Elijah, God prepared us for something more. Maybe after this difficult path, we will help others, he said... I realized his words began to come true in our lives. That day I also realized it was exactly SEVEN weeks after Elijah's passing. It was a sign for me that God was leading us in our life; I believed seven was His number of completion.

After this conference, I was invited to speak at another women's conference. I did not understand what God was doing in my life, but I did what I felt I had to do. Later, God showed me why He wanted me to speak and share. After the conferences, I met with mothers of disabled children. I listened to them, encouraged them to stay strong, and reminded them everything happens according to the will of God. Surprisingly, I had answers to many of their questions, because earlier I was going through similar situations. During those days, I realized that through my words and testimonies, God was answering people's questions and healing their crying hearts.

....

After a couple of weeks, I was invited to share my story on our local Russian Radio 7. I agreed. It was difficult for me to tell what we went through. A couple of times I stopped and took a deep breath, as emotions overwhelmed my heart. It was difficult to refrain from bursting into tears. In the end, I reminded listeners to trust God and not to fight with Him, because they will never win. It is better to accept their situation, glorify God and wait until the sun comes out from behind the clouds. At the end I read my poem.

After my testimony on the radio, I received a phone call from one mom, who had five children, two of which had died. A year after her last baby's funeral she still kept crying and could not look at her baby's pictures or go to his grave. She also felt her relatives did not understand her. Her husband also had a hard time. She thanked me for my story she heard on the radio.

"Olga, by listening to you, I realized I took the same steps as you did," she said. "My baby had been hospitalized also and died in my arms. I could not find my peace, but listening to you on the radio, it helped me realize what had happened. It reminded me I have to move on, make peace with the death of my baby and concentrate on my family."

She also said that she loved my poem and asked if she could use a couple of its verses to write on her baby's grave plate. I didn't mind and promised to bring her my poem and CD with my testimony the next day. When I hung up the phone, tears filled my eyes as I realized that the words "God may be preparing you for something" were coming true. I thanked God for giving me strength to listen, encourage her and help this hurting mom.

The next morning, I took my poem and the CD to her house and showed her Elijah's book. We just talked and, at the end of our conversation, for the first time since her baby's death, this mom took out his pictures and showed them to me. He was a beautiful baby and I encouraged her to frame his pictures and hang them on the wall low enough, so she could come and kiss him whenever she wanted. He needed to be present in her house because he was alive with God in heaven.

God showed me even though I did not understand why I testified, He healed the wounds of others through my testimony. I kept receiving more phone calls from mothers with ill babies or who had lost their baby. I listened to them and encouraged them not to go into depression, but to continue living for their healthy children and for their husband.

A week later, Lyubov asked me to help her for a few months on Russian Radio 7, while her assistant would be out of country. This was another new opportunity, and I felt God wanted me to be there. We conducted weekly radio broadcasts about families and children. Sometimes I was asked questions and I could answer them only because of my experience with Elijah. With Lyubov, we went to other cities and states to hold women's conferences. I shared my testimony there and reminded women to appreciate their lives and their loved ones more. These were blessed times.

In those days, I noticed that my relationship with Oleg had changed and deepened. We respected, appreciated, and loved each other more than ever before. I told our children their father was the best. I saw how Oleg studied the Bible and I always listened with a great interest to him. I was happy for him and saw how God was changing him and preparing him for something bigger. Oleg blessed me for what I was doing and did not ask why I was going to the conference or who needed to hear me on the radio. I became more confident because my husband trusted me. I felt God's blessing on me because my husband blessed me. I was confident in what I was doing because my husband praised me, and that meant a lot to me. I grew spiritually and individually. And in the same degree, Oleg's confidence grew because I respected him, because I believed in him, and because I loved him!

....

Three months after Elijah left us, I went to our church children's camp as a Sunday school teacher. There were many children. Between them there were five orphan children who recently buried their mother. In my heart, I felt I should talk to them, embrace them and ask them what they needed. During the day, I had the opportunity to spend a few minutes with each of them. With tears in their eyes, the children told me how much they missed their mom. Their answers touched my heart.

Late in the evening, I talked with their three-year-old sister. When I asked what she remembered the most about her mother, she said her long black hair. The little girl looked so much like her mom and wished to see her again. I hugged her and said that my little son was also in heaven, and her mom probably took care of him while I took care of her. The girl hugged me, kissed me, and wished me a good night. When I went back to my cabin, I cried and thanked God for reminding me to take good care of orphans. I realized I was hurting from the loss of Elijah, but the grief of others may be even worse. Everyone endures struggles.

24

Meet challenges head on.

One of my challenges was to be around babies. Every time I saw a baby in somebody else's arms, I thought I should have a baby in my arms. I should be providing my baby with love and nourishment, and then I would realize that I would never have that experience. After Elijah's death, I tried to be as normal as I could and to smile, when my heart was really crying. I tried not to talk about Elijah a lot and live a normal life, but it wasn't that easy.

My sisters and sisters-in-laws had several children at that time and I was invited to the baby showers. I had often hosted other baby showers, so they asked me to do it again. There was nothing wrong with them asking. The problem was me, not them. Life was different now. The first time I was asked to be the hostess I said yes, knowing it would be very difficult---I was embarrassed to say no. I got through it, but cried after I left. I can't explain how painful it is to sit without your baby in a home, where other babies are alive and loved so wonderfully. The past year had changed my head, my heart and my soul. I felt I needed to explain to other people, when they asked me, that I could not do it at this time. It was still too soon.

When I was invited to another baby shower, I planned on going. I knew it would be painful to buy baby clothes as a gift, so I decided to buy only a baby card and give money. When I was choosing a card, I realized if I read the cards for babies, I would start crying. Therefore, I just bought a card without reading it. Before I even got to the baby shower, I was in tears. I called my older sister, Tanya, and asked her to come outside, take my gift into the house, and give it to my younger sister. The pain of not having Elijah with me was so strong that I couldn't be there.

From then on, I made the choice to not attend baby showers and simply explain to individuals why. Acknowledging my limits was the best coping method I could manage for this situation. Some days I had to avoid a problem, and other days I had to protect myself from stealing another person's joy.

When my sisters' new babies were born, I had the hardest time meeting them. When I met the first baby, I stifled the scream: "I can't handle this." I politely excused myself, telling my sister I needed to leave. I hurried to the car crying and drove quickly home.

I met my other sister's baby at our family's prayer meeting. While we prayed, it was a good time for me to cry it out. So much pain was in my heart. At home, I told Oleg that it might be better for me to avoid my family with all the little babies.

The next week my sister, who had the second baby, called me and asked, "Olga, how are you?"

"Thanks for asking. I am actually going through a hard time," I said. "Can you please do me a favor?"

"Sure," my sister said. "What is it?"

"Can you please come with your baby, so I can meet him. I am afraid that I may cry, and I don't want my family to see me cry."

My sister came. I held her baby, but did not cry. He did not look like Elijah. Since then, I have been able to hold any baby because I realized there is no baby like Elijah. Every baby is someone's baby, but only Elijah was my baby. There never was a baby like him and there never will be. It is a special bond which is always with you. It never goes away and, overtime, it becomes better. Meeting my fear of holding babies has been an important event, which lead to my ability to participate in activities that I would otherwise not be able to do, had I not faced the issue.

....

Often, Oleg and I imagined what might have been if Elijah were alive. We knew it would not be, but we imagined it any way. For example, I found Oleg crying in the garage one day. I asked him why he was crying. He explained to me that he imagined when Elijah would be grown up, he would probably have the same hobbies as Oleg. They could have worked on cars together, but Oleg knew it would never happen because Elijah was not with us. Other days, Oleg and I would start a conversation about what life might have been like with Elijah and, sometimes, we would decide not to continue the conversation. What would it accomplish? We could wish, hope, we could want and remember... nothing would ever make that dream reality.

We tried to replace the pain in our hearts with joy. We did activities such as bike rides, walks to the park and family trips, which allowed us to be with each other, listen to each other, and return to the joys of our new normal life. When we had hard moments, we bought coffee or ice cream, prayed, read the Bible with the children, listened to uplifting music, or just watched a family movie. We did everything possible to survive those difficult days. We found it important to have quiet and frank discussions, so all of our family could have a better understanding of what had happened to Elijah. It is amazing what quiet conversations, hugs and hot chocolate can do.

We also understood that keeping busy with new activities was the best way to ease our pain. Oleg continued to study the Bible and repaired cars. That summer, he bought a wrecked mustang, repaired it and drove it to work.

I continued with the radio and women's conferences. David began his physical training for football; Kristina was busy with her piano lessons, and Michael was involved with basketball. We tried to do things that brought joy to our hearts. Friends and family were praying for us.

Still having panic attacks, which had started during my pregnancy, I had difficulty with breathing and was afraid that one day I might have a heart attack. I understood I needed to calm down and take care of myself before it became too late. My friend Katya felt my pain and tried to support me. With her sister-in-law, they invited me to join them on a-week-long Seattle-Alaska cruise, just us, without the children and husbands. Oleg let me go. He saw that I needed to gain my strength back after such grief. With girls we were able to rest and relax and gain new energy and health. I was so grateful to my friends, who during my difficult days could, for at least a while, take me away from tears. I was also so grateful to my dear husband for letting me go. I am convinced this vacation and stress-free time prolonged my life by about ten years.

Oleg also had a great support. His cousin, Eddie, took him out to a Chinese sauna for a whole day. They often met for coffee. Oleg also found that conversations with his brothers, friends, father-in-law, relatives and pastor were ways he could express himself during his grieving time and find understanding about what had happened.

·······

Four months after Elijah's death, in August, I received a call from WIC. They asked me if I wanted a job as a Breastfeeding Peer Counselor. At that time, my blood pressure was still elevated, and I had no desire to go through the stress of job interviews. It was a job where I knew the people, knew what to do, and it would be a part-time job from home. I decided I wanted the job, but working with mothers and babies scared me. I didn't know how well I could do the job, but I still applied and was hired. For the first few weeks I tried hard to be okay. I tried to be positive, have a smile on my face while my heart cried.

After a few weeks, I started wondering if I should quit my job. I needed help. I knew Patti would understand me and give me an honest opinion, so I called her. She had returned to work with babies at OHSU just ten days after her baby died. So, when Patti heard my concern, she said, "Olga, you are stronger than you think you are. Keep the job. I know that your experience with Elijah will help many mothers!"

Patti's advice proved to be right; I kept the job and I am glad I did. Later, I was able to help many mothers with ill babies. Who could understand them more than me? I was helping someone else and my confidence grew again. As I met with other parents, I found that I was able to provide words of encouragement and understanding by telling them my story. I could explain to them what I had experienced and how I could identify with their pain and struggles. Sometimes I could give them an advice, by telling about our family's experience. These mothers and fathers were sometimes the parents, who had to provide 24-hour-care to a child. These were the parents who wondered whether or not they could continue, as it seemed a never-ending battle. Being able to serve others in this manner brought great purpose and joy into my life. It was a way I could heal myself, add meaning to Elijah's life, and do good for others.

To help my healing I felt it was important to help others. It became a motivating factor in my life. We feel better when we help someone else. What I used to be scared of before, now became part of me. I was no longer scared of death or to hold a Down's Syndrome baby. I became a much stronger person. I found listening was more important than telling. Being truthful and honest about what happened to me was helpful to others. It allowed me to grow as a person. And being positive is important. It allows you to see the best in difficult situations.

Whether I was working with individuals or groups at work, or presenting a message at a large conference or speaking on the local radio station, I found my personal experiences with Elijah were so valuable because I could speak from the heart. The more I shared the truth of what happened to me, the more my confidence grew. I realized my message was important and the people wanted to hear it. The more I helped people, the more I was healing and could understand the importance of Elijah in my life and how much he had given me and my family.

....

Five months after Elijah's funeral, in September, his first birthday was coming up. Elijah's grave plate finally had been installed. When we saw it, we were all in tears again. It was hard. As Elijah's birthday grew nearer, I dreaded the inevitable crying surge. We always looked forward to celebrating each of our children's birthdays. Elijah's birthday brought us another "first" and raised many questions. What should we do for Elijah? Do we do anything special? Should we celebrate it or not? Should we buy a cake?

I knew that Elijah's nurses would understand me, so once again, I turned to them for suggestions. Their advice was to celebrate Elijah's birthday with a cake, release balloons into the sky, and go to the coast for a day and relax.

Buying a cake at the store was hard.

"Can I please have that small blue baby cake?" I asked the worker in the bakery department.

"Yes. Of course," she said.

As the worker was reaching for the small blue cake in the refrigerator, I changed my mind. I thought a small baby cake would remind me of a baby.

"Can you actually get that chocolate cake?" I asked.

"Yes, no problem," the worker said, reaching for the chocolate cake. While she was reaching for it, I changed my mind again.

"I am so sorry. Can I have that blue baby cake?"

As the worker was reaching for it, I broke into tears.

"Why are you upset?" she asked.

"It is a birthday cake for my baby, whom I dearly love, but who died five months ago."

I did not know that worker, but she embraced me with her hands and replied tenderly, "It is okay. Sad things happen."

When we ate that small blue baby cake at home, we were quiet, while tears slipped down our cheeks. There was nothing anyone wanted to say out loud. I almost choked on the cake. It was a cake of grief, rather than a cake of celebration. In my heart I knew I could never buy a birthday cake again for Elijah. We went to the coast and had a good time, but that was the last time we celebrated Elijah's birthday. What is the point of it? He is no longer with us. We recognize and honor his birth on September 9th, but we do not celebrate.

....

Elijah's death anniversaries have been different. When April, the month of Elijah's death comes, I feel it in the atmosphere a few weeks before. Often, I experience anxiety. I want to be farther from people and often want to be alone. I just want to have my personal time and remember my baby the way I want. He deserves to be remembered and I want to do it for him. Unfortunately, not everyone understands me. During those days I am very

294

sensitive. This is my time of remembrance. It is almost as if I am selfish. I don't want to share him with others. The experience is so personal. When people are really trying to be nice, sometimes it just doesn't feel that way. It hurts. It is impossible for them to comfort my loss. How can they know what I feel.

On the anniversary of Elijah's death, it has become our family's tradition to go to the Oregon coast. We don't hide that day. We simply visit the grave yard, bring flowers to Elijah, give him a moment of silence and remembrance. Then we leave for the coast. We cry, we pray, and we talk. We celebrate what Elijah gave us. Somehow our family is different and happier. We find more joy in life. We thank God for Elijah. On his anniversaries, I often find quiet time and write poetry. This is something that I have rarely done before. It seems like my emotions just flow to the paper and, in doing so, I find comfort and healing. Through this I often receive answers to my questions.

....

Each of us is still healing, but overtime, my family and I have made progress. We have developed a new life for ourselves. There are days that I cannot control my feelings, or my actions, such as tears. For example, I find it difficult to answer simple questions, such as "How many children do you have?" What do you say? Do I say "three" or do I say "four"? Should I explain one of my children has passed away? The important thing is to be honest with ourselves and do those things that make us comfortable and happy. We must assume what others say or ask is not meant to offend us. They simply do not understand how certain words, unintentionally said, may hurt us and evoke unexpected emotions. I had to realize that it was not their problem. These are good people. It is my problem and I still have to learn how to solve it.

25

God works in our life in different ways.

As we understood later, Elijah became our guide to a completely new life. Thanks to the changes that have begun to take place in us, we have also begun to rethink our religious views. Gradually, step by step, we began to return to our Jewish roots, which at that time we didn't even know about.

One case I will remember for a long time. Four weeks After Elijah's funeral we made a family trip to a Wildlife Safari, an Oregon zoo four-hour away from our home. For two hours we watched the animals walking around our car. It was a pleasant and relaxing time for our family.

On our way back, we ate at the restaurant "Noah's Ark", which had been built by a Jewish family. In addition to the restaurant inside, there was a replication of the layout of the Moses' Tabernacle, and a bookstore. By this time, we had learned a lot about the Jewish roots of Christianity, so seeing the Tabernacle of Moses, Priests, sheep, knives in blood from the burnt offerings and Mount Sinai made a great deal of sense to us. Murals of the Israelites' journey through the desert were painted on the walls. We were touched and felt the people of Israel deeply in our hearts.

We realized that we had become different and saw things in a new way. With great interest we went for a tour of Moses' Tabernacle and learned new things. We also visited the Noah's Ark room and listened to a familiar story. Then, we went to the book store. While I was looking at books, Oleg found his own treasures, a shofar and tallit. He knew the meaning of these items and wanted to have them.

Later I read in the Bible that when the Jews blew the shofar, God remembered them. The tallit helps people to separate themselves from the world when they pray and cover themselves.

The owner also gave us her book "From Paralysis to Praise", wherein she wrote how God healed her, how God worked in her life, and how her husband and she built the Noah's Ark restaurant. They had no money and support, but God helped them. They started building the "Noah's Ark", while having only faith. Then God sent them money and people to help. With "Noah's Ark" they were able to touch the souls of many people and tell them about God.

While we drove home, I read most of her book, which has really encouraged me. By this time, it was dark outside, so I closed the book. Oleg was driving, the music in the car was on and the children were nearly asleep. Tears rolled down my cheeks, but I tried to be quiet and not let Oleg know that I was crying. Sitting quietly, I looked at the dark sky and talked to God. In my heart I said, **"God, I love you so much and You know that. Even though our experience with Elijah was very hard, You see that we love You even more than ever before. God, I want to do something for You. I am ready. Use me..."** I prayed, but I didn't know that God really listened, and that the good changes will start happening in my life so soon.

That evening was also a new beginning of a big change in Oleg's life with his new shofar and tallit. Time came when Oleg decided to make some important changes in his life, faith, and love towards God. I saw that God was with Oleg, teaching him the truths. The changes in Oleg were similar to King David from Psalm 119. Oleg's soul was weary with sorrow; but God strengthened him according to His word. Oleg was learning the ways of God's decrees and tried to follow them to the end. Trouble and distress have come upon our family, but God's commands were our delight.

We did not want to be just religious and continued to study the Bible. Something incredibly beautiful was happening in our hearts. Jewish songs about the God of Abraham, Isaac and Jacob always played on Oleg's phone. We had goose bumps when we listened to them. Often Oleg went outside, looked at the stars, raised his hands to Heaven and just cried before God. He thanked God for our family and for our beautiful home, which we did not think we deserved, but God gave it to us. We had everything because God loved us. Who were we? We were the immigrants, but God blessed us.

In those days, Oleg lived with God, spoke of God, and was filled with the Word of God. I saw that Psalm 1 from the Bible finally came true for my husband, who day and night studied the Law of God. There it is written: *"Blessed is the man who walks not in the counsel of the ungodly, nor stands in the path of sinners, nor sits in the seat of the scornful; But his delight is in the law of the LORD (the Torah), and in His Law he meditates day and night. He shall be like a tree planted by the rivers of water, that brings forth its fruit in its season, whose leaf also shall not wither; and whatever he does shall prosper..."*

I could not see my husband in this Psalm before, because we did not even know much about the Law of God and never learned about it. We were taught to live by the New Testament. But for some reason, Oleg began to be disturbed by the following questions: "Why we do not follow ALL of God's Commandments? Who canceled some of them them and when? Since when has it become possible to eat non-kosher food, when the Bible prohibits it? Why do we know almost nothing about God's Festivals, holy days, appointed by God?"

In the process of studying, we learned there is still a Jewish calendar, countable as God instructed, and many people still celebrate God's Festivals on the appointed days, as it is written in the Bible. We also learned that there are so many pagan holidays, with which we came into contact, without even realizing it. In Daniel 7:25, we read that Satan's plan was to abolish God's Law and His Festivals, and we wanted to know what it meant. These were the important things that God was gradually revealing to us. We understood there is more than we already knew, and we continued to study the Bible.

....

Going to our church was very hard. I often hid my tears when I saw two other babies who had been born at the same time as Elijah. They were healthy and happy, but Elijah was not with us. I also saw tears in Kristina's eyes as she looked at other babies. On days when prayers for babies were performed, I walked out from church in tears. Our children often wished for Elijah to be with them. They wanted to carry him in their arms and take care of their baby brother, but this opportunity had been taken from them.

One evening, I took our children to our church's children's choir practice. While they were singing, I attended the Bible study. The topic was, "How harsh should we be on those who sinned?" I couldn't understand why? I thought that we had no right to judge them. I knew that Jesus wanted us to love each other. If someone sinned, they had already cried and asked God for forgiveness. Why do we want to be harsh on them? The leader of the Bible study continued, "When the sinners don't confess their sins, God gives them ill children…" That was enough for me to become very angry inside. I didn't agree with that teaching. I didn't sin and God didn't punish me with an ill baby. I knew we needed a change in our life in order to heal...

The values of our church became different than ours. We wanted to find the church that would represent our values and bring joy into our lives. One evening, while praying with the children before going to bed, I heard Oleg's unusual prayer, **"God, You see all my questions. As you sent Phillip to Eunuch, to explain the Word of God to him (Acts 8:26-40), please send a person to our house, who could help us find satisfying answers to our questions."**

What happened three days later was a real miracle for us. Our son, Michael, came from school and asked if his new friend, Avi, could come and play. We said, "Of course." When we heard the last name of his friend, we were surprised because we heard that his father was a Pastor of the local Russian/Jewish Messianic congregation. They worshiped God on Shabbat (Sabbath) which for them was Saturday, ate kosher food, celebrated God's Festivals with a great joy, and believed that the Son of God, Jesus, was the Messiah of Israel, whom they called Yeshua in Hebrew. Oleg often listened to this pastor's sermons on the radio and liked them very much.

An hour later, this pastor came to our house to pick up his son. Oleg asked if he had time to stop by and answer our questions. The pastor took his son home, came back and spent the whole evening with Oleg, answering his questions. After their conversation, Oleg was so grateful to God that through this pastor God answered many of his questions.

The next day, after work, Oleg told me that he was ready to stop working on Saturday, start celebrating God's Festivals and eat only kosher food. Changes in my husband alarmed me, but I liked it. I saw how my husband was transforming. He was becoming a real "Priest of the

House." He WANTED to read the Word of God, LOVED God with all his heart, and WAS a perfect example for our children.

Whenever Oleg spoke of God, his face was shining with joy. The wound of Elijah's loss in Oleg's heart was deep, but gradually it was being healed and filled with God's love and His Word. I was not ready to make any changes yet. I realized that I needed time to research and find answers to my questions. I wanted God Himself to teach me and to show me this in the Bible. I knew Oleg had found something very meaningful for himself, but what my parents taught me and how I was raised was also important to me. Although I did not understand everything to the end, I supported Oleg.

....

The following Saturday, Oleg did not go to work, he stayed with us at home. After breakfast, he began to read the Bible to us. That Saturday he taught us so much, reading about Aaron, Miriam and Moses and comparing them to our children, David, Christina and Michael. He also told us about Jesus and His crucifixion, and explained we no longer needed to make offerings and animal sacrifices, because Jesus died for us once and for all, and now intercedes for us before God. In the end, Oleg explained the Bible is the Book of God's Instructions for Life. We must respect its words, read it and study it often.

The children and I listened to Oleg with great interest. As we prayed, tears of joy rolled down my face. I could not believe that instead of asking Oleg to read the Bible to our children, he WANTED to read it and our children WANTED to hear it. We no longer did it because we had to.

Because Oleg chose not to work on Saturdays, he lost a portion of his income. Myself and our children also decided to give up our activities on Saturday. As a family, we began to honor the Sabbath on Saturday. Oleg's excitement about God and His Word expanded and extended to all of us. We could see our family growing not only in faith, but in love and respect for each other.

....

A week later, on Saturday, July 5th, 2011, SEVEN weeks after Elijah's passing, we visited the Jewish Messianic Congregation for the first time. Their service was something I had never seen before. I experienced so much joy when I heard how they sang meaningful and touching the soul songs in Russian, American and Jewish language; when I saw how they praised God with gestures; and when I heard the meaningful message of the messianic Pastor/Rabbi. After their service, we had even more questions about God and about life, which we had to explore.

Time was going by slowly. More often we visited this new congregation on Saturdays, while still attending our church on Sundays. We knew we needed to change something in our life in order to heal. **We also began to understand it was more important to know what we thought of ourselves, than what other people thought of us. And what was most important was what God thought of us. We accepted the fact that it was our responsibility to determine for ourselves who we were, what we would believe, and what we would do.**

All our changes were preceded by many personal signs that were not clear, but which clearly indicated that something unusual was happening.

For example, my FIRST dream about Elijah. I dreamed he was at the hospital and a nurse was taking care of him. I asked the nurse if I could hold Elijah and she let me. I held Elijah, talked to him and he smiled at me. Then, I just sat with him for a while, held him close and cherished every second with him. It was such a good dream...

When I woke up early in the morning, sadness covered me like a blanket; it was only a dream. I laid in my bed and remembered my precious moments with Elijah. Then, I realize what day it was, and was shocked to find out that it was exactly SEVEN MONTHS AND SEVEN days after Elijah had left us.

At first, I was a little scared and tried to reconcile what was happening. Earlier I heard that if the same number keeps repeating in your life, it may mean something bad. But then I understood that nothing happens without God's will. I thanked God for working in my life, for staying close to me, and for being kind to me by showing me my baby in a dream.

And such coincidences were repeated again and again. I started wondering why this adversity happened when I was 33 years old? Why was I born in 1977? Why was I married in 1997? Why Oleg's prayer for God to show Who He really is, was in 2007? Why Elijah lived exactly SEVEN months and SEVEN days? Why he went to God on the SEVENTH day – the Sabbath? Why exactly SEVEN weeks after Elijah's passing I was testifying at a woman's conference? Why exactly SEVEN weeks after Elijah's passing, our foot stepped into the Messianic Jewish Congregation? Why exactly after SEVEN months and SEVEN days I had my first dream about Elijah? And, why this book has been in writing for exactly SEVEN years?

I knew that Jesus was crucified at 33 and seven was God's Holy number. Looking back and putting all these pieces together, **I clearly realized that God planned our life long before we were born. God had His dates and terms already written for us**. I also realized if I wasn't writing my book, and wasn't trying to remember when what happened, I would probably never have noticed such close Hand of God in my life.

As Oleg and I continued to study the Bible, we became aware that the Bible is filled with the numbers 4, 7, 12, 17, 70, but mostly with the number 7, a number of God's completion, which is written 700 times in the Old Testament. It is great to see God work in our life!

....

Once there was another incidence that showed us that we were on a right path. I went to a doctor's appointment. It was going to take 45 minutes to check the nerve function of my injured hands, which I injured two years prior and still experienced pain. The doctor started the nerve study and we just talked. Usually, I didn't talk about Elijah a lot, but for some reason that was the topic I started with. At the end, I said that we made some changes in our life. We stopped working on Saturday, as we understood the importance of keeping that day holy. We stopped eating pork, ham and shrimps, and ate only kosher foods because we understood that God still wanted for our souls to be clean. We were looking for truth and were in a process of looking for a different church. We wanted to learn how to celebrate God's Festivals and tried to follow all of God's Commandments. As I was telling him that, I didn't even ask him if he was a Christian or if he believed in God.

I told that doctor how Oleg had been studying the Bible for three years at that point and how God was teaching him. God opened our eyes on things that we never even thought of before. And I told him that we were not sure about lots of things yet, but clearly saw that we had to make some changes in our life. It was not easy and we were not understood by many people, but we had to do what we felt God wanted from us.

The doctor stopped what he was doing and, with wide opened eyes, he asked, "Really? Those are the changes you are making? You know, Olga, God sent you here! I am a Seventh Day Adventist and go to church on Saturdays, but I go there because of my friends and because my wife wants me to. People in our church are not supposed to eat pork, but they do. Couple of years ago I started asking myself if God was real. I no longer feel that I believe in God. Your story touched me so much. You lost your child and, instead of growing apart from God, you love Him more now. You showed me that God is real. Now I have something to think about. I better make some changes in my life!"

I walked out from that appointment and could not believe what had just happened. Then, I called Oleg, told him what had happened, and Oleg answered, "See, God showed something to that doctor. But also, God is showing you through this doctor that we are on a right path!" It is hard to make a change, but sometimes we have to do what is inconvenient for us. We have to risk it, if it is what God wants from us.

....

26

You have to decide for yourself. Another person's value may not be your value.

Few months later, while regularly visiting the Jewish Messianic Congregation on Saturdays, we noticed after their service we were full of joy and felt we were doing something right! We had already learned much from the Bible and always wanted to learn more. For some unknown reason, God led us to this new community. We left our former church and became members of this new congregation.

We learned that ten years prior, God instructed our new pastor to open a congregation and serve Jews in our community. The goal of this congregation was to build a "bridge" from Christianity to Judaism, because most Jews do not believe in Jesus Christ who "abolished God's Law and Commandments." This congregation, to the contrary, shows the Jews that Jesus is their Messiah, who lived by the Law of God and by God's Commandments, who kept the Sabbath day holy and ate kosher food. The Bible also says that Jesus will not come until the Jews will call unto Him. *(Matthew 21: 9)*. For some reason, God led us to this congregation. Being there helped us heal, while we were learning more and more exciting doctrine about our God Almighty and His Rules for our life.

One day after the sermon, the pastor invited those who needed prayer to come up to the front. I went forward, knelt before God, and said, **"God, please reveal the Truth to me. I want to love You as much as Oleg does. I want to know more about Your Festivals and the Sabbaths, and** how important it is for me to eat the kosher food. I don't want to do this because people tell me, but I want You, God, to teach me and reveal this to me."

After a few days I felt a great desire to research the Bible. I took the Concordance and, using the King James translation and the translations of a Russian Jew, David Stern, I wrote out all the verses from the Bible about God's Law, about the Sabbath, about food, about praise, and about everything that interested me. I learned from the Bible that the Law of God is *SACRED* and *ETERNAL and* is written *FOR THOUSANDS OF GENERATIONS*. I also realized I need to obey not two or nine, but all of God's Ten Commandments. To my great surprise, I did not find the word "Sunday" in the Bible. The whole Bible was filled with the word Sabbath, the day of God's Rest, and the day of our joy before Him.

I was also surprised to see how one translation was so different from the other. It made sense why there is so many different religions in the world. I believe it is due to different translations and explanations of the Bible.

I was surprised when I read online that about 300 years after Jesus' resurrection, the Sabbath day was changed from Saturday to Sunday by the Roman emperor, Constantine. He made Sunday the official day of rest for the Roman Empire. Jews, who kept the Sabbath day holy, were put to death *(www.JewishRoots.net.)* It was scary for me to realize it and I cried. At the same time, I was relieved to know the truth.

I also wanted to know if we still needed to celebrate God's Festivals? I learned there are Seven of God's Festivals, the holy days, appointed by God for his people to celebrate with a great joy. They are: Pesach, Unleavened Bread, First fruits, Shavuot, Rosh Hashanah, Yom Kippur and Sukkot. These festivals are still celebrated by many people and half of them were fulfilled in Jesus. I realized the words of the prophet Daniel 7:25, *"And he shall speak great words against the most High, and shall wear out the saints of the most High, and think to change times and laws (God's Festivals and Sabbaths): and they shall be given into his hand until a time and times and the dividing of time"* came true because we, the generation of believers, knew almost nothing about the Festivals of God or His Law. Satan's goal of abolishing God's Law and His Festivals was successful because many people no longer read the Old Testament. They have no idea what God's Festivals are, and no longer keep the Sabbath day holy.

I realized that Jesus himself and his Apostles taught only from the Old Testament because at that time they did not have a New Testament. They lived according to God's Law and fulfilled all His Commandments! I realized I should live not only by the New Testament, but read all of the Bible and fulfill all that is written there.

It took me about three weeks to write down all these verses from the Bible. I finally saw how God revealed for as the "GREAT PUZZLE". I began to understand what happened, why Elijah came into our lives, and what God was trying to teach us. While writing these verses down, some days I cried because I did not know many things, but found them written in the Bible. On other days, I praised God with great joy because He revealed to me something new with great meaning!

I also visited my maternal Grandfather, who told me both his and Grandmother's parents were Jews. When I discovered this part of my heritage, I shed tears of joy for two hours and thanked God for such exciting news! The blood of Abraham was in us! Jesus was of my people, the descendants of Abraham! Later, I found out that Oleg's Grandfather used to tell his sons, "You don't know who your

308

ancestors are", but he never told them who. And Oleg's Grandmother still spoke the Yiddish language. I learned that not far from us lives a Jewish Rabbi, Daniel Lapin. I guess, our Lapin name is Jewish too? We really wanted to know more about our Jewish roots, but for some reason that information was hidden from us for a while. Finally, it became clear to us why God brought us into the Jewish Messianic Congregation!

Our transition to this congregation was an important event of our lives. The pastor is very understanding, and people are full of love. They come there from different nations and different faiths, but have one thing in common: Jewish roots. We have new friends and a new life, celebrating God's Festivals and observing Shabbats. New members have time to learn about God and draw closer to Him. A lot of broken hearts come and stay here. Jesus said, "I have come to the lost sheep of the house of Israel" (Matthew 15:24). In this congregation, the door is always open to sinners, who receive support as they find their way to God.

From the first days in this congregation, Oleg began translating the pastor's sermons from Russian into English. Many Americans thanked Oleg and said that God answered their prayers because they had been praying for a good interpreter. Looking back, I realized that Oleg's studies of the Bible in English and Russian languages prepared him for the responsible translation of God's Word. A little later, Oleg began to teach children's Torah classes. And a few years later, Oleg was elected as one of the leaders and elders of the congregation. I could not believe my husband was becoming a completely new person. God had worked a miracle in Oleg's heart, which helped Oleg learn the power of God to change lives.

In our congregation, I work with women and organize God's Festivals. God has taught me much through my work with people. I have learned to pray with faith and have seen even more miracles of God. I realized when it is His plan, He answers and heals us. But in some situations, God does not heal, and we must accept His will. I understood it is very important to pray to God in the name of Jesus, who shed his blood for us and atoned for our sins. Also, if we use the Bible verses in prayer, for example, "By the wounds of Jesus we are healed," then they have a great power. It is very important to believe what we are asking God. God loves us, hears us and answers our prayers.

During those days, I came to know what it means to have the Holy Spirit within me. It's to have the character of Jesus. How? To live as Jesus lived, to say what He said, and to do what He did. And how did Jesus live? According to the Word of God. What did He say? God's Word was in His tongue. And what did He do? He healed people by His words and deeds. I realized that I should be hands, words, and Jesus' actions on Earth. I must help people, wipe their tears, feed the hungry, hug them, and do the will of God on earth. I also realized that most of the time God helps people directly through people. So, if we see a situation and do not help others, we will answer for this on God's judgement day (Hebrews 10:30.) Our deeds, not our words touch people's hearts. What we give to others, sooner or later, we will receive it back.

Our children also understand the importance of serving God, not because of fear, but because of the great love we have for Him, so it is not difficult for us to fulfill exactly what God has asked us to do. With great joy they attend the Torah classes, participate in the life of the congregation, and often go on missionary trips to Mexico. David is a very good helper of the director of the mission. And when

Kristina visits orphans and ill children in Mexico, she is ready to adopt at least a few children each time. She loves them and is not afraid of children with disabilities. Our children are strengthened by life. They know how to love and take care of others.

Our association with this new congregation has blessed us and made our faith and our family stronger. We thank God for His blessing. We continue to this day to use Scriptures as a foundation for our decisions. Each of our choices are important as we believe it will reflect in who we become.

....

When I continued to study the Bible, I learned that in the last days (which may be our days), God will awaken all Jewish descendants. Today many people do not even know about their roots and do not realize that the blood of Abraham flows in them. The Bible says that in the last days all the nations will come to the Jews, pull them by the edge of their clothes and say, "Teach us!" *(Zech. 8:23).* And the prophecies of Jeremiah and Ezekiel tell us that in the last days God will bring the Jews back to Jerusalem *(Jer. 16: 15, Ezek. 37).* It is not easy to return to Israel if your heart is not ready.

After the days of Hitler and the Holocaust, many Jews changed their names and no longer told their children they were Jews. They didn't want their children to be bullied and cursed. Therefore, we did not know anything about this until we asked. According to statistics, in Kiev, where I lived, 60% of people were Jewish, and in Odessa, where my paternal Grandfather was born, 80% of people were Jewish. They came there after God scattered them around the earth.

With the group from our congregation we visited Israel in 2014. It was very eye-opening to see the dry land and the traces of the former waterfalls. When the people of Israel left their land, the land withered. I was so moved by this landscape. I realized you cannot joke with God. God gave His Rules and Commandments, but the people of Israel did not follow them. For that reason, God scattered them among the nations and dried up their land. In 1947, after the pogroms and the Holocaust in Eastern Europe, and the accompanying death of Jews, the state of Israel was formed. Jewish survivors began to return to their land. The earth responded to its people and began to blossom; green fields appeared, trees flowered, vineyards flourished and water sprang from the ground. If we had the opportunity, we would happily move there to live. In *Genesis 12:3,* God said, "I will bless those who bless Israel and will curse those that curse Israel." We always bless Israel and love these people.

....

Over the years, we learned more about God's Festivals. It is impossible to comprehend everything at once. Each year we learn and understand something new. One day, when this book was already close to publication I wondered if the dates of Elijah's birth and death meant anything on the Jewish calendar? *To my* tremendous surprise, **I learned that the birth of Elijah, on September 9th, 2010, fell on Rosh Hashana** (ראש השנה), the Feast of Trumpets, the Jewish New Year, the day of Creation of the World and the First man, Adam! And **Elijah's death, April 16th, fell on Shabbat a-gadol.** This is the Great Sabbath, preceding Pesah (Passover), when God performed miracles for Israel.

So, every time it's a Pesah time, we remember Jesus's crucifixion and what He did for us. We also remember Elijah and the gift of a new life that he gave us. I remember, one Sunday, still at the old church, we had a special service, where we remembered Jesus' death, ate a piece of bread, drank a sip of wine, and sang many songs about the crucifixion of Jesus and His resurrection. While singing about Jesus' suffering, I remembered Elijah lying in blood after his surgery and began to compare his wounds with the wounds of Jesus. I also imagined Mary, Jesus' Mother, and how her heart bled when she saw the sufferings of her son. Mary had a choice to accept God's Will or to protest and ask Jesus not to die on the cross. But Mary did not. She knew her Son was born to die for the sins of all people. God chose Mary because He knew she could and would bear it all. During the crucifixion, Jesus was still a man and it was painful to imagine Him suffering. On that day, I appreciated the sacrifice of Jesus, His wounds and His pain. I also realized how strong Mary was. Throughout the service tears streamed down my face and I could not stop thanking Jesus for His suffering and for our redemption!

....

This is our journey with God and Elijah. I hope you have seen the wonderful hand of God in our lives. I hope together with us, you will agree that God heard Oleg's prayer from 2007, when Oleg asked God to reveal Himself to him. Who is He, the Real and Powerful God? God came and began his work in our life. Even though it was painful, we discovered many beautiful things about our God Almighty.

The following verse from the book of Sirach in the full Bible, 2:1-6, came true for us. It says there: *"My child, if you come to serve the Lord, prepare yourself for testing. Set your heart straight, be steadfast, and don't act hastily in a time of distress. Hold fast to God and don't keep your distance from Him, so that you may find strength at your end. Accept whatever happens to you, and be patient when you suffer humiliation, because gold is tested with fire, and acceptable people are tested in the furnace of humiliation. Trust Him, and He will help you; make your ways straight, and hope in Him."*

Since we wanted to serve God seriously, He tested us and taught us to be sincere in heart and be steadfast and patient in the times of difficulties and sorrows. We accepted it, humbled ourselves and learned to be patient. Today we feel like that gold, which was tested in the fire and in the furnace of humiliation. Only a loving Father can lead us through pain to help us and save us. He knows what is best for us and how to lead us to a better future.

I know if Elijah had not been born with a heart defect, there would have been no real reason for us to turn so deliberately to God. We would not have had the faith building experiences that brought us to our knees, so God could lift us up. We would still be the same "warm" Christians we had always been. Although Elijah endured so much pain, and we endured it with him, all this led us to a better future. I hope that our story will remind every person about God, why He left the Bible for us, and what He expects from us. Only God can change us, strengthen us, teach us and use us for His Glory!

Today, SEVEN years later, Oleg and I thank God for every second of our lives with our son Elijah, for the miracles of God, for all life lessons, and for the fact He has shown Himself to us, who He really is! The work of God in our lives was very painful, but it was worth it. Our life before Elijah could easily be called prosperous, but, it is God Who prepared us both "for something more". It was the time of our spiritual growth and the knowledge of the real God through the study of His eternal Word. Today we love God, each other and our children much more than ever before. We cherish our family and know the price of health and happiness. And most importantly, we understand the difference between religion and the true living God.

DEAR READER

I hope that you will never go through what we did, but life happens. Remember, no one can tell you what to do. It is up to you to make those decisions. If you asked me for advice in a hard situation, I am not sure if I would give you any answers because each situation is unique. I have experienced only one side of this life. Someone else has experienced more than I did, but decided to keep it only to himself. For some people, it is too hard to talk about their personal challenges. Others may have experienced a lot more tears and sorrow in this life, and I have to learn from them. Each of us is so different. I am trying not to teach anyone, but just hope that my information will help someone to get up and keep going, no matter how hard this life may be. I have answered a few questions, which I have frequently been asked. If this information is helpful, thank God. If you don't agree with me, it is okay. We are free to make our own choices and decisions. May God help each of us in our journey.

1. *How do we deal with the loss of a loved one?*

I can only talk about my child. I cannot speak precisely for those who have lost their spouse, parents or siblings. I don't know what they go through. I can only imagine their heartache. You lost your child. What is next? What do you do? How do you react? Do you go into depression and refuse to see anyone? Do you become angry and blame everyone? Do you feel like you might lose your mind.? What should we do?

No one can give you an answer. You do what you think you should do. I can only tell you life is still beautiful. You can find joy again, even though it may take a long time. I chose to manage my feelings, to hide my tears, to stay positive, and to live for my beautiful three children, for my husband, and for other people around me. I chose not to cry for what I no longer have, but to be happy and cherish every moment with my loved-ones, whom I have today, because I may not have them tomorrow.

2. Can we trust the doctors?

Our doctors are a beautiful vessel in God's hands. We should trust them, not be afraid to tell them what we think, or to ask a question. We should work together as a team. When our loved ones are critically ill, we are under a lot of stress. We may see things, which really didn't happen. We may become very angry, when there is no reason. The doctors and nurses care for our loved one. We are blessed to live in a country with highly trained doctors, with advanced medications and medical equipment. People in poor countries don't have what we have. The doctors are our blessing from God here on earth. Thank you, Doctors.

3. Would we make the same choice if we had no medical insurance?

Probably, not. Oleg and I were blessed to have medical insurance and to be double-covered. Elijah's medical cost exceeded $2,000,000.00. We would have $200,000.00 out of pocket expenses, if the state insurance did not co-pay for Kaiser. We were lucky not to have out of pocket expenses, otherwise our life today would be totally different; we would have debt in addition to our tears. Elijah might have not lived for as long as he did. If three Open-Heart Surgeries and a Heart Transplant were not covered by the medical insurance, then it would probably not be an option for Elijah. Good health insurance is important.

Our wealth controls many aspects of our life. If we have little money, we have fewer options in life. It is the same with medical insurance. If you can't afford to pay for it, then you may not have the choices we had. Hospitalization and the doctors' care costs money. In America, we are blessed to have medical insurance which pays for our medical needs. Other countries don't have it. Even though we or our loved ones hurt sometimes, we are still blessed to have the best care we can possibly get!

4. How do we face the death of our loved one?

I used to be so scared of death. I never wanted to face it or to deal with it, but I had to, and I survived. Surprisingly, it wasn't as scary as I thought it would be, because God was with me. He carried me through my whole journey and never left me alone. That is what made all this process easier for me. There are two categories of people. Some are scared to die, and others are not. Why? Some people live righteously, and have no fear of death because they believe in a life beyond the grave. Others live believing death is the end. Some are able to find contentment in a life well lived; others have no anchor, so they struggle with dying.

So, what can we do so we can die peacefully or let our loved-one go without fear? We need to live righteously, be good people and not sin. How do we know what sin is? By studying God's instructions for life (the Bible), by knowing His Commandments, and by fulfilling His expectations. God gives us a choice of blessings or a curse, and He asks us to choose a blessing (Deut. 30:19). We have freedom of

CHOICE! Let's choose life and blessing, then nothing would scare us.

5. What if we make a wrong choice?

We make choices and sometimes we make mistakes. That is how we learn. We deal with consequences. Sometimes we have no choice. What if we make a bad choice? How can we live with it? How can we forgive ourselves? Remember, no one is perfect. Make the choice you think is best and move on. If you made a mistake – forgive yourself. Why be miserable? It is not worth it. Love yourself and be nice to yourself – you deserve it. Life is not easy.

Oleg and I were so lucky to have a supportive family and employer. If your employer doesn't give you enough time off work, if you don't have support from family, if your spouse leaves you in the hardest moment, if you don't have good medical insurance and have to lose everything in order to save a life of a loved-one, what should you do? Do the best possible in your situation. And remember, never blame yourself.

Life can be very harsh sometimes and can hit you from every side possible. Who can help us? I can help myself. You can help yourself. You can make a positive difference in your life! Treasure the gift of your life and the life of loved ones, but also be able to let them go when the time comes. During those days we may not have a choice, but still have to be able to move on.

6. Will my life be the same after the loss of a loved-one?

No. It will never be the same. Why? Because you will become different. You will start seeing things differently.

After feeling so much pain within yourself, you will feel the pain of others. After being mistreated and not understood, you will start understanding others. You will value your life and the life of your loved-ones more. You will treasure every second of your life and will make every second valuable. You may change the church you go to, change a job, or even sell your house in order to erase painful memories. Counselors and therapists suggest making no major life changes for a year after the death of a spouse or a child.

In the time of sorrow, we are so sensitive. It takes time to heal. Changing something in life helps. It may not seem as the best choice to others, but for you it may be the only choice at that time. You do whatever it takes to heal your wound. Instead of crying and feeling sorry for yourself, you may start helping others in similar situation. You may end up being where you had never been before and start doing new things in life. Hopefully, you will be able to find the best in the worst situation and continue enjoying your life.

One of many changes in our family was to become organ donors. When it was time for us to renew our driver's license, the question if you want to be an organ donor wasn't scary anymore. If we die, who cares about our organs? We would not. But there may be a father, a mother, a child or a sibling at a hospital waiting for that donor heart or liver. I may no longer be alive, but by choosing to donate my organs after my brain is no longer functioning, I may save other lives. Why not to do that? Elijah could have been one of them.

I also became a blood donor. Every six weeks I donate my blood at the local American Red Cross. Elijah needed so much blood and I have no idea who donated it for him. It was definitely not me. Thank you, everyone, who donated blood for Elijah. I used to be so scared of needles and didn't even want to think of death. Today, I see life from an opposite side. I know that I will not live longer than my God has planned for me. But I also know that while alive, I can do a lot more than I ever thought I could.

7. After such an adversity, how can I continue loving God?

"Does God really exist? Why didn't He come to help me?" These used to be my questions. In our situation, we were at an intersection, not knowing which way to go and which turn to take. We were blind and had no instructions...and, of course, God was quiet. People couldn't help us. In similar situations, people commit suicide, get a divorce or just lose their mind. You need a moral compass or code, i.e. God, to make decisions. Every person has a different code. It is up to each individual to uncover that question for him or herself, but for us the Bible was our answer and God was our support.

If Elijah wasn't born ill, Oleg and I would probably had stayed the same "warm" Christians. Having Elijah ill, nudged us to search for knowledge. We searched for answers in the Bible. The more we read it, the more we understood that it is a nirvana of knowledge. We realized it is a book of instructions for life. It gives us answers to our questions, tells us the characteristics of God, uncovers our future, and gives us hope to meet our loved ones again. We found more happiness in serving God the way He wants us to serve Him, loving Him the way He wants us to love him, and living this life the way He wants us to live it. Surprisingly, in our situation, instead of growing apart from God, we stuck to Him. Even though, our situation with Elijah was so painful, God was with us. He never left us. At the end, He took our baby back to His Kingdom, but in exchange He gave us knowledge, love and experience.

8. How do we deal with stress?

Our life may be so stressful sometimes that we don't know how to deal with it. We wail, cry or blame someone. Under stress, we hurt others and ourselves. So, apparently, stress is our enemy! Why stay friends with it? I chose not to stress out. When I feel overwhelmed, I turn the music on, have coffee or ice cream, or just go for a walk. It is good to be alone in such situations. Then, you can connect with God.

It may be easier to do it outside, while seeing beautiful nature and talking to God. It may also be a good idea to put sunglasses on and go for a long walk. Then for sure, no one, except God will see your tears or hear your cry. Yes, we need to cry it out – that is the healing balm for our hearts. But we also don't want to concentrate on our pain a lot. Sometimes, we just need to be strong and let it go, scoop it out from our heart and throw the pain away. Yes, the scar will always be there, but fill your heart with happiness, with what we still have – with the beauty of this life and with our loved-ones!

9. Can we control what happens in someone's life?

We can tell our children what to do until they are probably 18 years old. Then, we can just give them advice, and then let our children make their choice. After they are 21 and have their own families, they are on their own. Friends and family can give them advice, but they cannot make choices for them. Each adult has to take his or her own steps in their journey. Why does sorrow happen? No one knows. That is our life. Today we struggle and tomorrow we help those who struggle.

When Elijah was ill, I was scared to death. I didn't know how to handle my situation. But because I had God to rely on, I made it through. I realized when no one here on earth can help us, we have to give up and let God take control. It is always good to let God be in control, which is not an easy thing to do. In order to do that, we have to "die" for ourselves, we have to "bury our I" and become an individual with characteristics of God – love others, treat others with respect, be wise, don't lie, don't steal, be polite, live by God's standards, serve others, help others, and love yourself and your neighbor, etc. It is not easy to let God be in control of our life. But trust me, once we give up our control and start trusting God, our life becomes so much easier. Our stress dissolves, when we let God carry us in His hands. He takes care of things and performs miracles. God loves us!

In our journey with Elijah, I understood that our children are not really ours. They come from God. He numbers their days, controls their life, and plans their future, We parents do God's work on earth, by teaching our children and by loving them. Still, we need to trust God to be in those situations where we cannot be. We have to rely on God. He is alive! He will always help us, if we trust Him and if we ask Him to.

10. How do you remember your loved ones?

Do you hide their pictures? Do you never talk about them again or do you always talk about them? Do you always cry or do you stay positive? How do you celebrate their birthdays and their anniversaries? How do you survive those days? How do you celebrate holidays or take a family photo without them present? HOW? I cannot tell you how. Each of us is different and just deals with it when time comes. For example, even me and Oleg dealt with Elijah's death in our own way, and we respected .our different ways.

Elijah's birthdays, death anniversaries and holidays have been very hard for our family. Those are the days of remembrance. Sometimes they are days of tears, and sometimes just quiet moments. Elijah's pictures are on our walls. He is not hidden. We talk about him. We miss him. He is still with us in our hearts and he will ALWAYS BE! I know that there are not many books like mine, but this is one of the ways I want to remember our baby Elijah.

Grieving takes time. Working through your grief, i.e., writing, is okay. It is okay to ask for help. Sometimes, people need to see a counselor or talk to a friend or a pastor, in order to learn how to deal with grief. It may take years and it is okay. You do your best to survive such hard situations. Life moves forward. Do not get buried by or stuck in the past. Yesterday is not today – you have the future. Learn to share your story. Your experiences can help others, if you allow yourself to do so. Your family needs you to be considerate of them. Know they may say or do things they don't mean. They are hurting also. You need personal time. Don't put a time limit on grief. You have to deal with everyday life, while all this is going on.

11. When the doctors don't give any chances for life for our loved-ones, what do we do?

Having no more choices may be a lot easier than having choices. On one hand, we want our loved ones to live, so we battle for their life. On another hand, we are so tired and just want to give up. We want our normal life back. We can no longer do it. Oleg's and my motto was to help Elijah as long as he had chances for a normal life. So often, I had no more energy left in me and was just going with the flow. So many times, I was ready to give up, but thank God for Oleg, who was still strong in his belief to give Elijah all his chances for life. Thank You, God, for my husband Oleg. Together with him, we made best choices we thought for Elijah. It was our baby and we fought for his life. We were even ready to raise a disabled child, if he could only be with us. Life is a precious gift and we have to fight for it.

Also, there are people, who are in hospice for years. They have no chances for life. Their brain is no longer functioning, and their heart is barely beating. They cannot talk, cannot smile or love us. They are probably miserable, but cannot tell us, and we are miserable for them. We cannot bring them back to life and cannot let them go. They are on life support. The machine breathes for them and keeps their lungs working, but they are no longer there. What do we do? How much longer do we wait? Can someone judge us if we let them go in peace?

I have not been in this situation. Elijah was growing, smiling, breathing on his own, and his heart was beating weakly. Elijah still had chances. Elijah's story was different, and I am glad we did everything possible to give him a chance to live for seven months and seven days. Even though those were very hard days for all of us, at the same time those were the days of life, happiness and blessing of being able to hold our baby close to our heart, and enjoy every moment with him together! Thank you, God, for those moments!

What would I do if the doctor told me: "Olga, Elijah has no chance for life. His brain is not functioning properly. There is no surgery to help him. He will never have a normal life. This is it. It is time to let him go."? I would just let him go, as we did when that time came. If you are in such a situation, let your loved-one go. Disconnect his or her medication. Let them rest in peace. Keep pity to yourself. You have been through a lot. It is time for a change. It is time to bring your happiness back. It is time to continue living. It is time to let go?... you can do it. No one has a right to judge you. No one! If they do – don't listen. They haven't been in your situation. It is your decision to make, not anyone else's.

12. What if I am not understood, but hurt by others?

It is your loved one's birthday or anniversary. You feel it in the atmosphere. You become nervous, agitated, stressed-out and don't even know why. You are trying everything possible to deal with your stress. You tell your friends about your worries, but their answer is: "Stop worrying. Don't be nervous. Your loved one is with God. It is better for him to be there." It is easy for people to say that, but for me it is agitating to hear that. All I want to hear at those moments is probably NOTHING.

It is better to be quiet, than to say something that may hurt someone. They haven't been in my shoes. Their child is healthy. He brings them joy every minute. What would they do if they lost him? Would they say: "Oh, it is better for him to be with God?" Probably not. I do understand that it's better for him with God and I am not complaining. I agree with God's will. But it is hard to go through our loved-one's birthdays and anniversaries when they are not with us.

From year to year, those are the days of remembrance. We don't forget them. They stay with us forever. We have to learn how to remember our loved-ones and not to stress out excessively. Also, we have to forgive those who don't understand us. If you can, explain your feelings to them. And if you can't, you don't have to. Sometimes, we just need to have a quiet day far from everyone. Do what helps you live...

13. How losing our loved one can affect us?

You lost your loved one. Your life has changed. What do you do next? Do you want to stay in the same crowd of people, in the same church, at the same work place, or in the same house? There are lots of things that remind you of your loved one and bring you pain. Some people may come up to you and tell you that God is punishing you, for whatever it is, by taking your loved-one away from you. Others may feel too sorry for you and you just can't stand it. You are trying to survive because you are stronger than people think you are. People, who haven't been in your situation, can never understand you. Sometimes, you may need a change in your life to be able to deal with the loss of your loved-one. Expect the unexpected.

Even though, the change in our life may be painful and scary, at the end it is always good for us. Why? Because, when circumstances change in our life, even though we don't like it, we always learn something new. We gain knowledge and become stronger and better. Change may not be easy because we have to make choices. People may not approve of our choices. So what? It is our life. We have to do everything possible to deal with our loss and move on. People cannot do it for us.

Spilling my emotions on paper is not easy. After losing our loved-ones, we hide our tears and don't want to talk about it. We don't want others to pick at our wounds and, sometimes, we cut-off ourselves out from this world. I can tell you, I would never wish for anyone to go through the path that Oleg and I did, but I know that it is not in our control. I know that so many people travel even harder paths in their lives. Some cannot survive a divorce, others are ready to die after having a Down's syndrome baby, and others think that their life has ended after their mother or a spouse has passed away. Some children are born blind or deaf, and mothers have no choice as to become stronger and live with it. Life can be miserable, but we have to deal with it and move on. I did it and you can do it. It will be hard, so try to have God by your side. Let Him carry you in His hands when you can't do it on your own.

Death can be a terrible thing, but at the same time it can be an amazing learning experience. After losing our loved-one, our life will never be the same. Even though we expect it to be much worse, I believe it will only become a lot better, if we let it. We are in control of our choices, our feelings and our life. Sometimes, we may not have a choice, but most of the time we do. We chose to live in heaven on earth, or in hell on earth. God said "I give you a choice: a curse or a blessing. Choose blessing." (Deut. 30:19) Let's choose a blessing, love, and happiness, no matter what happens in our life. Life is still beautiful!

We never know when the pain of losing our loved ones may hit us again. We try to handle our loss as best as possible. We seem positive and strong, but sometimes, all of a sudden, we are reduced to tears and cannot stop them. Sometimes we hurt, but we don't show it. We hide our tears, and no one knows that we hurt. Sometimes we just don't talk about it. That side of our life is private. *Every individual deals with something private in their life. They can't tell everything that is in their heart. They have secrets. We have to respect every human being. Every life is strong and fragile. Every life is beautiful and painful. Every step in our life may have roses or thorns. We have to learn how to survive every situation in our life and not be broken by it.*

....

ACKNOWLEDGEMENTS

From the experience of our family's story, we are eternally grateful to so many people. You know who you are. Your phone calls, prayers, visits, hugs, words of love, cards, help with the meals and the child care were so special. These things let our family understand the importance of others in our lives and the importance of us to being involved with others in their lives.

A special thanks to my husband Oleg and our children. You were always there when I needed you and your support, love and comfort. Your love, help, and understanding kept me going and enabled me to heal. Together, we did everything possible for Elijah.

And lastly, I would like to thank my precious baby, Elijah. Thank you for choosing us as your parents. You only spent seven month and seven days with our family, but you live in our memories and are reflected in our daily lives. You changed us forever. We now have a new and better life. You have taught us to be braver, so that we can grow as individuals. You have taught us to understand other people's pain, and to know there is always someone who has more problems than us. Because of you, we began to ask questions about God, and about ourselves. We recognized we could do better. We learned happiness could grow from sorrow. And we began to understand we should be open to change and we should base that change on what we believe to be true. We found we had to trust in the Lord, and trust in ourselves.

We were the lucky ones to have you in our lives. We know in our hearts you were released to God. Today, I imagine you sitting on Jesus's lap, listening to His stories, asking Him questions, and experiencing the presence of God in heaven.

We love you, Elijah!
You are always in our hearts!

Dear friend,

I will be thankful if you could leave your reviews at my Amazon page at **http://a.co/ccrmv8u**

Also, you can share your review on my Facebook page:
https://www.facebook.com/olga.anischenko.3

or at my website: **www.olgaanischenko.com**

*My poems, this book, and my other books you may find at my **Amazon page** under my name, **Olga Anischenko.***

*You are welcome to record a testimony and add to my YouTube **"Olga Anischenko English Channel".** I am posting many other testimonies there.*

Made in the USA
San Bernardino, CA
20 May 2018